Weekend Walks

*in Dutchess and
Putnam Counties*

Weekend Walks

in Dutchess and Putnam Counties

History & Nature in the
Eastern Hudson Valley

Second Edition

Peggy Turco

The Countryman Press
Woodstock, Vermont

An Invitation to the Reader

Over time trails can be rerouted and signs and landmarks altered. If you find that changes have occurred along the walks described in this book, please let us know so that corrections may be made in future editions. The author and publisher also welcome other comments and suggestions. Address all correspondence to:

Editor, *Weekend Walks* Series
The Countryman Press
P.O. Box 748
Woodstock, Vermont 05091

Library of Congress Cataloging-in-Publication Data

Data has been applied for.

Cover design by Dede Cummings Designs
Text design and composition by Chelsea Cloeter
Cover photo © Carr Clifton
Maps by Moore Creative Designs, © 2005 The Countryman Press
Illustrations on pages 250 and 275 by He Who Stands Firm
Illustrations on pages 78, 153, 186-187, and 210 by Alex Wallach
Interior photos by the author unless otherwise credited

Published by The Countryman Press, P.O. Box 748, Woodstock, Vermont 05091

Distributed by W.W. Norton & Company, Inc., 500 Fifth Avenue, New York, NY 10110

Printed in the United States of America

10 9 8 7 6 5 4 3 2 1

This book is dedicated to the individuals and organizations that safeguard our natural landscape; the volunteers who design, construct, and maintain the footpaths in our parks; the scientists and naturalists whose research increases our knowledge of our ecosystem; and to my father, Rudy Turco, who first guided me.

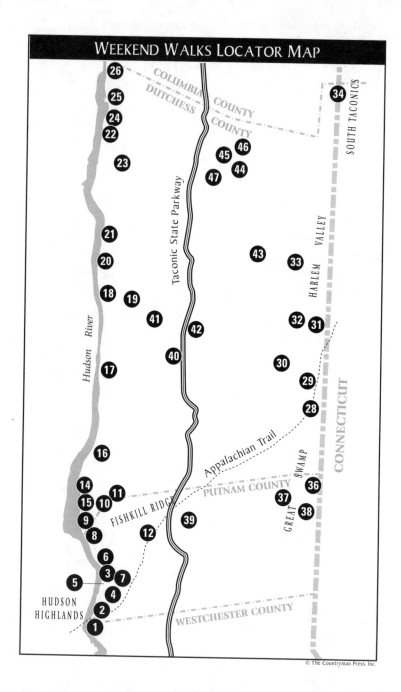

Weekend Walks Locator Map

Contents

The Hudson Highlands / 19

Millionaires' Row / 109

The Harlem Valley and the South Taconics / 193

The Inland Hills / 239

Introduction

I grew up in the Hudson Valley, in northern Westchester close to the Putnam County line, on top of a high hill. Our house was on a dirt road with one neighbor across the street—an old Italian couple—who had terraced their five acres and lived off their own vegetable plots, putting up tomatoes, green beans, and peppers in canning jars for the winter. There was a dairy farm at the bottom of the hill. Every now and then the black-and-white cows would break through the barbed wire fence and come walking up the hill on the road, udders swinging. It was all woods until my parents' house, and there they'd lie down on our lawn to chew their cud. My mother would ring the farm to come get their cows. The nearest store was in the next town. Every Sunday my father would drive there for the newspaper and fresh rolls and crumb buns. A local freight train ran in the valley, and you could see it from my backyard. My mother recalls one of the early words I learned was "caboose."

I spent most of my free time every day roaming over hundreds of acres of woods and fields, streams and marshes with the family dog. The older I got, the farther I explored. Yes, there were some houses, but mostly it was unoccupied land. I learned most of my natural history from the land itself, by observing and exploring. It was such fun! When I tell folks this story they find it peculiar, but I thought it was normal. All I had to do was run out the back door, across the lawn, and there the old trail started down the knoll into the woods. There were stone walls to walk atop, paths that led to more paths and old woods roads, and all sorts of foundations, collapsed farm buildings, and white, pitted bones of long-dead cows among the grasses.

I'm not all that old, but I've finally lived long enough to notice that the natural systems I grew up with have changed, along with the freedom to roam where one will across a natural landscape. Thank goodness for parks! And for the individuals and organizations that preserve them for us!

This book is a short guide to places where you and your children can roam and explore. I've had even more fun walking all the parks a second time for this second edition. In the fifteen years since this book first came out, thousands more acres have been set aside as parkland. Dutchess and Putnam are two of the state's fastest growing counties, with more housing and industrial development, more pollution, more agricultural abandonment, and just plain more people. That dirt road I grew up on is long since paved, and the high hill is covered with houses. That farm at the bottom of the hill is a housing development. Even the natural places themselves have changed. The forests and wetlands continued along the passage of eastern woodland succession. From my childhood backyard, I can no longer see the valley floor where a rail trail now runs along the old freight line, because the forest grew back. That's only natural, but other changes came as shocks. The stunning hemlocks, one of the hallmarks of the region, are being destroyed by an alien insect, the woolly adelgid, just as is happening up and down the entire East Coast. Zebra mussels from Eurasia, introduced to the Hudson River, are changing the entire estuarine ecology.

Things change. It's only natural. Not only do the signs of these changes remain with the landscape, but also the appearance of the natural systems is the *result* of past changes. Look at a section of woods, a mountainside, a plot of plants, a pond, and in that glance you can read its history and, to a certain extent, its future. Now that's fun!

As you explore, here are a few things to keep in mind.

Putnam and Dutchess Counties

Dutchess and Putnam were once one county. They split in 1812 along a seemingly natural separation, perhaps suggested by the old patent lines. Putnam County is all hills: the cordillera of the Appalachian Mountains known as the Hudson Highlands (in their larger sense), the ridges like fish backs running southwest to northeast. It's a tight fit, living in Putnam

County. Narrow roads snake around, up, and over endless knolls, ravines, and hills, and every tenth or so homeowner, it sometimes seems, has at one time or another dammed the little highland brook in the backyard to create a pond. Reservoirs of New York City's drinking water system also abound.

More diverse, Dutchess County, to the north, contains north-south tending Appalachian ridges, some quite high, but there are also broad, flat valleys, lowlands, even plains.

Putnam County is nearly all metamorphic, resistant, Hudson Highlands Precambrian granite and gneiss. Again more diverse, Dutchess contains schist and sedimentary limestones, sandstones, shales, and slates of various ages.

Both counties lie within the eastern deciduous woodlands biome of North America. Certain plant communities are, to some extent, predictable according to soil type. On the slopes one expects to find oak and sugar maple forests; in the cool ravines, hemlocks; in the swamps grow red maple, ash, and elm; and in the marshes, cattail and phragmites. "Expect," however, may be too strong a word. It seems any time you establish a "rule" in ecosystems, exceptions to that rule abound. Natural communities are still far too complex and unpredictable for the dismissal of human description.

It is the Hudson River—not actually a river here but a tidal estuary—that sets these two counties apart as special among eastern woodlands. The region is rich in flora and fauna as well as recreational, industrial, historical, and aesthetic resources. Putnam County contains practically *all* of the world-famous, river-hugging Hudson Highlands of the east bank. Dutchess County contains almost *all* of Millionaires' Row, the estates of America's early industrialists.

Poison Ivy

The Hudson Valley is famous for its poison ivy *(Rhus radicans)*. Nowhere else does the soil, humidity, and temperature combine for such excellent and luxuriant results. Expect it in the parks you walk. Learn the plant.

Avoid it. And be glad it grows. Poison ivy berries, white and ripe by fall, are a major food source for over sixty species of birds as well as for deer, black bear, mice, rabbit, muskrat, and fox. It keeps them alive. Can you imagine, *eating poison ivy berries?*

Mosquitoes

When Swedish naturalist Peter Kalm visited the Hudson Valley in 1749, he wrote in his journal, "I never saw the mosquitoes more plentiful in any part of America than they are here." He was specifically describing the upper Hudson, but we get our fair share here in the mid-Hudson.

Especially in the lowland (but not the highland) parks that border the Hudson River, expect a summer nightmare of mosquitoes when temperature and rainfall lead to a big hatching. You may want to save those parks for some other time of year.

Bushwhacking

Trails buffer the walker from the woods. Though a great convenience, trails prevent a true experience of the habitat they pass. Once you are used to trails and become more experienced in the woods, try bushwhacking now and then.

A bushwhack is the best way to see the woods. For instance, it's one thing to walk through a laurel thicket on a trail, another to bushwhack through it. Bushwhacking through a laurel thicket will open your woodland heart and eyes. You'll know mountain laurel to the core of its ecology and gain a deeper understanding of its relationships with its environment, even though you curse and call the thicket a laurel hell. Bushwhacking will lead you to intimate groves and deep hollows that will be all your own.

Some preserves require that you keep to trails since they funnel compaction and minimize damage. Many of these parks contain rare or endangered plants and animals. Even a little trampling in the wrong spot can be devastating. At sites where you know the flora is fragile, such as on top of mountains or steep shorelines, never bushwhack. But on forested slopes with thicker soils, fields, and in valleys, with care and attention to footwork, the walker can bushwhack occasionally with little harm to the soil and flora. New York State Forests are prime bushwhack territory, as is the vast landscape of Clarence Fahnestock Memorial State Park. Make it a habit to step between plants, not on them. Duck beneath branches rather than break them. So long as you do not visit the same site regularly, there should be little disturbance to wildlife. However, if you find yourself near a hawk or owl nest, quit the area.

Lyme Disease

Adult and nymph deer ticks are tiny creatures, often no larger than the dot over this "i." A high percentage of deer ticks are infected with the spirochete that causes Lyme and three other diseases. If you are bitten, gently remove the tick whole and intact, and ask your doctor for a two-week antibiotic prescription. Left to run its course, Lyme disease can cripple you.

Prevention is the best cure. Spray your shoes, socks, and lower pant legs with a pesticide containing DEET. After a walk, check your body for ticks.

Hunting Season

If you walk in a state forest during hunting season use extreme caution and wear bright orange clothing.

Trail Conditions

Trails change, boundaries move, once abundant plants and animals can disappear. There is much "here today, gone tomorrow" in any ecosystem. If you find a change in things as described in this book, write and let me know. If you do not find one of the plant species noted in a chapter, keep an eye out for it elsewhere; sooner or later you will come across it in your travels where conditions match those described in the chapter.

Be prepared and equipped when you enter a park, especially on a full-day hike. In a light pack, take food, water, a trail map, compass, and extra clothes. Carry rain gear if the weather is questionable. Wear sturdy hiking shoes or boots. Remember that high, exposed places such as Brace Mountain, South Beacon Mountain, and Anthony's Nose can be much colder than the surrounding lowlands. A warm spring or autumn day in the valley may become a cold, windy, raw day on the mountaintop. In both these seasons, carry a hat and gloves. Also be aware that the same day's weather in northern Dutchess County can be different from that in Putnam or southern Dutchess counties.

Many people prefer to hike the high hills when the leaves are down, the better to see the views. This is especially true of places like Hell Hollow in the Fishkill Ridge Conservation Area, which is at its best when the cold and the wind make things dramatic. There also aren't any bugs.

For each park, I have noted the route distance and approximate walking time. This is my own walking time, which allows for plenty of exploring and stops for scenic admiration. Should you gallop through, you can complete these walks in shorter time.

Remember not to smoke when you hike and never to litter. Please, take good care of our parks.

Trail maintenance crews stack small logs or branches across trails to indicate the paths are closed or undesirable. So long as you are on a well-blazed trail, you are safe from trespassing. Otherwise, respect "posted" signs.

The Hudson Highlands

Deepened by glaciers, the flooded Hudson River gorge is a true fjord (a tongue of the ocean) reaching inland clear to Troy. For 15 miles, the Hudson River breaches the Appalachian Mountains. From the North Gate at Storm King and Breakneck Ridge (truly a gate, the old Wey Gat or Wind Gate, where the river flows into a narrow gorge) to the South Gate at Dunderberg and Manitou Mountain, the river narrows and twists past the Hudson Highlands, the eroded roots of high mountains formed 200 million years ago. Wecquehacki, the indigenous Lenape called these highlands, which in both the Unami and Munsee dialects translates as "end of the land."

What a remarkable river: an estuary, a gigantic riparian ecotone between salt- and freshwater and terrestrial habitats, rich, adorned with mountains. Enter through one of the gates in a sailing ship, and instantly feel the Highland's infamously treacherous winds. The Hudson runs at its deepest here, up to 200 feet deep.

Ecologically, the Highlands are the heart of the Hudson Valley. Here is a major divide between northern and southern ecosystems of the eastern woodlands. North-facing slopes and shady ravines are suitable for northern birds such as Blackburnian warbler, Canada warbler, and brown creeper. Southern birds such as fish crow, cardinal, mockingbird, blue-gray gnatcatcher, tufted titmouse, and turkey vulture are near the northern limit of their ranges, as are opossum, fence lizard, and eastern minnow. Goshawk and golden-winged warbler, birds of the north, are near the southern limits of their ranges. Prickly pear cactus grows on dry sunny outcrops, while glacial relicts such as tundra bog moss and subarctic black spruce grow on top of the heights, at the southern limit of their ranges.

The river channel through the Highlands is deep and turbulent. Strong currents wash over the rocky bottom. This deep channel is the major spawning area for Hudson River striped bass. The only other such area on the east coast of the United States is in Chesapeake Bay. Half of the year, during spring and early summer, the Highlands stretch is fresh water. Come late summer, salt water intrudes in a wedge shape upstream. At different times of year either freshwater, anadromous, or marine fishes are found here, or all of them at once.

The Hudson River and its Highlands have been a catalyst, even a cause, of some of America's most important historical events. For ten thousand years, this wild, beautiful, bountiful land was the home of an indigenous people who developed a culture that was married to the landscape. The misunderstandings, intermarriages, and genocidal wars here between Natives and Europeans were typical of the early colonial period. This river and these hills were the geographical pivot of the American Revolution. Almost one-third of Revolutionary War battles were fought on or near the Hudson River. Inaccessible and stony, the Highlands were left unsettled for centuries while Europeans clear-cut the lowlands for agriculture.

Then came the industrial age. Mining and quarrying blasted Breakneck Ridge, Anthony's Nose, and Bull Hill. Railroads were built on both banks. Storm King Highway was blasted into the face of Storm King Mountain.

In turn, a new appreciation for nature found expression in the Romanticism of the Hudson River school of painters and artists, which made the Highlands and the river famous throughout the world. Preservationists vied with industrialists. The American park and preservation movement began in the Hudson Valley with the crusade to save the Palisades from the quarrymen. Thus was inspired the national park system, the model for national parks around the globe. The battle to save Storm King from Consolidated Edison started the national environmental movement. And Sloop Clearwater's battle to save the Hudson River initiated America's search for clean water.

There are those who linger in the old view of the Hudson as an open sewer hopelessly contaminated with PCBs, used only by trains and ships. People stare at me when I say I swim in the river. But with organizations such as the Open Space Institute, Scenic Hudson, the Nature Conservancy, and the Hudson Valley Greenway Commission, along with concerned cities and citizens, the Hudson is now guarded and triple-warded with concern and care. It's time to patch up past damage done, preserve what we have before it is lost, and plan for careful development. The river is busier than ever with recreational boaters. And, on every weekend, the shoulders of NY 9D are lined with parked cars, hundreds of cars. Hikers go up into the Hudson Highlands to explore and weave kinship with the landscape upon which they live.

1 · Anthony's Nose

Location: Bear Mountain Bridge
Distance: From NY 9D: 2.5 miles, 2 to 3 hours; from
   South Mountain Pass Road: 4 miles, 3 hours
Owner: State of New York, part of Hudson Highlands
   State Park

Anthony's Nose straddles the Putnam-Westchester county line. There are two approaches in Putnam, one murderously steep but short, the other longer and steep but at least less so. Either way you'll need a couple of hours to complete our walk. From the summit, the entire stretch of the Hudson Highlands is visible. In autumn, Anthony's Nose is one of the best lookouts along the Hudson flyway for migrating hawks.

A mountain named for someone's schnozzle has given rise to all sorts of nonsense as to the origin of the name Anthony's Nose. The mountain was already so named in the 1697 deed that described the north boundary of Van Cortlandt Manor. Washington Irving wrote how the sun shone off the great nose of Peter Stuyvesant's trumpeter, Anthony von Corlear, and shot "hissing hot" into the water where it killed a sturgeon sporting beside Anthony's vessel. From the father of tall tales, we expect such stuff, but others insist Anthony's Nose is named for St. Anthony, or for an old Dutch Hudson River captain with a mighty honker. Historian and engraver Benson Lossing had it right when he wrote, "the true origin of the name of this promontory is unknown."

Access

For the steep way, park in pull-offs along NY 9D immediately north of the Bear Mountain Bridge on either side of the road. For the less steep but

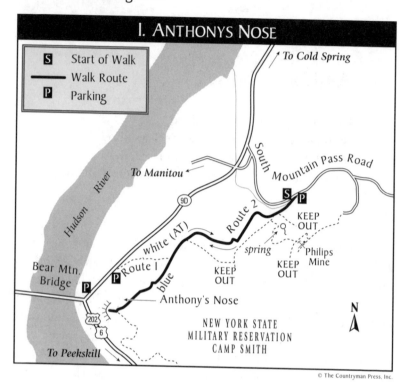

I. ANTHONYS NOSE

S Start of Walk
— Walk Route
P Parking

To Cold Spring

To Manitou

South Mountain Pass Road

9D

Route 2

S P

KEEP OUT

spring

Philips Mine

white (AT)

KEEP OUT

KEEP OUT

Hudson River

Bear Mtn. Bridge

P

P Route 1

blue

Anthony's Nose

202 6

To Peekskill

NEW YORK STATE
MILITARY RESERVATION
CAMP SMITH

N

© The Countryman Press, Inc.

longer route, from the Garrison stoplight at NY 9D and Putnam County 403, travel 2.9 miles south on NY 9D to a left onto South Mountain Pass Road. Drive 0.6 mile to parking in pull-offs. Dogs are allowed. Information: Fahnestock State Park headquarters, 845-225-7207.

Trail

No matter what your route, begin with a walk out onto Bear Mountain Bridge via the pedestrian walkway. Sugarloaf stands upriver and all the Highlands spread out to the North Gate and South Beacon Mountain. Downriver is Peekskill Bay and the South Gate. Opposite is Popolopen Gorge, Bear Mountain, and Iona Island. And behind rises the steep rock face of 900-foot-high Anthony's Nose.

An unmarked trail leads down to the river right to where the First Great Chain—the Revolution's first defense against the British sailing north from New York City—was attached. Listen for predatory screams of *ke-ree, ke-ree* and you may see one of the peregrine falcons that nest in the bridge tower, small and swift, with pointed wings and dark-hooded heads. These are the fastest animals in the world.

If going for the steep path, from the bridge walk north on NY 9D to the road sign for the Appalachian Trail (AT), where the white blazes begin on the right, up stone stairs. Climb steeply, angling north through xeric (extremely well-drained or dry soil) chestnut oak and mountain laurel. You will meet the wide old military road marked in blue blazes. Turn right. The walk from here is nearly level. Pass a woodland pool, and you are soon at the summit.

From South Mountain Pass Road, the Appalachian Trail begins as a level, old, military trail practically paved in Hudson Highlands granite pebbles. Follow the white blazes as the AT uses footpaths and other old logging and mining roads as it leads up and over knolls, past other military trails, and along the crest of the ridge until it finally runs into the blue trail on the left. Sign in at the register. Some of the comments from hikers can be amusing, such as the suggestion to "Make the trail flat." Climb the blue trail to the summit, which is actually just before the road ends. Watch for a herd path on the right that leads past the cement foundation of a tower long gone, where there are benchmarks. Continue to a bedrock outcrop with an 1852 benchmark. Here is a view upriver.

At the end of the blue trail turn right for the cliff edge and the view. The Hudson River bends around Anthony's Nose in a triangular-faceted way. Before the Pleistocene Epoch, the river ran on the west side of Iona Island. See the old channel, where the Timp Brook curls through Salisbury Meadow? Originally, Anthony's Nose was a wider mountain. Iona Island was the foot of its slope. But there was a notch on the slope of Anthony's Nose. The most recent glacier severely eroded this notch and sheared off the foot of the mountain. Into this new channel the Hudson flowed, past an Anthony's Nose with a new look: triangular, known as a truncated spur.

Upriver, the glacier gouged out the sides and bottom of the Hudson, creating a deep gorge hundreds of feet below sea level. The Bear Mountain Inn sits on a terrace that was the bed of the ancient Hudson River when it flowed in its old channel. Glaciation hollowed out the terrace where Hessian Lake now glints in the sun.

When the glaciers melted, the sea level rose, flooding the Hudson gorge and creating a true fjord. The only other fjord in the eastern United States is Somes Sound outside Acadia National Park in Maine.

Between Bear Mountain and Anthony's Nose, the Hudson River is up to 165 feet deep and is almost its narrowest: three-eighths of a mile wide. This is the deep and swift tidal Devil's Horse Race, or Horse Race, or simply the Race, the fastest and most dangerous section of the river for sail navigation, also known to skippers as the Crescent or Cook's Reach because of its crescent curve around Anthony's Nose.

The wind on top is strong as you survey a panorama that includes New York City, Croton Point, and Haverstraw and Peekskill Bays, clear up the entire range of the Highlands. There is Manitou, a tiny village squeezed between the river and the railroad. Look what a huge mountain Bear Mountain is. Directly opposite, just north of Bear Mountain Bridge, is Popolopen Gorge.

In 1777, on the south side of Popolopen Gorge, stood Fort Clinton. On the north side stood Fort Montgomery. American generals George and James Clinton, brothers, commanded the forts and redoubts. The First Great Chain was a raft of floating logs that supported a chain of huge iron links stretching from Fort Montgomery to Anthony's Nose. There were also log booms set out ahead of the Great Chain. Impenetrable, surely. Five various ships rode at anchor above the chain. With two forts, two brothers, two frigates, two galleys, a sloop, and a Great Chain, let the British just try to get through!

Sir Henry Clinton, second-in-command of His Majesty's troops in New York (no relation to the brothers Clinton, nor had he yet earned the title "Sir"), wanted the Hudson River. He knew, and George Washington knew, that with this key valley the British could split the American colonies in

The Hudson River flows out of South Gate into Peekskill Bay. That's Dunderberg Mountain across the river from the rocky, xeric oak slope of Anthony's Nose.

two, and finish them off. Whoever controlled the Hudson River controlled America, and the Revolution. Sir Henry Clinton sailed with his fleet from British-held New York City. He landed two thousand men near Peek's Kill in a feint on General Israel Putnam's Fort Independence on the south slope of Anthony's Nose. It worked like a charm. Putnam sent most of his forces to the attack. The fog came in. Under cover, Clinton crossed the Hudson and landed two thousand more men just south of Dunderberg. They split into two groups, one for each brother's fort. One group crept over Dunderberg as the other snuck through Timp Pass. At Lake Sinnipink, one group met Fort Clinton's picket guard and a detachment of rebels. The fight was bloody. When it was done, the British had won. They threw the bodies into the waters of Lake Sinnipink, so many bodies that the lake turned red with blood. Since then it's been called both Bloody Pond and Hessian Lake.

Sir Henry Clinton's Hessians continued toward Forts Clinton and Montgomery. When their main commander was killed, Beverly Robinson (see Arden Point chapter) took command of one section. By now, the Clinton brothers knew they were in for it. They were outnumbered, and their forts, vulnerable from the rear, fell to the British. The brothers escaped. George Clinton slid on the seat of his pants down the steep slope from the fort to a boat on the river. James, bayoneted in the thigh, escaped into the hills. The British climbed down the cliffs to the Great Chain and destroyed it, breaking up the wood rafts and sending the chain to the bottom of the Hudson. Some of the dredged links can be seen in various museums today. The two rebel frigates stationed above, along with the two galleys and the armed sloop, gave battle until the loss of the forts, then they turned upriver to flee. But the tide was on the ebb, and the wind too weak to sail. Only the galley Lady Washington managed to escape. The others were either run aground or, to keep them from British hands, set afire as the rebels jumped into the river.

Triumphant, Henry Clinton sailed up the Hudson. He planned to sail clear to Albany, where he would meet General Burgoyne coming south from Canada and, together, they would secure the Hudson corridor and the north. But, frustratingly, Clinton was recalled to New York City. He sent the good news of his success to Burgoyne written on a slip of paper concealed within a hollow silver bullet in the hands of a spy. And he sent his armada under one of his officers to sail upriver, burning and looting to Poughkeepsie, then on to the state capital at Kingston where they burned "that nest of rebels" to the ground. Then on to Clermont, likewise burning it to ashes. Just started on his way, the spy was stopped by some soldiers in red coats and, confused, he asked to be shown to General Clinton. If you're confused by the plethora of Clintons, imagine the poor spy when he was shown not to Henry Clinton but to one of the American rebels Clinton! As for the reaving British fleet, they took too long. Benedict Arnold saved the day at the Battle of Saratoga. Burgoyne surrendered, and the fleet had nothing to do but return to New York City. The Hudson River, the key to the colonies and to the war, was left to the rebels. After this near disaster, George Washington reprimanded General Israel Putnam, reminding him of the importance of the Hudson Highlands and to see to their better fortification and defense.

On top of Anthony's Nose you can see all these places laid out like a map: Dunderberg, the distinctive hump of The Timp, the notch of Timp Pass, Hessian Lake, and the sites of the forts on either side of Popolopen Gorge.

In autumn, stand at the top of Anthony's Nose to watch the hawks. Down the ancient flypath of the Hudson Valley they zoom. The broad-winged hawks travel in large flocks that soar in a tight boiling pattern. Single falcons and accipiters shoot overhead. Bald eagles winter at Iona Island where the Hudson remains ice free and they can continue to hunt for fish.

Iona Island, used by Native Americans since as early as 3500 B.C., once a resort and then a military camp, now is the Doodletown Bird Conservation Area. You are likely to spot bald eagles here in winter. At Iona Island the sea breeze stops. This is about as far inland as the mediating influence of the Atlantic Ocean reaches and is the dividing line between north and south ecosystems. South of Iona Island, the annual mean temperature is higher. Only 14 miles north of Iona at Newburgh, spring comes two weeks later. South of Iona grow southern arrowwood and oblong fruited pinweed. North grows striped maple.

Back at the military road, the blue-blazed Camp Smith Trail continues southward for 3 miles into Westchester County. There are many other trails to explore if you are headed back to South Mountain Pass, such as a trip to elusive Philips Mine. Most of the old woods roads are not marked and it is easy to get lost. Also, take care not to trespass onto National Guard property, which is actively used for military training. Trespassers may be in danger and are subject to arrest.

Philips Mine

Philip Philipse was the great-nephew of Adolph, the first patent owner of today's Putnam County, sibling to Susannah and Mary who were banished from America for their Tory leanings. His sisters and ultimately the new state of New York inherited Adolph's lands, while Philip got only the mining rights. Peter Hasenclever of Bear Mountain–Harriman State Park fame opened this mine in 1767 looking for iron ore, but the sulfur content was too high. The ore was mined for a sulfur plant located in the hamlet of Manitou during the late 1800s and early 1900s.

Finding your way here is a challenge along numerous unmarked old military trails and footpaths. Attempt this only if you are an experienced map reader. Respect private property. Be careful not to stray into Camp Smith Military Reservation. And of course respect the fence that keeps people out of the mine; anyone falling in that gaping maw with its cold breath will not come out again. Of interest are the tailings dumped from the mine; the rocks are all yellow and rusted, those laden with ore heavy in the hand.

Side Trip of Historical Interest

Fort Montgomery has been preserved as a ruin within Fort Montgomery State Historic Site. There are walking trails throughout with excellent displays and descriptions of the 1777 battle. Drive over the Bear Mountain Bridge. At the traffic circle, keep right for NY 9W north. The park will be on the right. Parking is 0.2 mile farther on the right.

2 · Manitou Point Preserve

Location: Manitou
Distance: 1.5 miles, 2 hours
Owner: Scenic Hudson and Open Space Institute

The Open Space Institute and Scenic Hudson bought what was known as Mystery Point. They leased the mansion and property to Outward Bound for their national headquarters. By this arrangement, the bulk of the property is a nature preserve open to the public. Mystery Point was renamed Manitou Point. Manitou is pure Native American. The word means "spirit" or "deity" in most all the Algonquian languages (which make up about two-thirds of the Native peoples of North America), including in the local Mahikan and Lenape languages. Manitou is a catchall phrase loosely and variously applied to many religious things, since in native culture "spirit" is inherent in all aspects of the ecosystem and in everyday life: spirit of human beings, spirit of stone, spirit of animal, spirit of plant, as well as the higher spirits of Our Elder Brothers the Sun and the Thunder Beings and, highest of all, He Who Creates All of Us With His Thoughts. These are just a few.

A new public place, Manitou Point is wild looking and little used, the trails fresh with untrammeled plants. It is not a completely quiet place, since trains pass nearby regularly, and some of the views across the river are of unrestrained development. Even so, the best part is the cliff walk along the Hudson River.

Access

From Bear Mountain Bridge, drive north on NY 9D 1.8 miles to a left onto Mystery Point Road. From Garrison, drive south on NY 9D 2.6 miles to a

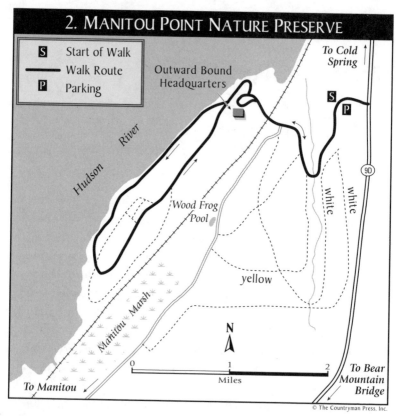

2. MANITOU POINT NATURE PRESERVE

S Start of Walk
— Walk Route
P Parking

Outward Bound
Headquarters

To Cold Spring

Hudson River

Wood Frog Pool

white

white

90

yellow

N

0   1   2
Miles

To Manitou

To Bear Mountain Bridge

© The Countryman Press, Inc.

right onto Mystery Point Road. There will be a sign for Outward Bound USA. Drive in; parking is on the left. Dogs allowed on leash. Note: Outward Bound buildings closed to the public. Information: 845-473-4440 or visit www.scenichudson.org.

Trail

Pick up a trail map at the kiosk. Trails lead from the parking lot, but what was once a stunning hemlock forest is now dead and dying, being replaced by ironwood, sugar maple, and red oak, home to the hooded warbler, the great crested flycatcher, and the Louisiana waterthrush. Explore these areas if you wish, or head on down the road for the river.

Go all the way to the mansion (closed to the public) and take the right fork in the driveway. When you are opposite the mansion's front door, take the trail on the right. This brings you to a phenomenal view of the Highlands, looking from right to left, of the pointy mountain Sugarloaf and West Point's gray towers with Crow's Nest and Storm King in the distance behind. Opposite you on the other side of the river is a long rocky hill called Bare Rock Mountain, and another point slightly north with marsh, headland, and green buoy. That is Con Hook. Green buoys tell ships to pass them on the ship's port or left side. To the right of the buoy the channel drops to 87 feet deep, but the buoy itself marks seven feet of water over a rocky bottom. The Highland section of the Hudson is especially treacherous for modern ships unfamiliar with the sudden twists and turns, obstructions such as Con Hook, the shifting sandbars, flats, and the currents, especially in a fog or a stiff wind. This is why taking on a local pilot familiar with the river is so important. At the shore find red cedar or juniper and northern white cedars, sometimes misidentified as Atlantic white cedars.

Follow the path. At the fork choose the river-hugging footpath on the right. This fabulous rocky headland trail looks similar to the white trail

Red and northern white cedars frame a view upriver of the distinctive cone of Sugarloaf.

at Mills-Norrie State Park far to the north in Staatsburg, but since it's lesser known it's in better shape. White pine, hemlock, pitch pine, mixed deciduous trees, mountain laurel, and lowbush blueberry grow in a xeric or dry-soil environment, even though the Hudson River's water is only yards away. Vibrant green mosses carpet the ground. The delicate, flat groundcover is partridgeberry, each oval green leaf with a white vein down its center. And there's wintergreen, the small evergreen herb of the north that tastes of its name.

Before reaching the point's end, the trail strikes inland and meets the woods road. If you are visiting when the leaves are down, you may wish to continue on the white trail. There are views through the trees of Bear Mountain, Anthony's Nose, and the village of Manitou. Manitou Marsh stands blond with Asiatic phragmites reeds much of the year, green only in summer. Return to the mansion via the woods road, then back up the entrance road.

If you are a student of history who reads the landscape for clues of the past, or, in the spring, if you've come to see the wood frogs singing, then after crossing the railroad tracks turn right on the dirt road. Just past the old brick carriage house on the right is a low stone structure with a cement roof. Inside, three cisterns are sunk into the edge of the swampland, thus intersecting the water table and filling with clear water for drinking. When in use, these would have been kept clean of leaves and sticks. For the past few hundred years, most farms and estates used cisterns for their drinking water. The poorer farmsteads of the Hudson Valley would have had something simpler, perhaps one cistern with a board for a roof, or no roof at all.

For early spring frogs, continue along the road. Before the ruins of the oxen barn, you'll pass a pool on your right frequented by wood frogs and peepers. They are alert to the passage of humans on the road and may fall quiet. If you approach the pool they will dive out of sight, but simply follow the steps described in the Clarence Fahnestock Memorial State Park chapter, and you'll get to see them up close. If you continue to follow the dirt road it will lead you all the way to the riverside hamlet of Manitou.

3 · Philipstown Park

Location: Garrison
Distance: Less than half a mile, 30- to 45-minute leisurely stroll
Owner: Town of Philipstown

This park provides the only public view, short of climbing a nearby mountain, of dramatic World's End from the east bank of the Hudson. Even if you do climb a mountain, this big S-curve in the river as it rounds West Point and Constitution Island is often hidden in a fold of the land. But, unless the view at this park is maintained it will soon be possible to see only when the leaves are off the trees. Also at this park, Philipse Brook dramatically waterfalls through a steep ravine to meet the Hudson.

Access

From the stoplight at Putnam County 301 in Cold Spring, take NY 9D south for 2.9 miles. The park is on your right on a blind curve just after the Hastings Center. Open 8 AM to dusk from mid-spring to fall only. No dogs allowed. Information: 845-424-4618.

Trail

Go left to the southwest corner of the parking lot for the Trail of Trees, past soccer fields, straight down a lane of trees headed for the Hudson River. On the left grows a white pine plantation. On the right stands a row of red pine and larch, also called tamarack, a conifer whose soft needles turn gold in autumn and fall just like a deciduous tree's. Some days you can hear the West Point Military Academy band playing on West Point's parade

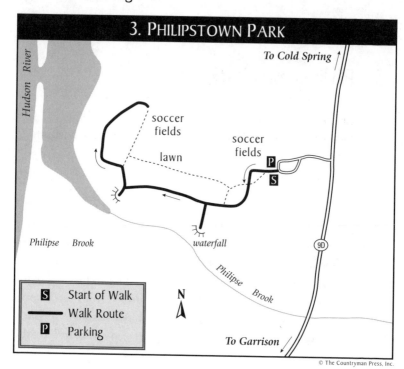

3. PHILIPSTOWN PARK

Hudson River

To Cold Spring

soccer
fields

soccer
fields

lawn

P

S

Philipse   Brook

waterfall

9D

Philipse   Brook

N

S — Start of Walk
— Walk Route
P — Parking

To Garrison

© The Countryman Press, Inc.

ground across the river. At the end of the lane turn left to follow the field edge toward the basketball court. Where a black fence on top of the ravine wall ends find the unmarked footpath that leads down into the ravine.

Towering tulip trees and mixed deciduous woods with moosewood and dying hemlocks populate the ravine wall. Skunk cabbage and spicebush mark areas of wet soil. Shortly, a side trail leads left to a view of the splendid waterfalls, best in spring. Do not go down the bank to the stream at the falls; such trampling causes soil compaction and erodes the bank, causing severe damage. Return to the main trail and follow to a bedrock outcrop that overlooks the brook's mouth. You can see part of the Military Academy, especially Trophy Point, famous for its view across World's End.

From here, a rough footpath follows the brink of the river bluff while another fork goes right to return to the lawn areas. Pass glacial erratics

Tulip trees

(boulders). The view of World's End will be through the trees, with Crow's Nest behind it, Constitution Island on the opposite shore, and the Highland hills all around. Constitution Marsh is to the right with Bull Hill behind it. Across World's End was strung the Second Great Chain during the Revolution. Links from it can still be seen at Trophy Point.

The trail leads uphill and doubles back. Head left on a side trail into the soccer field, follow along the field edge, and you'll get another Highland view. The yellow house is private property; please respect its boundaries as marked across the lawn. Make your way across the playing fields to a bench where the view of the hills is even better.

4 · Sugarloaf

Location: Garrison
Distance: 1.5 miles, 2 to 3 hours
Owner: State of New York, part of Hudson Highlands State
Park

Smack in the center of Revolutionary War history stands Sugarloaf
Mountain. Tales swarm thick around this hill. Benedict Arnold
betrayed his country at Sugarloaf's foot. George Washington breakfasted
often with his staff in its early morning shadow. Heart of the Highlands,
the mountain is practically divided along a dotted line into north and
south vegetation due to a change in microclimate, a microcosm of the
Highlands themselves as a continental biome divide. Sugarloaf was
named by the Dutch colonials who likened its pyramid shape, as seen
from the south by someone coming upriver in a boat (or by a hiker walking across Bear Mountain Bridge), to an old-fashioned loaf of sugar—a
suycker broodt, hung by a string in the center of Dutch household tables.

Just the right length for an afternoon's walk.

Access

Park at Castle Rock Unique Area. Just south of the intersection of NY 9D
and Putnam County 403 is a country club. Opposite the green are fields.
A castle with slanting red roofs stands atop the ridge. Watch the stone wall
that lines the east/left side of the highway for the state sign for Castle
Rock. Drive in through two stone pillars; one says "Wing & Wing 1857,"
the other "Castlerock 1881." Follow signs for parking in the designated
area behind the red barns. Dogs are allowed. Information: for Castle Rock

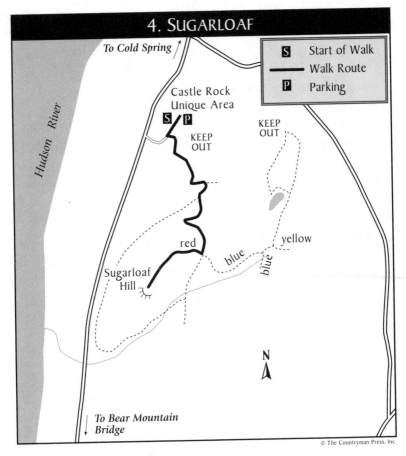

4. SUGARLOAF

To Cold Spring

S Start of Walk
— Walk Route
P Parking

Castle Rock
Unique Area

S **P**

KEEP
OUT

KEEP
OUT

Hudson River

red

blue

blue

yellow

Sugarloaf
Hill

N

*To Bear Mountain
Bridge*

© The Countryman Press, Inc.

Unique Area, Department of Environmental Conservation at Stony Kill
Farm, 845-831-8780; for Sugarloaf proper phone Fahnestock State Park
headquarters, 845-225-7207.

Trail

Walk back the way you drove. At the first fork turn left. At the gate and sign
for "Wing and Wing" turn right. This name comes from the original farmhouse, which was purchased in 1855 and enlarged many times with addi-
tions until it became a castle with thirty-four rooms.

It is important to keep in mind that the castle, the winding entrance road, and the land immediately around the castle are private property. Built in 1881 by the first William Henry Osborn, president of Illinois Central Railroad, Castlerock (the name for the house itself is one word) housed five generations of Osborns in the focal point of a 2,500-acre estate. In the 1970s, the property was offered in parcels on the real estate market. The contents of the mansion were auctioned off. New York State expressed interest but, in the end, the castle itself remained in Osborn family hands. The Osborns donated the bulk of the properties to the state, a priceless gift for the public. Castle Rock Unique Area is a small portion of what the state acquired, the rest being the adjacent 1,371-acre Osborn Preserve portion of Hudson Highlands State Park, which extends from Castle Rock south, including Sugarloaf, to the slopes of Anthony's Nose. The Appalachian Trail follows the ridgeline along Osborn Preserve's hills. Our trail to Sugarloaf links up with that system, including the trails at Manitoga Preserve, so you can make a longer hike if you wish.

The hiking trail begins on the left with a walk through fields straight back toward the woods of Castle Rock and a cedar gazebo where you can take your ease. The huge view back the way you came shows the gray towers and turrets of West Point, Crow's Nest to the left, Breakneck Ridge, Bull Hill, and the Fishkill Ridge hills to the right. On a clear day the tilted ridge of the Shawangunks show blue on the horizon over the Wind Gate.

Facing the gazebo, turn right toward Sugarloaf on the red trail and follow as it turns left and uphill alongside the highland brook. Once, this was a hemlock-clad slope. Now, the hemlock giants lie dead on the forest floor, killed by the woolly adelgid insect infestation. At the T-intersection turn right, then shortly bear left, still following the red trail. The entire character of Osborn Preserve and Castle Rock has changed from a shadowed hemlock landscape to an open deciduous woods. Moosewood, also called striped maple, grows thick in the new sunny openings among the fallen hemlock trunks. It is moosewood's place or niche to close gaps in the forest, but it is usually only seen in cooler climates to the north. Putnam County lies at this tree's southern limit. In warmer spots in Dutchess County, and in

Viewed from the south, Sugarloaf forms a perfect cone in silhouette.

points south of Putnam County, black birch is the closer of such gaps. The cool microclimate of the north slope of Sugarloaf fosters more northerly conditions. Moosewood grows here as vigorously as in the Adirondacks.

The trail switchbacks up Sugarloaf's flank, and you get good views through the trees when the leaves are down. You can see the sharp bend the river makes around West Point called World's End, where the Second Great Chain was stretched during the American Revolution (see Arden Point chapter). Pass a man-made pond on the left. Step to the shore to spook the spotted newts and tadpoles so numerous the water will writhe. Shortly, you'll arrive at a four-way intersection with the blue trail (if you come to another cedar gazebo, you've gone too far). Turn right on the red trail to steeply climb the mountain.

Pass chunks of Hudson Highlands granite stained here and there with rust that marks the historically desirable iron magnetite. The trail follows what was once an ecotone: to the right, hemlock; to the left, sugar maple and oak. The annual mean microclimate changes just enough to support totally different forests on the cooler, moister, river-facing, northwest slope and the warmer, inland-facing, southeast slope. With the fall of hemlock, that line will become invisible. Yet, since the microclimate will persist, what vegetation will the future foster?

The trail reaches the summit, but trees block the view. Follow along the narrow arêtelike crest. At nearby Fort Hill, two of the many Hudson River Revolutionary War cannon redoubts were kept. General Israel Putnam's men evidently became bored when the British stayed away. One day they rolled a boulder off the top of Sugarloaf and with glee watched it crash down the mountain, crushing huge trees. They claimed it landed in the river, and they named it for their general, who, it is said, jumped on top of it and proclaimed it rightful American territory.

At the end is the ledge with the view. The Hudson spreads wide below. There's Anthony's Nose, Bear Mountain, and Bear Mountain Bridge spanning the chasm between. Manitou Marsh and Point are on the east bank, and the Highlands all around. In 1778, Dr. Dwight, a chaplain of a Connecticut regiment stationed at West Point, described the view as "majestic, solemn, wild, and melancholy." Other early writings state that the Beverly Robinson house at the north foot of Sugarloaf was visible from the summit. Beverly was the manor house for a 60,000-acre Tory estate that was confiscated and used as a busy rebel headquarters by Washington, Lafayette, Hamilton, and Benedict Arnold.

If you look about the ground carefully you will find . . . is that cactus? Prickly pear cactus, yes: *Opuntia humifusa* with showy yellow flowers, maroon fruits, and extremely annoying hairlike spines that adhere to the flesh at the slightest touch. The only cactus found in the East occurs along the Hudson River on warm, exposed rocky and sandy sites. Normally, prickly pear is a coastal plain plant, where it grows in dry sunny habitats. The Hudson River, as an extension of the ocean, mediates the local climate. As a trough, the river allows warm air to funnel inland. This allows coastal and southern species access to the Highlands, not only prickly pear cactus, but also fence lizard and Carolina wren.

On the return, you can lengthen your walk by circling Sugarloaf's base. After the descent off the summit, turn right onto the blue trail, then take the next right onto an unmarked trail around the mountain. This will return you to the red trail. Turn left to retrace your steps to your car.

5 · Arden Point

Location: Garrison
Distance: 2 miles, 1.5 hours
Owner: New York State, Town of Philipstown, Garrison
Institute, Open Space Institute

George and Beverly were boyhood school chums, best of friends. They'd grown up together, so when Beverly confided to George that he'd fallen in love with the beautiful Susannah from New York colony, perhaps it seemed only natural for George to fall in love with her even more beautiful sister, Mary. Wouldn't that be the high life? A sister for each! They'd marry and move up to their new wives' estate on the North River, today's Hudson Valley. They could each build a manor house. Yes, the sisters were very well-to-do. It was their grandfather who had secured the vast lands, granted a patent for settlement by the crown itself. Oh, there was that native chief, Sachem Ninham, or whatever his name was, who had made such a fuss over unfair land deals, but that was all over now, so Beverly went ahead and married beautiful Susannah. He moved to her father's estate in New York colony, while George—well, poor George was shunned by the even more beautiful Mary. Not interested, she said. She married a dashing colonel instead.

The years went by, and George moved on to other endeavors. But friend Beverly thrived, lord of his manor, master of mills, homesteads, and farms, of slaves and land-bound tenants (serfs, really). When the Revolution came, why would Beverly the landlord have wanted anything to do with it? He did what any loyal manor lord would and sided with the crown, but in short time the common people overran the Hudson Valley. Beverly's manor, his lands, his house, all were confiscated by those

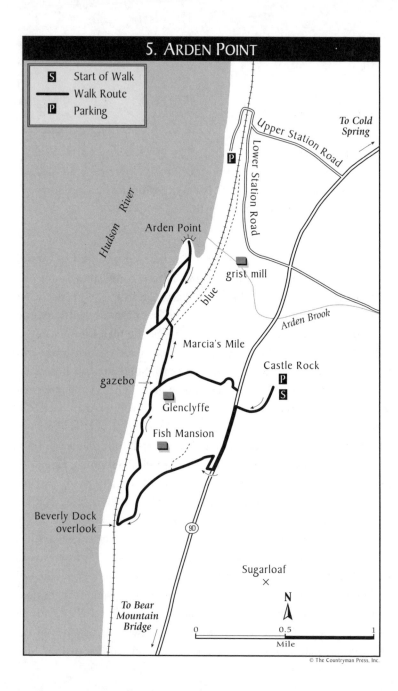

5. ARDEN POINT

S Start of Walk
━━━ Walk Route
P Parking

To Cold Spring

Upper Station Road

Lower Station Road

P

Hudson River

Arden Point

grist mill

blue

Arden Brook

Marcia's Mile

Castle Rock

P
S

gazebo

Glenclyffe

Fish Mansion

Beverly Dock overlook

9D

Sugarloaf
×

To Bear Mountain Bridge

N

0   0.5   1
Mile

© The Countryman Press, Inc.

rebels and their general, who promptly set up *headquarters* in his house. Beverly and Susannah fled to New York City, but what was this? A defector? Indeed, the very one presently posted to his house? Would Beverly kindly help escort Major John André to General Benedict Arnold commanding from Beverly's manor house at the foot of Sugarloaf Mountain, and see what Beverly could do to ensure that the capture of West Point went smoothly?

Well, history knows the rest. Major André was snared while Benedict Arnold grabbed an aide's horse and rode like a madman from Beverly's house down to Beverly's dock and escaped unscathed to New York City. Send Mary, they said, beautiful Mary surely will be able to win André's release. After all, it was her old suitor, George, who was holding him. George? George Washington, who met with Mary once more years after his love for her had nearly led him to marriage into the Philipse family that his boyhood friend Beverly Robinson had married into, beautiful Mary came to Beverly's house and pleaded with George. To no avail. André was hanged as a spy while Beverly, Susannah, Mary, and her dashing colonel husband were banished from New York colony under pain of death.

William Denning got most of Beverly Robinson's properties. Upon Denning's death, the estate was broken up and passed to several owners, including Thomas Arden, who kept several farms around the place. In 1898, Beverly Robinson's house burned without a trace, yet that road that Benedict Arnold rode is still there today, and you can walk it, down past the same brook through the same ravine. Long in private hands, the Open Space Institute has made this historic road available for all to walk, along with the rest of the point.

Maps of the 1800s show it as Ardens Point, along with Ardens Dock and Ardens Brook, and the numerous homes of the Arden family. From here are the closest views of West Point nestled within the Highlands of Revolutionary War stories. Two historic houses grace Arden Point. Glenclyffe was a Capuchin friary for 80 years, built in 1929. It is now home to Garrison Institute, a nonprofit, private, interreligious center for social change. On the south tip of the point is Hamilton Fish's estate built in 1861. Neither building is open to the public, but they can be viewed from the outside as you walk through the woods. The main attraction for the hiker is the fabulous river views and woods and rocks of Arden Point itself.

Access

For our walk, park at Castle Rock Unique Area (see Sugarloaf chapter) since it is a permanent parking area, and other parking spots may change. You can also park at the Garrison train station (free on weekends) where you can access Arden Point along the blue trail at the south end of the parking lot, but be sure to check signs for any restrictions. Residents of Philipstown can park at the town's community center by the old Fish mansion. In addition, plans call for a hiker's parking lot just inside Garrison Institute's main entrance off NY 9D. As of this writing, the only road signs are for Philipstown Community Center and Garrison Institute, and public access issues are still in discussion, so stay tuned for changes. Dogs will probably be allowed on leash just about everywhere except the golf course. There is no one phone number to call for information, but you might try the Open Space Institute, which started it all, at 212-629-3981.

Trail

From Castle Rock parking, walk back down the entrance road, admiring Sugarloaf off to your left, and turn left for a short walk along NY 9D. Cross Beverly Brook (a tiny thing); you'll see Putnam County's historic marker "Arnold's Flight." (Beverly's house stood a bit farther south and is marked on NY 9D by another historic sign.) Cross the road and follow the unmarked old woods road downhill.

After a lifetime of hearing the Arnold betrayal story, on my first walk here on this road I felt much the same awe as Buddhist monk Thich Nhat Hanh when he wrote: "We met in space, but not in time." Benedict Arnold and all the rest of the Revolutionary War personages walked right here and elsewhere at Arden Point. Was this the spot where Alexander Hamilton ran up, out of breath, to break the news to Washington? Was it here that Washington questioned the trust he put in his closest friends? Could Arnold's wife, Peggy Shippen, see all this from her window as she not only watched her husband flee and plotted how she and her baby could delay Washington's pursuit, but next heard her former lover, Major André, brought to Beverly House for questioning?

Abloom with celandine in spring, Beverly Dock Road takes you past a pond and an old water pump house. Keep straight, headed toward the river. At the next fork bear right, still following Beverly Brook. The brick Fish mansion stands on the bank above a second pond. At the bottom of the ravine the lane becomes a footpath as the historic road dissolves into swampland. Follow the footpath along the bank and then head right into the woods, up and over a knoll to a lookout from atop a cliff under a viewing platform toward the site of Beverly Dock. If the trail has become obscure from lack of use, simply follow the markings. An "overland" road once was the main thoroughfare from Beverly House to Beverly Dock, and it was on that road Alexander Hamilton ran up to hand Washington the fatal news. Arnold used the side, lesser-used road to the dock along the ravine purposely to avoid running into Washington. But they both led to the same dock and Washington was on his way there. It seems a miracle Arnold got away at all on such slim timing.

The view is possible only when the leaves are down off the trees. Sugarloaf Mountain rises behind you. Downriver, Anthony's Nose looks every bit the truncated spur it is, shorn off by the last glacier. Its cliffs plunge straight into the Hudson at the Race or the Horse Race where the river bottom drops to 47 feet right at the Nose's foot, and as much as 157 feet in the Race itself. Across this narrow channel at Bear Mountain Bridge in 1777 was stretched the famous First Great Chain, made of huge iron links mined and forged locally, floated atop a boom of logs. In 1776 George Washington first ordered the fortification of the Highlands and all passes to them. As you know from the Anthony's Nose chapter, the First Great Chain was not successfully defended. From your pleasant chair at Arden Point you can see The Timp and Bear Mountain when the leaves are down, those two places that figured in the great blow dealt the rebels on that night in October 1777. What a scare Washington and his rebel leaders had when the British overwhelmed the forts and destroyed the Great Chain, and with an armed and pillaging armada took possession of the river clear to Albany. They had split the colonies in two. It was largely only Benedict Arnold's heroism at Saratoga, and the fortuitous interception of a spy's note that was never to reach Burgoyne, that led the British to abandon the river and retreat back to New York City.

That's Con Hook on the west side of the river in the foreground, with the blonde phragmites reed marsh between the rocky island and the mainland. At your feet across the railroad tracks rises the other side of the original rocky headland of Arden Point, topped by pitch pines. Backtrack slightly, then take the left fork to follow the cliff edge. Shortly, the trail descends slightly into hollows and past knolls, then switchbacks up the ravine wall near the Fish mansion. Follow the trail as it wends its way past an old chain-link fence, nearing the river cliff top. At the dirt road, bear left and watch for the path as it turns off on the left headed again for the cliff edge. From on top bedrock you view a large, yellow building across the river. Built as Cranston's Hotel, a famous steamship landing, it became Ladycliff Academy for Franciscan nuns and today houses the West Point Museum. Directly across the river behind the old Ladycliff is the aptly named Bare Rock Ridge and just south of that is Crown Ridge. Just left of Ladycliff is a waterfall that runs only in spring or after heavy rain called Buttermilk Falls.

Continue. You'll pass the Georgian brick friary, Glenclyffe, and arrive at a gazebo with an overlook of West Point to the north, Bull Hill showing behind. Keep straight onto the orange-marked Marcia's Mile Trail headed upriver on what becomes an old carriage way. You'll meet the blue trail coming south from the Garrison train station. Cross the bridge over the railroad tracks onto the state-owned portion of Arden Point proper. Turn left onto the red trail. At the next fork, bear left on an unmarked path through oak and white pine, a xeric or extremely dry (well-drained) soil overlaid by lowbush blueberry and vibrant green moss. Bear right to a small cove and shingle beach. Rejoin the red trail and pause a while on the bench overlooking the river on top of the rocks.

West Point Military Academy, Bull Hill behind, as seen from Arden Point.

Follow the red trail as it climbs a small slope. Watch carefully for the fork where you bear left to follow along the headland edge, getting views the whole way when the leaves are down. Arrive at a rocky overlook darkened by hemlocks and pitch pines, reminiscent of the rugged Maine coast. In a stiff wind, the Hudson's waves crash on the rocks. It is interesting that no northern white cedars occur here.

As you continue, chunks of Arden Point's bedrock, Hudson Highlands Precambrian granite, the iron magnetite ore rusted, can be seen in the trail. The red trail joins the blue. Keep left on the red for the rugged tip of the point. There's always a breeze here, and you may feel a bit like a historical spy peering out at the fort from beneath the pitch pine, hemlock, red maple, and mountain laurel. The view of West Point is best from here, and it is easy to see Garrison as simply a river landing opposite West Point. The river appears to dead-end, but actually it turns sharply around the gray-walled fortress of West Point in a stretch known as World's End. The riverbed drops up to 175 feet deep.

Following Washington's orders in 1778, the army forged a Second Great Chain and stretched it this time across World's End from West Point north to Constitution Island. To defend the chain, they built a system of forts and redoubts armed with cannons. Ships must tack to make the turn, against a sharp current with swirling eddies, to boot. By the time a ship bumped up against the chain, it would have no momentum and the forts could easily blow an enemy British ship out of the water. The British planned to conquer these seemingly impregnable defenses with treachery. But the Second Great Chain and its forts never saw battle. After Arnold's duplicity was discovered, the British did not try the Hudson River again. You can see some of the original links of the Second Great Chain preserved at West Point at the Trophy Point overlook.

Return to the railroad bridge via the blue trail. This route is little used and may be obscure in places, so watch out for the blue markers. Trout lily blooms throughout the point in April. On the other side of the tracks, the blue turns left to return to Garrison, while you go right on Marcia's Mile. (If you wish to extend your walk, go to the Garrison train station to see the sights on the river—refer to the next paragraph—then follow Lower Station Road uphill past the historic gristmill to NY 9D.) Follow until you are abreast of the gazebo. Marcia's Mile turns left. Follow past unmarked trails to the entrance road. Cross NY 9D and cut straight through the fields to your car.

You may enjoy a visit to historic Garrison's Landing. As you motor out of Castle Rock, turn right onto NY 9D, proceed to the stoplight, and turn left onto Lower Station Road. Drive slowly. The first house on the right is the white clapboard Mandeville House, a contemporary of Beverly House that miraculously still stands and is in fine shape, too. As you wind downhill, a left turn into a state-owned dirt driveway will take you to a historic gristmill open by appointment only (call Open Space Institute at 212-629-3981 to schedule a time to visit). The adjacent golf course is actually laid out within what used to be an old farm that may date from the Dutch colonial era (no one's really sure just how old the buildings are). The barn, certainly, is one of the oldest in the county, and you'll also see the farm pond and the Dutch-style farmhouse. Continue to the train station (be careful of a sudden stop sign on a blind curve), cross the tracks, and enjoy the public park on the river's edge.

6 · Constitution Marsh Sanctuary

Location: Garrison
Distance: Less than 1 mile, 2 to 3 hours
Owner: New York State (part of Hudson Highlands State
Park), managed by National Audubon Society

There are two parcels to Constitution Marsh Sanctuary: the marsh itself, and the Indian Brook ravine. The visit to each is one-way, so you may either first walk uphill to see the ravine and the waterfall, or downhill to the Hudson for the boardwalk through the cattails.

Access

From US 9D, south of Cold Spring and just south of Boscobel Restoration (a place to visit after you walk), turn west/right onto Indian Brook Road, a dirt road. Drive 0.5 mile to the sanctuary sign. No pets are allowed. The trails are open every day from 9 AM to 6 PM. The nature center is open 9 AM to 5 PM Tuesday to Sunday, closed on Monday. Information: 845-265-2601.

Trail

Henry Hudson did not get on well with some of the Native people who lived along the river that today bears his name. He sailed north to the future site of Albany, and by the time he returned to New York Harbor, he'd killed, for various reasons, fourteen or so Native people. The natives weren't happy about this. On Hudson's trip downriver, he anchored in Newburgh Bay for two foggy days. An unarmed party of sailors went ashore near Glenham. They were attacked by local natives, an undocumented but persistent local tale says, and Jacobus Van Horen was wounded and captured while the rest fled back to the *Half Moon*.

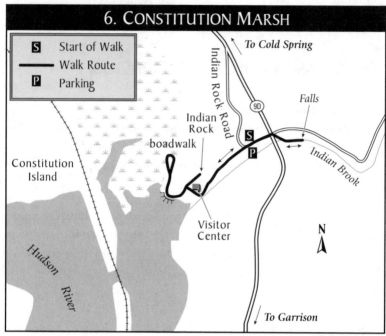

6. CONSTITUTION MARSH

S Start of Walk

— Walk Route

P Parking

To Cold Spring

Indian Rock Road

9D

Falls

Indian Rock

boadwalk

Indian Brook

Constitution Island

Visitor Center

N

Hudson River

To Garrison

© The Countryman Press, Inc.

Van Horen was taken into the hills around Matteawan, today's Beacon Range, and we cringe to think what his captors contemplated. Princess Manteo, daughter of the chief, saw the captive, fell in love with him and pleaded for his life. He was given to her, their marriage planned for a year hence. An excellent fisherman, Jacobus was allowed to roam freely in the Indian Brook area, each day bringing in a supply of trout.

But one day, when they were swimming in the pool below Indian Brook Falls (a spot still popular with young lovers), Henry Hudson's man spotted a European ship on the river. Jacobus abandoned Manteo and bolted for the shore. He was seen and picked up. Manteo's body was found in the pool. Some say Jacobus murdered her to escape. Others say that after her lover fled, Manteo walked brokenhearted and weeping up Indian Brook, a white flower springing up where each tear fell to earth. At the falls, she hurled herself from the cliff top to her death in the pool.

This tale, while totally European in origin, does give insight into the numerous misunderstandings and intermarriages typical of the early contact between Europeans and natives.

From your car, go up the narrow dirt Indian Brook Road along the top of the ravine. Pass beneath the NY 9D bridge and then turn right past an old estate gate. Follow the old driveway until you cross Indian Brook. Be careful not to continue on the driveway any farther than this as it soon becomes private property. On the far side of the bridge take a hard left onto a rough footpath. Follow upstream along the waterside to the falls. It is best to keep as close to the water as possible; some herd paths needlessly try to climb the impossible ravine, damaging the slope. In 1833, there was neither driveway nor trail when the young and famous actress Fanny Kemble, walking atop the ravine wall with a male friend, glimpsed foam and heard the waterfall's roar. It made her "wild to go down." When you reach the foot of the falls, do not feel as Miss Kemble did: "an uncontrollable desire seized me to clamber up the rocks by the side of the fall, and so reach the top of it." She nearly killed herself and her companion helping her. Indian Brook Falls for a time was known as Fanny Kemble's Bath. In summer, watch the rocks beside the falls and you might see a nesting Louisiana waterthrush.

Return back down the road to your car. Continue on the dirt road that follows the top of the ravine wall of Indian Brook, going steeply downstream. Over halfway down the road to the river watch carefully on the left for a footpath. It is marked by a green diamond on a short post. This leads to Indian Brook sparkling in the sun within the coolness of the ravine. The cool, moist microclimate once supported the growth of hemlocks, but now they are dead and soon will be gone due to an infestation of the imported woolly adelgid insect. Follow the path downstream to the canoe launch and the James P. Rod Audubon Visitor Center. After viewing the exhibits, pick up the blue diamond trail behind the museum headed for the boardwalk at the marsh.

Shortly after the right-hand turnoff to the rock shelter (described a bit later during your return), green-twigged cat brier *(Smilax rotundifolia)* twines by its tendrils and drapes the woods in a tangle beloved by small birds, which can sleekly slip through the mazed fortress that no large predator can penetrate. Hooked, sharper than the claws of cats, the thorns of the cat brier are the most vicious the hiker can encounter. They are strong, and tear not only clothing but flesh, too. The male and female vines are separate, one bearing pollen, the other eggs in green flowers that ripen into blue-black berries, also beloved by birds. The round leaves with their parallel veins often remain green far into autumn. In protected spots, they grow evergreen.

The first indication that you are nearing the marsh is a swamp of red maple, tupelo, alder, and ostrich fern. In spring and fall, color shows first in swamps. It is here that skunk cabbages bloom, often before the snow has melted, and it is here that the red maples fuzz out red and orange in April, while the hills are still stark and cold. As early as late August, the red maple and tupelo trees begin to turn scarlet. And nowhere are the fall colors more vibrant than in October when the sun shines upon an entire swamp of red maple saplings colored in brilliant red, orange, and yellow.

As you walk west, the tree and shrub height lowers. Cattail and loose-strife grow among the alder. Then the woody plants end, and it's all cattail marsh. This progression, red maple swamp to cattail marsh, is typical and corresponds to increasing soil moisture that leads to arrowhead, arrow arum, and pickerelweed, then open water.

Arrive at the river. Follow the bedrock up and over the granite knoll past cushions of moss and chestnut oak and pitch pine. It is amazing how a bone-dry plant community lies adjacent to a sopping wet one, the line between them no thicker than a trail. Water rules plant species. In eco-logical terminology, water is a limiting factor. Corresponding to this dif-ference in plant habitats are different associated animal species.

Rocky cliffs and outcrops such as this headland are common in the Hudson Highlands and always afford wonderful views. From the top you see Sugarloaf rising behind the mainland shore, and Anthony's Nose, the distinctive curve of The Timp and Timp Pass, and Bear Mountain.

The summit of Crow's Nest forms a sort of bowl that, from the river, might look like two separate peaks. Storm King is to the right.

Opposite stands West Point with Crow's Nest just to the north. Keep on the trail downhill to the marsh boardwalk with the North Gate of Crow's Nest and Storm King to the left and Bull Hill on the right. To the west is Constitution Island, for which the marsh is named. Both were named in colonial days before the Revolution for the British constitution. The earlier Dutch called the island Martalaer's Rock. While Constitution Island lies within Putnam County, public access is mainly from West Point with occasional special buses from Cold Spring (for information phone 845-446-8676 or visit www.constitutionisland.org).

Constitution Marsh is a tidal freshwater/brackish marsh of 270 acres. It is one of the largest undeveloped tidal wetlands on the Hudson River, supporting an unusual diversity and abundance of wildlife species. In late summer, the Atlantic salt front moves upstream past the marsh and you can find blue crab and shrimp among the cattails. Any time of year, this is a fantastic place for bird watching, though not at any time of day. Many birds are crepuscular, active at dawn and dusk. If you come here at noon, the place may seem dead.

Even during the day, spring and fall migration participants of up to two hundred species wing through in fantastic flocks. Can you imagine seeing the picturesque wood duck by the hundreds? Thirty-one species of birds use the marsh for breeding. In late summer, there are the hordes of swallows at dusk. In winter, there are usually bald eagles. In summer, the most common nesting bird is the marsh wren. But the red-winged blackbirds are the noisiest.

Our first bird of spring, the male red-wings return from the southern states up the ancient flypath of the Hudson River in middle to late February. On the first warm day of March, they disperse inland to the marshes of Dutchess and Putnam counties. They settle in among the brown cattail leaves to battle for nesting sites, using song and occasional ritualistic sparring as weapons. Two or three weeks later the brown females fly north to select the mates of their choice and raise their broods. The nests are built of cattail fibers that are attached to the stalks. The males perch upon the dipping cattail leaves, sing their territorial boundaries, and pluck insects off the cattail stems for their nestlings. Red-wings and cattails go together.

In 1837, Henry Warner, owner and resident of Constitution Island, decided to grow wild rice. He diked Constitution Marsh and dug the channels still visible today. In 1851, the railroad was built. In 1952, the U.S. Army Corps of Engineers built a factory at Cold Spring to produce rechargeable nickel-cadmium batteries. Under successive owners, the plant operated until 1979, polluting Foundry Cove with cadmium, nickel, and cobalt so badly that the area was listed as one of the most serious hazardous waste sites in the United States of America and one of the largest and most concentrated cadmium-contaminated sites in the world. Dredging of Foundry Cove to remove the toxins began in the early 1990s and was completed by 1996 by the U.S. Environmental Protection Agency. Constitution Marsh itself was left alone because the heavy metals count was too low to warrant destructive dredging. Even though there are hot spots within the marsh, if they were removed, then alien purple loosestrife and phragmites would enter, outcompete, and replace the catttail. The entire marsh flora and fauna would change.

A tidal marsh produces 10 to 15 tons of biomass per acre per year, as compared to our best farmland, which produces a paltry two to five tons per year at a greater cost in equipment, fertilizer, pesticides, and storage. A tidal marsh is the most productive of places. When the biomass of tidal marsh cattails and plants dies, it decays into detritus, the basis for fisheries that produce millions of fish per acre. Tidal marshes, Constitution Marsh among them, are the spawning and feeding grounds for perhaps eighty percent of all the species of Atlantic Ocean fish and shellfish.

On your return, you may want to visit the Indian rock shelter. A large glacial erratic (a boulder dragged from somewhere north by the last glacier and dumped here) is broken clear in half and forms sheltered areas used in historic times. A hunter or a fisherman out for a few days away from home would use this sort of camp shelter. Archaeological records from the late 1800s and early 1900s list native village sites at the mouth of Indian Brook by the visitor center, at Garrison, Cold Spring, and on Constitution Island.

Side Trips

West Point Foundry Preserve

Owned by Scenic Hudson. Site of the Civil War-era Parrott Gun manu-
facture and the U.S. Army Corps of Engineers battery factory. Historic
buildings, restored marsh, views, 87 acres. Access: From Constitution
Marsh, drive north on 9D to Cold Spring. At the stoplight turn left on
Main Street into town. Go for 0.3 mile to a right onto Chestnut Street.
Parking is along the street. Entrance is at the end of Chestnut Street at a
bridge. Plans also call for access from the south end of the train station.
Information: 845-473-4440 or visit www.scenichudson.org.

Foundry Dock Park

Owned by Scenic Hudson. A tiny park in a great location, between the
Cold Spring train station and delightful Chapel of Our Lady on the bank
of the Hudson River, which you'll want to visit, too. The park is perfect for
picnicking and a popular launch for kayaks and canoes for paddling in
the nearby marshes. 0.7 acre. Access: Follow Main Street in Cold Spring
over the railroad tracks to the end. Turn left on Market Street. Park on
the right. Free weekend parking is adjacent to the train station. Information: 845-473-4440 or visit www.scenichudson.org.

7 · North Redoubt

Location: Garrison
Distance: A little over 1 mile roundtrip
Owner: State of New York (part of Hudson Highlands State Park), managed in cooperation with Hudson Highlands Land Trust

Parking here is tight, but nowhere else does the public have such ready access to an authentic Revolutionary War redoubt on the east bank of the Hudson. Yes, the redoubt is still there. Well, the earthworks are there. The historic site today looks like an Iron Age hill fort of England, and there is a fabulous view through the trees of the river.

The second charm of this walk is that it is just the right length and steepness to tucker out small legs whose owners can then say they climbed a mountain, plus the excitement of visiting a real, live fort. Explain ahead of time that some imagination is needed to build the fort atop the remnant earthworks.

Access

There is no formal parking available for this trailhead. All you can do is pull off the road onto the narrow shoulder. From the intersection of NY 301 and NY 9D at a stoplight in Cold Spring, travel south on NY 9D for 3.2 miles to a left onto Snake Hill Road. If coming from the south, clock 0.8 mile from the Garrison stoplight at the intersection of NY 9D and Putnam County 403, with a right onto Snake Hill Road. Drive slowly along Snake Hill Road for 0.3 mile to the merest of pull-offs, tiny, suitable for one car, directly opposite Walter Hoving Road. There are no signs, but the trail is marked. Be sure your vehicle is completely off the pavement. Dogs allowed on leash. Information: 845-225-7207.

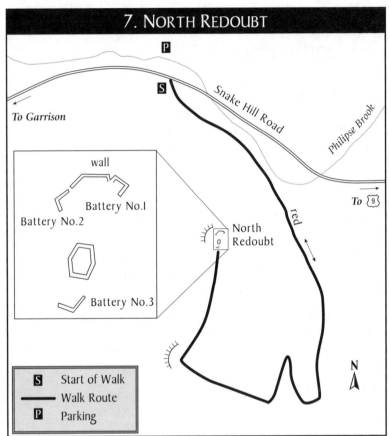

7. NORTH REDOUBT

To Garrison

Snake Hill Road

Philipse Brook

To [9]

red

wall

Battery No.1

Battery No.2

North Redoubt

Battery No.3

N

S	Start of Walk
—	Walk Route
P	Parking

© The Countryman Press, Inc.

Trail

The red trail uses the original cannon road for its entire path as it winds up to the redoubt. At first, it parallels beautiful Philipse Brook. Follow the red discs uphill to the top where you find those wonderful grass-like, woodland sedges, most commonly *Carex arctata,* a hallmark of the open, highland oak woods. They feel dry when run through the hand and have raised ridges. "Sedges have edges," the saying goes, to distinguish them from grasses, which do not. Neither sedges nor trees were much in evidence when the redoubt crowned the hill, nor for centuries afterwards when the land became pasture and farmland. You gain a deep view through openings between trees of the opposite shore of the river, of Bare Rock Ridge and its surrounding hills. How was some fort this high up from the river supposed to protect anything? The answer is, North Redoubt was part of a system.

After the British took Forts Montgomery and Clinton at Popolopen Gorge and destroyed the First Great Chain, George Washington ordered the sharp bend in the river at West Point fortified as the single greatest defense of the crucial Hudson River. With the British in control of both Canada and New York City, American control of the Hudson was vital to keep a route for supplies and infantry open between the north and south colonies. Most of the food for the army came from the southern colonies, while most of the infantry came from the northern colonies. Without that flow, the Revolution had not a chance. "Seize the present opportunity, and employ your whole force and all the means in your power for erecting and completing, as far as it shall be possible, such works, and obstructions as may be necessary to defend and secure the river against any further attempts of the enemy," Washington wrote to General Israel Putnam two months after the near disaster in 1777.

By 1780, West Point had four forts, seven redoubts, and two more redoubts on Fort Hill, on the river's east bank. All of these were designed on a central plan for one purpose only: the protection of that object of paramount importance, the Second Great Chain. A map of West Point's defenses drawn by the cartographer to Rochambeau, the French general destined to help defeat the British at Yorktown, shows not only the forts and redoubts, but also the line and length of fire from each fort's cannon. The map was a maze of crisscrossing lines that covered both river and shore, an impenetrable defense complex. (A copy of the map is in the files of the West Point Museum.) Any ship attempting to approach World's End would be blown out of the water by numerous cannon from forts and redoubts on the west bank and on Constitution Island. Any infantry attempting to sneak up on those forts along the flatland on the west bank would be destroyed by cannon from forts and redoubts high above West Point. Any troops thinking to creep up along the flatlands of the east bank would be decimated by cannon from North and South Redoubt, on what came to be known as Fort Hill.

How *could* Washington let the French make a map of these important defenses to show to any and all? And how *could* he allow the use of local Tory captives to build them, for goodness sake, and then simply release them so they could go home and blab all about it? Paul Ackermann, Revolutionary War curator at the West Point Museum, explained about "psychological warfare: Sir Henry Clinton knew all about the fortifications. Everyone did. It was no secret. Washington was making sure the British knew how impregnable West Point had become. Come ahead, he was saying, just try us."

And try they did, but with treachery rather than direct conflict. It appears that Benedict Arnold's plan was to let the defenses get run down. Instead of maintaining the forts and redoubts, he sent the troops out to cut wood. He let the log rafts that floated the Great Chain get waterlogged. Part of the chain began to sink. To André he gave in writing a full description of current conditions, especially where the troops and guns were stationed at the moment, along with the promise that he would send most of the regiments out again on another useless woodcutting expedition. If not for the fortuitous capture of André, the British perhaps could have taken West Point, the Hudson, and the war under these circumstances.

What is a redoubt? It is a detached stronghold that acts as a satellite to a main fortification, in this case, West Point's forts. It is a classic European defense that uses land with hills to advantage. All West Point's redoubts are the same, consisting of a central fort surrounded by batteries. From the river or the west bank, it is easy to see South Redoubt atop the hill, with North Redoubt somewhere there atop the small, wooded knob to the north. In some accounts South Redoubt is called Middle Redoubt, because another was planned for Sugarloaf. But it was never built. South Redoubt today is on private property where the landowner has exposed the stone and earthworks, cutting down the trees and removing debris.

This view from nearby South Redoubt (private property) clearly shows the river's curve, called World's End. The view from the north is the same, though somewhat obscured by trees.

This actually can be fatal to historic sites due to ensuing erosion, which causes the stonework to collapse. Believe it or not, North Redoubt hidden away in the woods and buried under soil is in better shape for survival, so long as NOBODY takes a shovel to it. Don't even THINK of disturbing this national treasure.

After the first view, the old cannon road and red trail climbs higher to the redoubt itself. First pass piles of stone and dirt. This was the south battery, or gun emplacement. Note the skeletons of ancient red cedars that grew when this was an open hilltop. The squared earthworks were the main building, or redoubt, the infantry stronghold. The trail ends at three red discs at a view through a forest opening, below which were two more batteries connected by a wall. There's Constitution Island and Marsh and the North Gate opening onto Newburgh Bay. The Shawangunks show on the horizon. Directly across the river, you glimpse West Point and World's End through the trees, that sharp bend in the river where the Second Great Chain stretched across the water.

To build North Redoubt, and all the other redoubts, the crown of the hill was first leveled and a stone wall built around it. This is called a scarp. It is the redoubt's foundation, on top of which is built a wood floor. The redoubt is then built on top of the scarp using ancient European defensive structures called gabions and fascines. A gabion is like a big basket, taller than a man, woven of saplings. Line them up atop the scarp and fill them with dirt. Voila! You've got a big, fat wall. One of the privates working on the construction of North Redoubt wrote that it was bombproof: a cannonball fired at the fort would just thud into the gabions and the shock would be absorbed by the earth, whereas the wood walls of other types of forts would splinter and fly apart. A fascine is a bunch of saplings tied together in a bundle and laid across the tops of the gabions, then covered with dirt. Voila! A lintel over a space between gabions for the cannon to shoot through. Since such works were subject to rapid decay in the Hudson Valley's climate, these redoubts needed regular maintenance and even periodic reconstruction. Also, since they were based on wood, they could burn, and sometimes did, from lightning strikes or stray sparks. Indeed, North Redoubt accidently burned to the ground and had to be rebuilt. So, what you see now is the dirt fallen from the gabions and the fascines. The original stone wall of the scarp is still there, inside the dirt.

Notice how the dirt undulates, especially at the battery. The low points are the embrasures where the cannon were stationed on wood platforms. Stand on top of the main redoubt earthwork. There would have been a wood floor, with a magazine for powder and supplies below, and the walls standing about 8 feet above the floor, creating a two-story structure. If an enemy took the guns at the battery, the troops were to fall back into the last defensive stronghold of the redoubt itself. Here all the supplies were kept. Since the batteries were open in the rear, where they faced the redoubt, the defenders would be able to fire on any enemy that took them. A redoubt such as North Redoubt was designed to be garrisoned by 150 men. They lived in primitive conditions in brush huts and tents around the redoubt. Rations from the southern colonies of bread, salt beef, salt pork, beans, and Carolina rice arrived regularly from headquarters. Every six men made up a mess, with one man chosen as the cook. A skeleton watch was always on duty within the redoubt's main stronghold. Should the alarm go out, whether by beacon or drum or cannon fire, to signal a call to arms, a sighting of enemy activity, or a commanding officer on a visit, all the men in the huts would go into the redoubt.

On the way back you can cool your feet in Philipse Brook, named for the Philipse family that held the original patent for Putnam County, partially bought from the local natives in 1697. You might also like to visit St. Philip's Church in the Highlands with its old graveyard that dates back to the 1700s. To see it, drive back down Snake Hill Road, turn left onto 9D, and you'll see the stone church on its knoll on your right. From here you can continue to a right at the stoplight to tour historic Garrison's Landing (see Arden Point chapter), ending with a picnic at the riverside park.

8. BULL HILL, BREAKNECK RIDGE & LITTLE STONY PT.

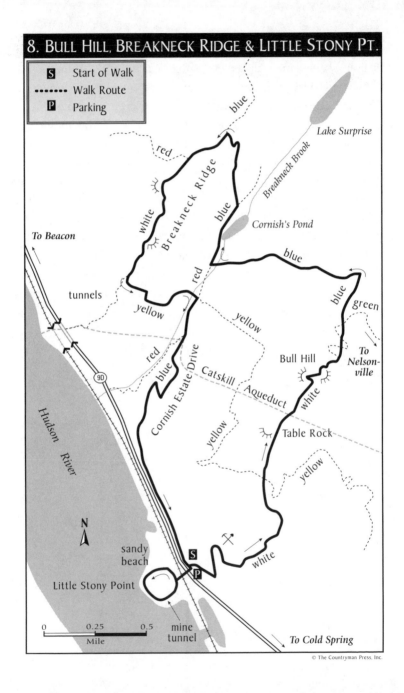

S Start of Walk
•••••• Walk Route
P Parking

Lake Surprise

blue

red

Breakneck Brook

Breakneck Ridge

blue

white

Cornish's Pond

To Beacon

blue

tunnels

red

blue

red

yellow

yellow

blue

green

To Nelson-ville

Bull Hill

Cornish Estate Drive

Catskill

Aqueduct

white

yellow

Table Rock

Hudson River

9D

yellow

white

N

sandy beach

S
P

Little Stony Point

white

mine tunnel

To Cold Spring

0   0.25   0.5
Mile

© The Countryman Press, Inc.

8 · Bull Hill, Breakneck Ridge, and Little Stony Point

Location: Cold Spring
Distance: 6 to 8 miles, 7 to 10 hours
Owner: State of New York (part of Hudson Highlands State Park)

Right around here somewhere in the early 1700s a wild bull caroused through the countryside, ravaging nearby farms when hungry, threatening woodcutters and hunters. The farmers decided it had to go. A posse on horseback with dogs hunted up the slopes of the bull's hill and chased the renegade clear down Lake Surprise ravine and up the other side to the very edge of the cliff. The bull fell off, breaking its neck, hence: Breakneck Ridge and Bull Hill.

It seems that these rocky hills have inspired other renegades. There is an old Lenape story that somewhere in these hills was the last haunt of the feared and ferocious Great Naked Bear, a species that ate humans. Hairless except for a tuft of white hair on the back, they originally lived over a wide area of Turtle Island (North America). Because their hearts were too small to aim at with a spear, they were almost impossible to kill. They could smell a solitary human all the way from the other side of a mountain, and villages were never safe from their attack. Nonetheless, one by one the Great Naked Bears were hunted down and destroyed, until there was only one left on the east bank of the Hudson. A hunting party climbed a steep cliff of rock for protection; the description fits Breakneck Ridge, but the exact spot could have been any number of locations. When the creature attacked from below, the men threw boulders, crushing its skull and breaking its back.

The Romanticism of the 1800s prompted an attempt to Victorianize the "coarse" name Bull Hill into Mount Taurus (an attempt that lives on), as was done to Butter Hill, which became Storm King, and Crow's Nest, which became Cro' Nest for a time.

There are various routes up these two mountains. Breakneck Ridge is famous for its stony, cliffhanging, death-defying path that begins at the train and road tunnel at its foot and scrambles straight up its face. The ridge even has its own train whistle stop on weekends on Metro North's Hudson Line. You could go that way, then climb Bull Hill from the north side and loop around. Or, if you want to climb only Bull Hill, you can park in a tiny pull-off along Putnam County 10 (Fishkill Road) 0.4 mile north of Nelsonville off NY 301, returning via the same trail. Or, you can access either mountain via the Beacons for some mighty long hill walks. There are plenty of choices, even whether to climb only Bull Hill or to continue onto Breakneck.

Or, if you want to tackle both mountains but are terrified of rock scrambling down the short section described on Breakneck (and I can't say as how I blame you but I climbed down it as if it were a ladder and if I can I bet you can, too), then follow this chapter backwards, starting with Breakneck, then go over Bull Hill to end at pleasant Little Stony Point for a picnic supper on the beach.

Choose the clearest, coolest, spring or fall day for this walk for outstanding views. Note: Breakneck Ridge is not recommended in wet or windy weather, and never when there is ice.

Access

From the stoplight at the intersection of NY 9D and NY 301 in Cold Spring, drive 0.7 mile north on NY 9D. Park in the pull-offs along NY 9D beside Little Stony Point. Dogs allowed on leash. Information: Fahnestock State Park office, 845-225-7207.

Trail

Little Stony Point is a joy. Despite the years of blasting that reduced its impressive granite cliffs to building stone, it contains the finest views from the river on the Hudson's east bank and the Hudson's best sand beach.

Cross the railroad bridge that leads to Little Stony Point and turn right. Keep straight on this road and it will lead you to Sandy Beach, a popular spot for boaters, picnickers, and sunbathers, with a fabulous view. Backtrack off the beach and continue on the road as it dwindles to a footpath past the remnants of Little Stony Point's cliffs (on your left; you passed a trail earlier that leads to their summit). Feel the wind? It's usually present in all seasons except the heat of high summer. That's the infamous Highland wind historically treacherous to sailing craft. It barrels down from the Clove, also known as Mother Cronk's Clove for the Cronk family who inhabited the valley between Storm King and Crow's Nest. Upriver stands the North Gate: Storm King to the west, Breakneck to the east, Pollepel Island in the center with the ruins of Bannerman Castle. And there is Bull Hill, with a quarry scar. We're going all the way up there?

At this northwest tip of Little Stony Point the water is 140 feet deep. Barges used to moor here at a dock awaiting loads of quarried and crushed mountain rock. Continue around the point. On the south side, there is an old mine tunnel from the iron-ore days of the early 1800s. Crouch and crawl in. The level tube curves into pitch blackness; you'll need a flashlight to find the T-intersection.

Cross back over the railroad tracks past your car and cross NY 9D for the white trail. Shortly, you'll come to a fork. Bear right to keep on the white (blue on the left is your return). The trail climbs uphill following the site of the tipple (huge crusher and rock processing buildings and chutes on stilts that extended from the quarry to the river) and you walk on top of piles of gravel. Scoop up a handful from the trail to see the granite of Bull Hill and all the Hudson Highlands made up of crystalline pink feldspar, white quartz, and sparkling black mica—gorgeous. Besides being pulverized to gravel, rock blasted from Bull Hill (and Breakneck Ridge) was used to build the Brooklyn Bridge, West Point, the Taconic State Parkway, and the front steps of the capital building in Albany.

Emerge out into the amphitheater of the quarry grown over with a black locust tree colony and little bluestem grass. The Hudson River Stone Corporation operated from 1931 to 1966, and the public outcry began

From way atop Breakneck Ridge, Sandy Beach looks like a mere line along faraway Little Stony Point.

as soon as they set up operations. It was the long public battle that finally closed the quarry down. Further public pressure by 1968 mobilized the state government to purchase, with matching private funds, Little Stony Point, Bull Hill, Little Sugarloaf, Pollepel Island, and what they didn't already own of Breakneck Ridge to form Hudson Highlands State Park.

Backtrack slightly. Notice that just before the quarry, the white trail turns sharply to follow up the steep south lip of the quarry through oak woodlands. The yellow trail crosses the white. You will be using a different section of that yellow to come down Breakneck, so if you would prefer to climb up Breakneck (which is safer), you may turn left on the yellow now and climb Bull Hill from the "rear." The disadvantage of this route is that you climb Bull Hill twice. Do not attempt to climb down Breakneck if you are afraid of heights or unfamiliar with rock scrambling (which means using hand and toe holds while going down a cliff as if going down a ladder).

Climb through the black, chestnut, and short scrub oak woods with some shadbush and hickory, lowbush blueberry, and sedges. Watch for ledges to visit for the growing view. When the leaves are down, you get glimpses the whole way up, but none compares to the open view from Table Rock: West Point, Constitution Island and Marsh, Sugarloaf, Crow's Nest, Storm King, and Breakneck. Continue. Soon you can see the distinctive curve of The Timp south by Bear Mountain. Crest the mountain. There will be no view at first. The trail widens, the remains of an old carriage road. Watch for a herd path on the right that leads to a view over the Fahnestock plateau with its communications tower, across Putnam County to Connecticut and Westchester. Follow the rock ledge down and look to the far right. On a crisp, clear day, you can see as far as the skyscrapers of Manhattan and the towers of the Tappan Zee Bridge. Smog and humidity often obscure this view, so you may only find Bear Mountain Bridge among the Highlands.

Look directly below at the foot of Bull Hill. See the green avenue of grass with a square brick pumphouse? Imagine, 1,000 feet beneath your feet, through the heart of Bull Hill inside a 14-foot-diameter tube, the finest public drinking water in America courses through the Catskill Aqueduct headed for the faucets of New York City. Five hundred million gallons a day, and it's not enough.

Return to the white trail and continue to an incredible view of all the Catskills, the Shawangunks with their horizontal strip of white cliff, the fire tower on South Beacon Mountain and the taller towers behind that are on Mount Beacon, Fishkill Ridge clear to Bald Hill, Storm King, the steep cliffs of Breakneck, all of Orange County (that's Stewart Airport there). If you know your hills, you'll recognize the profile of the Devil's Path of the Catskills, and to the left of that the clumping of the Catskill high peaks around Slide Mountain. Sam's Point and the low, south Shawangunk Ridge run on the horizon. Small aircraft, hawks, and turkey vultures ride the thermals below you over the Lake Surprise valley that falls away at your feet and rolls up onto Breakneck Ridge. To the far right past Bald Hill you can see another quarry scar, this one still in use, in the Fishkill Wind Gap, with the hills of Dutchess County beyond clear to the South Taconics and Brace Mountain. And, of course, there is Newburgh Bay as the Hudson narrows to enter the North Gate.

The carriage road now descends Bull Hill via switchbacks. Follow the white trail carefully; it leaves the carriage road and heads right steeply downhill cutting across the switchbacks. At the intersection with the green Nelsonville and blue trails, the white ends. Keep straight across this four-way intersection onto the blue trail, called the Notch Trail on NY–NJ Trail Conference maps. Head steeply downhill where stone walls announce past farmland use. Sight the blue blazes with care as the trail avoids an old farm road to jog right and head purposefully across and then along an old farm lane lined by stone walls.

The trail proceeds to take you on a tour of the old farm's stoneworks. You'll pass the house site on the right, a foundation of dressed Hudson Highlands granite. The farm lane, once level with its walls, has been washed out and eroded by centuries of rainfall and use. Cross an intermittent brook in an eroded gully of its own. Once within the valley floor, you encounter the stonework, foundations, and ruins of the Cornish

Estate. Cross Breakneck Brook and at the T-intersection turn right, still the blue trail (the red trail is to the left). Look at the spooky old buildings! You are on the original road that connected Beacon to Cold Spring, the old Lake Surprise Road that became Dairy Road when Edward G. Cornish built his estate.

Chairman of the board of the National Lead Company, Mr. Cornish could afford the best. His early-1900s estate was large. Walk up the road, past his farm. The barn ruin has some of the fanciest stone- and brickwork I've ever seen devoted to cows. You can still find remains of farm equipment and wagons lying around just as they were left. A dam holds back the farm pond, but it is leaking and will be breached with time. This is the pond you saw from atop Bull Hill. Now you have a choice. If you are ready to call it quits, then head back down the blue trail where it runs into the red trail, and follow Dairy Road on home to NY 9D. If you want to climb Breakneck, then continue on the blue to the end of the pond. The blue trail leaves the old road and turns left headed toward our goal.

And now, for the second climb of the day (though it's not as long, at least). Climb until the intersection with the white trail. The blue goes to the right downhill. We turn left uphill on the white. Be sure to make this turn. And voila! you are on top of Breakneck with great views and you see for the first time that the summit of Breakneck is really a sort of humping spine of rocky knobs interspersed with steep-sided saddles, like a broken neck of vertebrae. Any one of these would have been defensible against that last Great Naked Bear. Keep on the white, past Breakneck Bypass (red dot on white), down and up to the next, lower crest and onward. This pattern repeats itself as you go from knob to knob gradually losing altitude. Each knob also gives various windows of views of the summit of Little Sugarloaf with the Hudson River and Newburgh beyond. Keep your eyes peeled for open woods on your right with rocks visible. A seldom-used herd path leads to the award-winning view of the North Gate, Pollepel Island at your feet, Newburgh Bay awash with boats, Little Sugarloaf's summit, Denning's Point and the mouth of Fishkill Creek, the Newburgh–Beacon Bridge, the gas- and oil-powered power plants at

Roseton and Danskammer Point, and the Long Reach of the Hudson River clear up to the white towers of the Mid-Hudson Bridge at Poughkeepsie. Here take your ease. As you look at Storm King with the old Highway cut into its side, the long, supine ridge to the right and in the distance is Schunemunk (there are two short towers visible left of its summit). The mouth of Fishkill Creek spreads green with water chestnut. The light green lowland trees of the old brickyards of Dutchess Junction lie between Little Sugarloaf and Denning's Point. There is also interesting crevice vegetation here in between the rocks of paper birch, pitch pine, juniper, fire cherry, lowbush blueberry, and scrub oak.

Continue on the white trail, getting good views at each rock outcrop, still steadily losing altitude, sometimes steeply. Finally, arrive at the end of the summit crest with a view of the lower knob of Breakneck below. There is Little Stony Point way down by the riverside off to your left, and West Point beyond. It's easy to spot on a summer weekend when Sandy Beach's cove is filled with anchored pleasure boats and swimmers. Ah, and now we can see Little Stony Point's cliff remnants and imagine what the promontory once looked like.

Now, to get down there, continue precipitously downhill on the white trail. Be very careful. Use two handholds and two footholds at all times when rock scrambling. Beware of loose scree that moves on top of bedrock. Go down the cliff facing the rock as if you are backing down a ladder. This is just a taste of what the remainder of Breakneck is like were you to continue downhill on the white trail. Needless to say, it is not recommended, and downright suicidal in wet or windy weather. Once in the notch at the bottom of the knob, turn left onto the yellow trail, a well-designed and -constructed undermountain trail that takes you in a reasonable albeit steep manner down into the Lake Surprise valley. There is one spot where you go up and over a knoll before continuing to descend. Watch here for quarried blocks of Breakneck Mountain granite never shipped for sale beside an ancient red cedar. This is an old quarry. If you lose the yellow trail at this spot and find yourself on some unmarked herd trail, not to worry. Just follow it downhill, cross Breakneck

Brook, and turn right onto the red trail. The yellow trail comes downhill and crosses the stream farther upstream, so if you come that way turn right onto the red.

You're on Mr. Cornish's Dairy Road with more remnants of his estate. At the fork bear left onto the blue trail. Cross the grassy Catskill Aqueduct, which you can walk in either direction. The aqueduct originates in Ashokan Reservoir and, incredibly, passes beneath the Hudson River. Engineers drilled for four years through layer upon layer of silt, sand, gravel, and boulders, seeking the bottom of the Hudson at Storm King. Endless, they thought, bottomless; the gorge was choked with glacial debris. At 1,114 feet below the river surface, their angled east and west diamond drill borings met in solid rock.

Pass the big, round cistern for Mr. Cornish's drinking water, the wood remnant of the charcoal filter still standing. Dairy Road turns to concrete, still in perfect condition. How many new paved or concrete roads do you know that look so good? Mildred Eaton Carr, daughter of builder James W. Eaton, recalled how the very best of materials was used in building the estate, which is why things have lasted. On the right pass the ruins of the house and greenhouse. Built from rocks hewn from Breakneck Mountain, the house contained the luxury of indoor plumbing. The elder Cornishes died during the 1930s. Pending property settlement, the farm was boarded up and left vacant. The house burned in 1956, probably from careless campers.

Back at sea level, turn left onto the blue trail just before the gate and NY 9D. This returns you to your car.

9 · Little Sugarloaf

Location: Beacon
Distance: 2.5 miles, 2 to 3 hours
Owner: State of New York

This little, pointy, bald hill halfway between Beacon and Cold Spring with a mighty 360-degree view is chock full of historic stories and folklore. Also known as North Sugarloaf or Sugarloaf Mountain (not to be confused with the larger but similarly shaped Sugarloaf Mountain of Garrison to the south), this hill's hike is just right for a half-day's excursion: neither too far nor too rigorous, but, still, steep. For those who like more, the trail links up with paths to Breakneck Ridge and the Beacons.

Access

From I-84 just before the Newburgh-Beacon Bridge, exit south onto NY 9D and proceed through the city of Beacon for 6.1 miles. As you are going down a hill, parking for Little Sugarloaf will be in dirt pull-offs on your left. If you come to the Breakneck tunnel you've gone too far. The trailhead itself is opposite Metro North's Breakneck Ridge whistle stop. From the stoplight in Cold Spring at NY 9D and 301, the trailhead is 2.4 miles north on NY 9D. Dogs allowed.

Trail

Start at sea level. There it is: the Hudson River. You might want to mosey over to the train stop and have a look. Be careful. Approaching trains are surprisingly quiet, although those from the north do blow their whistles as they round the bend at 70 mph. There's Bannerman's Castle on Pollepel Island to your right, of which we'll talk more later. To your left is a

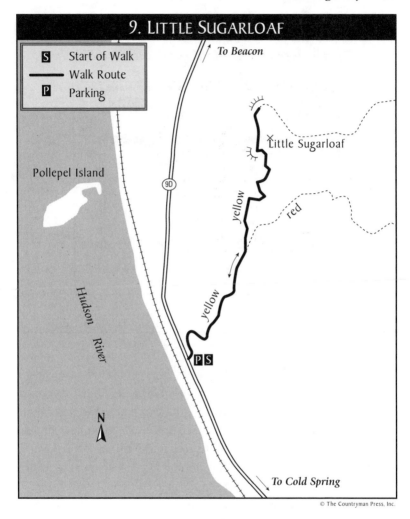

9. LITTLE SUGARLOAF

S Start of Walk
—— Walk Route
P Parking

To Beacon

Little Sugarloaf

Pollepel Island

9D

yellow

red

yellow

Hudson River

yellow

P **S**

N

To Cold Spring

© The Countryman Press, Inc.

pumphouse of the Catskill Aqueduct, which is pumping up drinking water from more than 1,000 feet below the river's surface, to get it from the Catskills across the river to New York City faucets. Why pump from so deep? Because the pipes needed to rest on stable bedrock. Problem was, as they started looking for the bedrock bottom of the river, all they found

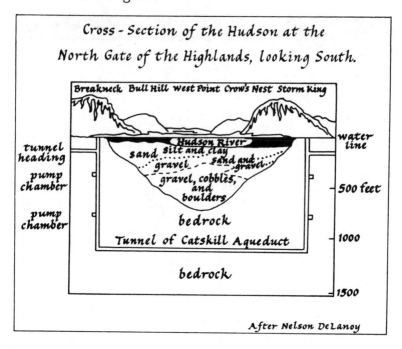

Cross - Section of the Hudson at the North Gate of the Highlands, looking South.

Breakneck   Bull Hill   West Point   Crow's Nest   Storm King

water line

tunnel heading

pump chamber

pump chamber

Hudson River

sand   silt and clay
gravel   sand and gravel
gravel, cobbles, and boulders

bedrock

Tunnel of Catskill Aqueduct

bedrock

500 feet

1000

1500

After Nelson DeLanoy

was gravel, boulders, and sand; the glacial gorge of the Hudson is choked with glacial debris. The bedrock doesn't begin in the middle channel until about 800 feet below the riverbed. Storm King across the water there stands 1,355 feet high at its summit. See how its slope plunges straight to the river? Well, for over half as the mountain is high, it keeps going down, straight down, more or less, sloping into the channel to form a wide, U-shaped glacial valley. When the glaciers melted and the ocean flooded this valley, it became a true fjord.

To the left of Storm King is Crow's Nest with the valley of Mother Cronk's Clove in between. Local spirits, it is said, inhabit the top of the Clove. They delight in sending sudden storms to sink ships. Newburgh Bay ends as the river enters the North Gate of the Highlands between Storm King and Breakneck Ridge. The winds, tides, and currents are treacherous for sailing ships. And, yes, there can be sudden, black storms.

The yellow trail (Wilkinson Memorial Trail) begins from the parking pull-off into the mixed deciduous woods past a stone foundation. Soon, the weedy woods of previous human habitation becomes a stunning mature woodland of tulip tree, sugar maple, oaks, hickory, and black birch. Cross a cascading mountain brook and follow along the ridge slope. When the leaves are down you can see bald Little Sugarloaf dead ahead, with what looks like people or some sort of sentinel on top.

Pass the Breakneck bypass trail on your right, marked with a red square on white. Keep straight on the yellow trail. Cross another mountain brook and begin the climb. In these rich, moist woods you may hear in summer the entrancing song of the wood thrush, or the steady *thunk thunk thunk* of a male chipmunk proclaiming his territory. In spring, warblers feed as they migrate. As you climb, red and chestnut oak become predominate, getting more and more stunted as you approach the summit. At a rocky knob, the trail passes between pitch pines and scrub oak. Above this, the trail levels as it crosses a saddle, and here the deeper soil grows tall oaks and pignut hickory, which is the hickory of dry or well-drained soils (as opposed to the savory shagbark hickory). Pignut's nuts are small and bitter, fit only for rooting swine.

Watch for trail markers that lead up the final ascent through the rocks and along bedrock channels; herd paths compact and erode this fragile slope. On top there is usually a breeze to blow the pesky, biting bugs away. The sentinel turns out to be a red cedar. Follow to the view at two blasted trees, the bones of long-dead, old red cedars, looking just like the ones we're always reading about in Romantic Era literature and seeing in Hudson River School paintings.

Pollepel Island lies at your feet. Pollepel is Dutch for "pot ladle." No one knows why the Dutch colonials gave the island this name, although the simplest explanation is that it reminded them somehow of a big ladle, much as the rocky knob on Storm King's western summit reminded them of a big pat of butter (they named it Boterberg, "Butter Hill") and the Sugarloafs a cone of sugar. Okay, I can see it: the island as a spoon resting at the bottom of a giant bowl whose sides are the North Gate mountains of

Breakneck Ridge and Storm King, a pat of butter melting on the west rim and a cone of sweetener on the east. No? Well, some say the name is from drunken sailors "off their ladle" who got thrown off their Dutch ships onto this island to sober up, which they did right fast because the island was inhabited by ghosts. Yet others say the island is named for Polly Pell, a local girl, and her amorous affairs. This plethora of stories and place names pervades the Hudson Highlands and largely came about during the Romantic Era. Dismissive of the aboriginal culture with its own stories, the new Americans populated the Hudson Highlands with tales drawn from European folklore, of storm goblins, ships and sailors, and Indian maidens in love. These tall tales adorn practically every stream and hill of the Highlands. A few native beliefs remain, along with a few native place names. And there are true tales, of course, some might say stranger than fiction.

After the Dutch, Pollepel Island went through several interesting owners. Moonshiners in the late 1800s gave way to a woman who believed she was the queen of England and used to sing opera into the North Gate winds. Francis Bannerman, a gunrunner whose stockpile of arms and powder exploded one night (after it had been sold to New York State), destroyed the 1908 replica of the family's supposed castle in Scotland. Those are the ruins you see. The island is part of Hudson Highlands State Park, and "hard hat tours" of the island are available by boat (visit www.bannermancastle.org).

Schunemunk is the long mountain in front of you. Then looking left you'll see the hills of Black Rock Forest, then Storm King and Crow's Nest. Breakneck Ridge rises across the valley from where you climbed.

Little Sugarloaf is prone to fire caused by lightning strikes, exacerbated by drought and the already naturally dry conditions. These periodic fires foster baldy vegetation; that is, a hilltop bereft of its tall trees, populated instead by grasses and herbs, some shrubs, and a few stunted trees, giving it a bald appearance. Along with the fire-resistant scrub oaks, there grow saplings of fire cherry, black cherry, paper birch, cottonwood, poplars, and aspens. In these field-like conditions also grow red cedar, the tall poverty or little bluestem grass, and meadow wildflowers.

One of Little Sugarloaf's famous blasted trees, the ramains of an ancient red cedar overlooks the North Gate to the Hudson Highlands.

Keep on the trail across the summit for views of Newburgh Bay and its city, the entire range of the north and south Shawangunks, and the Catskills. Behind Pollepel Island is the mouth of Moodna Creek, a romanticized version of the original 1600s name of Murderer's Creek where Dutch settlers were killed by local natives during the First Esopus War in retaliation for massacres committed by the Dutch. Plum Point, now a state park managed by Orange County, is the wooded land to the right of that. You can see the square indent in the tree line of the old slip for the Newburgh–Beacon ferry, the way to get across the river before I-84 was built in the early 1960s. Keep on for further views up the entire Long Reach from Danskammer, that sacred place spoken of with longing by many contemporary natives, now seat to a power plant, to Crum Elbow where the river curves out of sight. And there lies Denning's Point in front of the Newburgh–Beacon Bridge where once a native village stood. In the late 1800s native villages were also documented at Beacon near the river, along with traces of thousands of years of civilization stretching from Denning's Point south clear to Croton Point. Another village was across the river at Plum Point.

That's Mount Beacon with the communications towers, South Beacon Mountain with the solitary fire tower, the closer hill Sunset Point, and to the right of that Scofield Ridge as it runs into Breakneck Ridge. You might continue on the yellow trail across the valley up to Sunset Point, and onward to the hills you see. Or, there are lots of spots on Little Sugarloaf to loll on the rocks or in the grasses in the sun, enjoying the view.

10 · South Beacon Mountain and Mount Beacon

Location: Beacon
Distance: 3 miles, 4 hours
Owner: State of New York and Scenic Hudson

North and South Beacon mountains are the highest peaks between the Catskills and the Atlantic Ocean. The panoramic views from their summits are unparalleled. From the top of South Beacon you can see from New York City to Albany, from Connecticut to Pennsylvania. When the air is very clear, you can see even farther than that. As you drive around Dutchess County, the blue Beacons appear often on the horizon when roads top a rise.

A miscalculation of mountains is to judge them when standing at their feet. "Not so high, and ugly, too," purists might say of rocky Mount Beacon crowned by communications towers and scarred by old ski tracks, power lines, and a railroad. But seen from I-84 as you drive east out of Pennsylvania, the Beacons loom blue on the horizon tall and peaked as any mountain range. And you appreciate their slope and height when you start up the trail to climb them. They are tall, rising practically straight up from the sea level of the Hudson River, and they are old, 1,200 million-year-old granite-gneiss. The Beacons used to be much taller, of course, about as tall as today's Swiss Alps, at a time when no animals lived on the planet except invertebrates.

The mountain that looms over the city of Beacon, topped by towers, is commonly called Mount Beacon but is also termed North Beacon Mountain. It is 1,531 feet high. Taller at 1,635 feet and topped with a solitary

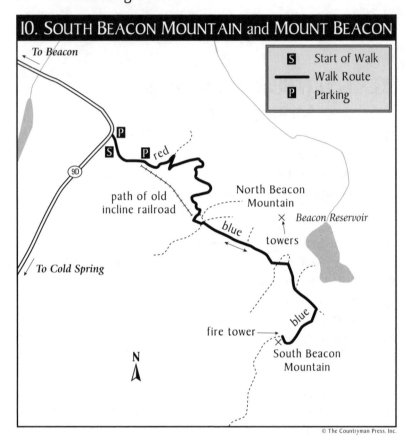

10. SOUTH BEACON MOUNTAIN and MOUNT BEACON

To Beacon

S Start of Walk
—— Walk Route
P Parking

red

path of old
incline railroad

North Beacon
Mountain

× Beacon Reservoir

blue

towers

To Cold Spring

blue

fire tower →

South Beacon
Mountain

N

© The Countryman Press, Inc.

fire tower is South Beacon Mountain slightly to the south. Three hundred feet of stairs are planned alongside the old incline railway climb the city-facing slope of North Beacon to a knob near the summit, and from here is an easy path to South Beacon.

According to legend, in 1682 Francis Rombout and Gulian Verplanck sealed a land deal on top of Mount Beacon. The story goes that the native Wappingers agreed to sell the pair "all the land they could see" on this side of the river. The Dutch businessmen then led the natives to the top of Mount Beacon to lay claim to 85,000 acres.

Since the days of Rombout and Verplanck, the mountains that run from Breakneck Ridge east to the Harlem Valley were named the Fishkill Range, and the little river dock near the Indian villages was Fishkill Landing, later Fishkill-on-the-Hudson, merely a depot for the important regional inland center of Fishkill. The most famous use of the Fishkill Range hills that shadow Fishkill Landing came during the Revolution. The British seized the river in 1777, but then let it go. In response, General Washington ordered the fortification of the Hudson Highlands. A system of beacons in an arch around New York City was constructed and kept in readiness, from New Jersey north to Butter Hill, Mount Beacon, and into Ridgefield, Connecticut. These were signal posts as calls to arms, visible for miles. The local militia was made up mostly of farmers and their sons who, when things were peaceful, tended their farms, keeping an eye on the Fishkill Mountains for smoke by day and fire by night. Should the British sail up the Hudson in another attempt to take the valley and split the colonies in two, the ancient British technique of communication throughout the realm was used: pyres were to be lit and the militia assembled. The British never succeeded in attacking the Hudson again, so the beacons, though kept prepared and manned, never actually got lit until, it is said, George Washington ordered them all fired to mark the end of the war. The name "beacon" stuck to the mountains and, as Fishkill Landing grew, it voted to name itself after the mountain that looms over the city.

The views from the mountaintops are best on clear, cool spring and autumn days. Since it is always windy and cooler on top of South Beacon, bring a sweater. If you visit on a humid summer day with a south wind funneling smog from New York City up the Hudson, you may be lucky to see Newburgh. While this walk is simple and short, from Mount Beacon the hiker has access to a vast landscape. From Bald Hill in the north, which looms over Fishkill, to the Beacons and south through the Hudson Highlands clear to Cold Spring in Putnam County, you could hike these hills for a week. The New York–New Jersey Trail Conference and New York State have blazed many trails through what is truly hikers' country. Trails climb straight up steep slopes. There are constant ups and downs, and views in all directions. Since the range has been used for centuries, there are roads and trails everywhere, many unmarked, which makes it easy for even the experienced hiker to get lost. Sometimes the marked trails are confusing or difficult to follow. Friends and I chuckle whenever we plan to spend the day in the Beacons "always getting lost." The trails sometimes change, and trail conditions vary tremendously. Do not venture into this area without a topographic trail map and a good sense of direction. The NY–NJ Trail Conference East Hudson Trails map is best.

Access

Park at the foot of Mount Beacon at the old incline railway, off NY 9D in the city of Beacon. Dogs allowed on leash. Information: Scenic Hudson owns the stairs and parking, 845-473-4440 or visit www.scenichudson.org. For the parkland, contact the office at Fahnestock State Park, 845-225-7207; for trails, NY–NJ Trail Conference, 201-512-9348 or visit www.nynjtc.org or info@nynjtc.org.

Trail

Plans call for stairs to go straight up. The red trail begins to the left of the railway and the stairs, and switchbacks up. Take your pick. I'm looking forward to the rebuilding of the railway, myself. The views come immediately either way. On the red trail, follow the markers. Keep in mind that you will pass many other trails. The Beacons and the Fishkill Range, more so than other Highland hills, are crossed by footpaths, herd paths, old farm roads, logging roads, military roads, and abandoned town roads, off-road-vehicle trails, city and utility roads, tourist trails, and hiking paths, all going in different directions. Don't get disoriented.

At the top of the railway is a vast view of the Hudson River and all of Orange, Ulster, and Dutchess counties. Before you is wide Newburgh Bay, which ends at Danskammer Point (that's the second power plant, to the right). From there north runs the entire Long Reach, just past the Mid-Hudson Bridge where the river appears to stop. Actually, it curves to the left out of sight into a stretch known as Crum Elbow. Starting with the hills to

The view from South Beacon Mountain.

the far right, there are the South Taconics on the horizon. To the left of that, Stissing Mountain rises like an island; it's amazing to think it is part of the same Hudson Highlands rock you are standing on at Mount Beacon. Across the Hudson stand the Catskill Mountains, with the Marlborough Hills in the foreground bordering the river. To the left and in front of the Catskills, the white cliffs of the Shawangunks climb southward to their highest at Sam's Point, then drop to a low, long ridge known as the southern Shawangunks. Keep looking left, and there is long, broad Schunemunk Mountain, and finally the Hudson Highlands, starting with the hills of Black Rock Forest, to the steep face of Storm King with Little Sugarloaf in front of it and Pollepel Island with Bannerman's Castle where the river just seems to end. Here the river looks every bit the true fjord it is, a glaciated channel lying below sea level, flooded by the ocean and adorned by steep-sided mountain slopes that plunge straight down into the water. To your far left is the fire tower atop South Beacon Mountain, your destination.

A few words about Danskammer. In the 1600s Dutch skippers saw Indians dancing by firelight on this flat rock that today houses one of Central Hudson Gas and Electric Corporation's coal and oil power plants. *Duyvel's danskammer*, or "devil's dancehall," they named it, although the Native people had, of course, no concept of any devil, let alone devil dances. Acreswide, perfectly level, only 2 or 3 feet above the Hudson waterline, natives continued to gather at this site for sacred ceremonies even into the 1800s, long after they had been forced to move from the area.

There are many trails from this point and as of this writing they are all unmarked. The trick is to look at the fire tower on top of South Beacon and choose level trails toward it. Head straight back from the railway toward South Beacon Mountain on a level old road. The vegetation is mostly oak. The tall ones are stunted red and chestnut oak. The short ones are bear or scrub oak *(Quercus ilicifolia)*. Spiky, squat, and gnarled, scrub oak grows no taller than a shrub, forming thickets. Bushwhack through this highland stuff and you'll get speared; the wood in those skinny branches is tough!

At an intersection with four trails, count from the right and take the second trail. This leads toward South Beacon and is blazed with red on white and blue paint markers. (The first trail on the right is also blue, and leads downhill.) You will bypass the communications towers and the summit of North Beacon Mountain on your left shoulder, gaining steadily on South Beacon.

If there's been a fire (and the Beacons are prone to them) you will pass sections sprouting new growth. Depending on how long it's been since the blaze, and how intense were the flames, you may find only bright green mosses and bracken fern, or meadowsweet and sweet fern bushes, or a thicket of paper birch and other deciduous saplings. Amazingly, cottonwood, normally a tree of moist, bottomland soils, can grow thick in these fire openings, its cottony seeds blown on winds from the river below up to the mountaintop. The various saplings flourish for a while, but above the height of a man they tend to get shorn off by winter storms. Eventually they will probably be replaced by the hardy squat and tough oaks, the lowbush blueberries, and the sedges of the highland forests. To survive, flora on the Beacons must be adapted to these three: fire, storm, and supremely arid soil. This is one rigorous habitat.

Over the centuries, these mountaintop scrub oak woods have seen little use (as compared to the lowlands), and probably look much as they did when Robert Juet looked at them from Henry Hudson's *Half Moon* on September 30, 1609, and wrote, "The Mountaynes looke as if some Metall or Minerall were in them. For the Trees that grow on them were all blasted, and some of them barren with few or no Trees on them."

Beacon Reservoir can be seen through the trees on your left, the city's drinking water. Originally called Fishkill Reservoir, it was formed in the early 1900s by damming natural springs to flood an abandoned farm and apple orchard. Shortly, the blue trail cuts right and steeply climbs up South Beacon, using bedrock as the trail to avoid further rutting the mountain slope.

The old state fire tower is signed as closed to the public and dangerous. Anyway, you hardly need it to appreciate an extraordinary 360-degree view. You can see all the Hudson Highlands, and the shorn-off slopes of the mountains where the glacier plowed the river channel. New York City is easy to see. From Manhattan looking left, or east, you view Haverstraw Bay of the Hudson River. Farther to the left is all of Westchester and Fairfield counties, the communications tower of the Fahnestock plateau in the foreground. Looking left still, on the horizon are the Housatonic Highlands of Connecticut, then the taller South Taconics at the Massachusetts border, and the Berkshires. Keep going left past the little, rolling bumps of the Taconics. There by itself is the two-hump profile of Mount Greylock, the highest point in Massachusetts, close to the Vermont border. On a very clear day it is possible to peek into Vermont, and north to the Adirondacks. As before from North Beacon, there stands the entire range of the Catskills. Follow that long, low ridgeline of the southern Shawangunks to where it gets high again. Those are the Kittatinny Mountains in New Jersey on the Pennsylvania border. And, as before, Schunemunk Mountain and all the great heights of Storm King and Breakneck Ridge are paled into small hills from on top of mighty South Beacon Mountain. Only broad and tall Bull Hill looks to impress you from where you stand. Behind Crow's Nest runs a long ridge on the horizon, topped with a tower. That is part of the Ramapo Highlands on the New York–New Jersey border. Sugarloaf Mountain, which looks to be so tall from the river, is just a bump, low among the hills in front of Manhattan. It is noticeable from here only because its conical shape causes it to stand out in shadow. And, I swear, once when I stood up here the sunlight angled just right to dance a silver line along miles and miles of the salt water of Long Island Sound; a dark ribbon of land behind that was Long Island, and a sparkling beyond that was the open sea.

11 · Fishkill Ridge Conservation Area

Location: Beacon
Distance: 5 miles, 4 to 6 hours
Owner: Scenic Hudson, managed by State of New York as
part of Hudson Highlands State Park

The maze of trails that characterizes the Beacons continues here at Fishkill Ridge. Thank goodness the New York–New Jersey Trail Conference and others have marked routes through the maze. Nonetheless, the hiker must stay on guard to follow the blazes through the labyrinth. Either that, or enjoy a jolly time using whatever trails and old roads the territory throws at you as you come upon them. There are great views throughout, bald hills, highland forests, an abandoned bulldozer in the center of nowhere, dark Hell Hollow, and the remnants of hardscrabble farms. Wow! What better place to have fun exploring?

Access

Just 0.2 mile past the junction of NY 52 and I-84 (exit 12) on the west end of the village of Fishkill, turn left onto Old Glenham Road. Go 0.8 mile. Just past the Glenham Post Office, turn right onto Maple Street. At the end of Maple Street, cross the bridge and turn left on Old Town Road. Turn right on Sunnyside Road and go to the end. Bear left, then right, and continue up the hill to parking. Dogs allowed on leash. Information: Scenic Hudson, 845-473-4440 or visit www.scenichudson.org; state park headquarters at Fahnestock, 845-225-7207; NY–NJ Trail Conference, 210-512-9348 or visit www.nynjtc.org.

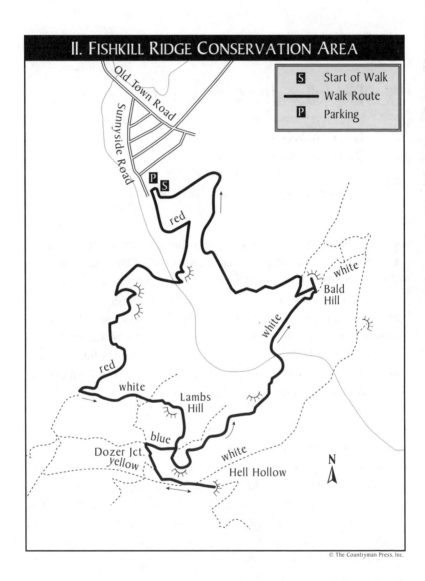

II. FISHKILL RIDGE CONSERVATION AREA

Old Town Road

Sunnyside Road

S Start of Walk
—— Walk Route
P Parking

P **S**

red

red

white

Bald Hill

white

white

red

white

Lambs Hill

blue

Dozer Jct.

yellow

white

Hell Hollow

N

© The Countryman Press, Inc.

Trail

From the parking lot, walk back along the entrance drive (a dirt road) to the kiosk on the left to pick up the red trail. Soon, you'll come to a fork. The left fork, on an old woods road, is your return. Bear right on the red trail. A moderate to steep climb leads you through open, mixed deciduous woods that abound in sarsaparilla in spring. Boulder fields cover the wooded slopes. Be sure you are always following the red blazes, since the path sometimes follows old farm roads for a span before turning off.

Finally you gain your first view of the Hudson River valley, in one glance seeing the entire Long Reach from the Newburgh–Beacon Bridge to the Mid-Hudson Bridge. At your feet are the state prisons and I-84. Straight ahead on the river's west bank stand the double boxes of Central Hudson's Roseton plants, and to the right or north of that is the Danskammer plant with its single, white smokestack. These supply power to the eastern U.S. electricity grid. The entire chain of the Marlborough Hills rises behind the river, behind them the Shawangunk Ridge, and behind them the Catskill Mountains.

On the east bank of the Hudson, to your right, you view the length and breadth of Dutchess County clear to the highest mountain in the distance: Stissing Mountain's wavy profile. To the far right rise the South Taconic Mountains.

Climb a bit farther and you enter a dwarf chestnut and scrub oak crest woodland that bears the brunt of storms. The trail becomes an escarpment path through the lowbush blueberry with wide views south along the Hudson of Newburgh, Beacon, and Denning's Point with a green cove of Asiatic water chestnut at the mouth of Fishkill Creek. Climb even farther into mountain laurel as you attain the crest. Taller oaks and maples grow along the top where the land is more sheltered from storms and the soil richer and deeper. Old stone walls evidence historic farming use. Continue. At the next outlook grow pitch pines. The Beacon Mountains come into view.

At the T-intersection, you can see the towers of Mount Beacon and the fire tower on top of South Beacon Mountain to the left, with Beacon

Reservoir at its foot. Turn left onto the white trail. You are entering that maze mentioned earlier. At this point you might want to offer yourself a little prayer for good luck. Follow blazes very carefully. There is one instance where the blazes indicate an obscure left turn off the beaten trail. If you miss this, you will find the way blocked by deadfall beside stone walls. Backtrack until you find the white blazes. This will lead you to the summit of panoramic Lambs Hill with its view of the Beacons, then steeply down toward Hell Hollow.

Whenever I find myself in this area, I cannot resist a visit to the edge of Hell Hollow, so, if you want, make a right turn onto the blue trail at Dozer Junction (location unmistakable) and at the bottom of the hill turn left onto the old overmountain or notch road, Hell Hollow Road, marked in yellow, that connected Mountain Avenue in Beacon with Albany Post Road (today's US 9). In the past, this was an important springtime route, when the lowlands around Fishkill flooded. Do not follow the yellow markings uphill to the right; those lead south to Scofield Ridge.

Hell Hollow Road brings you out to a view of what some say is the Fishkill Wind Gap. The north-facing slope of the hill opposite the trail is covered in hemlock. Sheer cliffs plummet into Hell Hollow, a wild and windy drop choked with talus, best seen when the leaves are down. Sometimes ravens are seen and heard here.

Now you have a choice. You can either return uphill past Dozer Junction to continue on the white trail, or keep on along Hell Hollow Road a bit more, going downhill, to intersect the lower loop of the white trail. Either way, head along the ridge to Bald Hill's bald summit and wide and windy views. You'll know you've found the summit because there will be a benchmark (a copper disc embeded in the bedrock) labeled "Bald Hill." You'll have views similar to those from Bull Hill (see that chapter) with the skyscrapers of Manhattan rising over the hills like a ghostly castle. The hills opposite Bald Hill (where the active quarry is) are also part of what was historically called the Fishkill Ridge.

Now, to find the return route to the parking lot is a bit of a challenge, because it is unmarked. From the benchmark at Bald Hill, abandon the

Fishkill Ridge Conservation Area

white trail and take the unmarked path on the right, which leads south toward the Beacons. It is a wider track than the newer white trail. Follow this just a short way, off the knoll, to a T-intersection. Turn right on another unmarked path. In a short while, take your next left on an unmarked old woods road. Follow this road all the way downhill to the parking lot. Whew! You did it!

12 · Clarence Fahnestock Memorial State Park

Location: Dennytown, Putnam Valley
Distance: 3.5 miles, 4 to 5 hours
Owner: State of New York

Within the last decade, Fahnestock has doubled in size and is still growing, largely due to the efforts of the Open Space Institute working with the New York State Parks Department through conservation-minded patrons, notably the Lila Acheson and DeWitt Wallace Fund for the Hudson Highlands, established by the founders of the Reader's Digest Association, Inc., to preserve for us all a vast public playground of wilderness.

Yes, this land was farmed in the past. Yes, it was mined, and used in myriad other ways. Entire communities have come and gone here. Now it is the hiker's domain, a wild place where you can wander and know that the distant views contain still more protected land to explore. In a day when natural areas are becoming islands within suburbia, it is a wonder to enter this, the fifth largest park in the entire state at 13,150 acres and growing, easily the largest in Dutchess and Putnam counties.

So large is Fahnestock that once you disappear into the folds of its hollows and wooded hills, there is silence. Only wind and birdsong echo off the hills. No constant traffic. No sirens. Only now and then the solitary sound of a car, or a plane, for a short time, and distant. This great silence, the endless woods with views now and then of blue hills, and the knowledge that one can just keep ranging onward rivals the Adirondack park. It even smells like the Adirondack woods here sometimes.

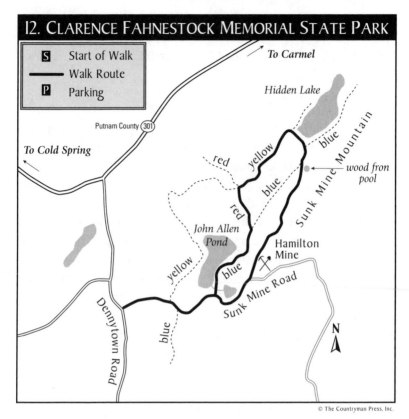

12. CLARENCE FAHNESTOCK MEMORIAL STATE PARK

In Fahnestock, there are recreational facilities where you can swim, camp, fish, picnic, or rent a boat. But the bulk of the property is for the bushwacker and the hiker. Trails lead through upland woodland that still bears the stamp of a mining and farming history, through wide fern glens, along hollows with secret brooks, and to wild lakes. There are enough trails for Fahnestock to have its own big guide book. Offered below is only a smattering of suggestions. The large number of marked trails hint at the even larger number of unmarked and slowly fading old trails and roads.

Though inland from the Hudson River, geologically the park is part of the Hudson Highlands and shares the hill region's special cold climate.

Those who commute the Taconic State Parkway during the winter know that everywhere else north and south it may be raining but climb the Fahnestock plateau and it's Winter Wonderland. Expect snow on the trails until the end of March.

Access

From the Taconic State Parkway, exit onto NY 301 west toward Cold Spring. Go 3.1 miles, past Pelton Pond (stop in at the park office on the left for a trail map) and Canopus Lake (boat rentals), until you see a large satellite communications tower on the hilltop in front of you. Turn left onto Dennytown Road. There will be a sign for the Taconic Outdoor Education Center. Go 1.7 miles to a dirt lot on your left at the "Road Closed" sign. If you own a vehicle with a high carriage and four-wheel drive and if no gate has been erected, you can turn left onto old Sunk Mine Road and drive 1.2 miles until the lake is on your left. Parking is in pull-offs. Do not block the road. For the rest of us, since this road is no longer maintained, it is best to park and walk on in. The woods are superb along this old road. Or drive in as far as you dare and park in a pull-off. Dogs allowed on leash. Information: park office, 845-225-7207.

Trail

If you're walking in from Dennytown Road, keep on for 1.2 miles on old Sunk Mine Road, a pleasant woodland walk good for birding and botanizing. Fahnestock is known for its bright and fragrant woods. A friend once commented to me that "woods don't get better than this." Which is remarkable considering what these woods have been through historically.

Soon as Europeans settled the land and right on up to the 20th century, the forests of Fahnestock were lumbered. The tannin in oak and hemlock bark was used to tan animal skins into leather. Wood was used for construction and for firing commercial brick kilns. Whole forests of logs were piled into great pits and slowly roasted into charcoal for home stove cooking fires and iron furnaces.

Even in colonial times, the Hudson Highlands were known to contain deposits of iron ore that was strongly magnetic, known as magnetic oxide of iron, or magnetite, but it wasn't until 1821 that exploratory cuts were made in the area you are walking. In the 1860s, five mines operated on Sunk Mine Mountain. Known as the Canada Mines Group, the largest was the Sunk or Stewart Mine: 1,500 feet long and 300 feet deep. Odelltown, an entire community, flourished nearby on Canopus Creek. A railroad on site transported the ore to NY 301 where horse and wagon carted it to the foundry at Cold Spring and then by barge to New York City.

These lumbering and mining activities changed the way the Fahnestock plateau looked. More change came with the Depression. Around 1935, the Civilian Conservation Corps dammed, among other waterways, Sunk Brook to form John Allen Pond, which you should be seeing through the trees on your left after that 1.2 miles of walking the road. It is the CCC dams you will walk on around this lake. You probably noticed the blue Three Lakes Trail that came in from the right and joined the road some ways back. Once you come to John Allen Pond, follow the blue trail as it leaves the road and turns left toward the lake. Go down the slope, across Sunk Brook that waterfalls over the ailing dam, and turn right.

The trail soon leads out on the shore of the lake at another, lower dam. Three-inch-long green-yellow "caterpillars," the spent male catkin flowers of the overhead oaks, litter the trail in mid-June. The trail leads downhill away from the lake. The land may have gotten a rest since the Depression and the woods may have grown back, yet a sharp eye will still find the slag heaps, ditches, and old roads from past use. The signs are everywhere. Fahnestock is riddled with foundations, old wells, pits, holes, cuts, charcoal heaps, ore dumps, and railroad beds. For a few yards on the blue trail, you walk on one of the old roads and, should you miss the right turnoff, you'll come to the stone foundation of a collapsed bridge. Just below this bridge, the trail passes a clump of gray beeches with bark stretched smooth as skin. Rejoin the old road and bear left at the tiny remnant of a clearing (John Allen's farmsite) closing in with blueberry and seedling trees. Pass foundations on both sides of the trail as you climb uphill.

Watch for a left turn at a cairn onto the red trail for a pretty walk in June through blooming mountain laurel and across a brook on stepping stones. At the next intersection, look on your left for two interrupted fern plants, so named because the dark brown fertile fronds hung like shriveled gills occur midway on the stalk that otherwise bears ordinary green sterile fronds. These two ferns (yes, there's only the two, and I'm mentioning them because, barring accident, they should survive in this spot for decades) grow on thick, black rhizomes hairy with rootlets. Watch for this species elsewhere as you walk the Hudson Valley, and you may come across that intriguing phenomenon of aged farm fields, the fairy ring. If these two interrupted ferns spawn more plants, it is possible for a clump of such individuals to grow outward from their place of origin for about 50 or more years to form a perfect circle of tall ferns around an empty center within which pixies were once said to appear on moonlit nights.

Turn right onto the yellow trail, the old mine railroad, well built and a pleasure to walk. As you pass a swamp the road is lined with highbush blueberry bushes. Late June and early July is the time when the berries are ripe and blue and bursting. At the next intersection turn right, following the yellow markers, to the earthen dam shore of Hidden Lake. Watch the water's edge for green frogs, pickerel, and bluegill. Damselfly and dragonfly adults hunt for insects in the air. Underwater, tadpoles and insect nymphs swim among spatterdock and pond lilies.

Each summer, female snapping turtles climb on the dam, painstakingly dig holes, and lay fifteen to fifty white, leathery, round eggs. The eggs are covered over again with sand, and you'd never know they were there unless you happened to see them hatch out. Raccoons find them, however, and each year dig for an egg feast. Infant mortality is a powerful control on reptile populations. Look for signs of this predation: disturbed sand and shriveled pieces of egg shells.

Wild blue irises bloom on John Allen Pond.

Continue across the dam (if there is no bridge you may have to make some fancy footwork to get across the brook) and into the woods. I've seen black rat snakes here in the past. Most readily spotted sunning in the grass, these large, harmless constrictors spend most of their time in the trees. They are common. One lying the length of a branch looks like just another extra-thick branch. At the intersection turn right onto the blue trail. See the sunny slope floored in what look to be grasses between dark, tall trunks of oaks and sugar maples? Those are sedges. Feel a sedge stem. It is triangular. Grass stems are round.

The blue trail leads back to John Allen Pond. Halfway up the sedge slope is a seepage area. At the end of this, leave the blue trail and head left. There is no marked trail. No trail is even apparent. Trust me. Follow the trickling water from the seepage upstream and uphill and you will shortly see a footpath heading right along a swamp. If you are walking here in early April you will already have heard a terrific racket from up ahead. It sounds like hundreds of sticks being clacked together. You're in luck! The wood frogs are singing in the swamp pools. They gather for only two weeks to mate and then disperse back into the woods.

To see a wood frog up close, walk to the shore where the water is deep. This is crucial. In drought years when the water is shallow, the wood frogs will be found only far out in the deeper center of the swamp, a difficult spot for you to get to. If the water is deep and they are croaking here by the shore, they will hear and feel you coming, and will dive out of sight. Get seated in a position that you can hold comfortably for the next ten minutes. Lean over and put one hand, palm up, in the water up to your wrist. Then wait, without moving, until the first wood frog resurfaces. It may take five or even ten minutes, but it's worth the patience. When one finally does resurface, keep still. Frog vision centers on movement. If you move, he'll dive. Stationary objects are ignored, so remain perfectly motionless, and more will come up. One will start to sing, then another. Finally, they'll be satisfied that you're no longer there, and they'll start in again with the racket.

A male wood frog sings by inflating two air sacs over his shoulders. He swims and glides through the open water, mounting anything his size that moves. Should he mount a receptive female, she'll lay eggs, and he'll fertilize them. More often it's an unreceptive female or another male, which results in a lot of splashing and croaking.

Once the frogs have gotten back into the swing of things, slowly move the fingers of your hand back and forth in unison. Do not move your palm. Your fingers will look the size of a frog, and the waves you send out will be frog-sized. This will attract the nearest males, who will come to investigate. Let them swim onto your hand. Then you can pick them right up.

Wood frogs are brown and cinnamon, with a black mask over their gold eyes. They come to your open hand because of the Laws of Frog Behavior: If it moves and is larger than you, run from it. If it moves and is smaller than you, eat it. If it moves and is the same size as you, mate with it.

In past decades, I have often seen the cloud jellies and strings of frog and salamander eggs floating in the numerous woodland pools of Fahnestock State Park. Sadly, the increased ultraviolet light of the modern atmosphere shining onto the eggs in the leafless spring literally fries the embryos and has contributed to the decline of these species.

Continue along the unmarked trail, which soon opens out into an old woods road. You are walking just west of the brink of Sunk Mine Mountain. When you see a clear spot, bushwhack to the edge of the cliff for the view. The phragmites reed marsh at your feet is all that remains of a millpond. The hills pile up along the horizon, wild and windy and dark. Below you lies a steep mountain slope riddled with sunken mines, holes, shafts, adits, and pits. Please do not explore these mines. They are treacherous.

Continue along the old woods road. At one point you may notice a trail that leads over the ridge to your left. Choose instead the right fork. The road winds down into a rocky hollow of open woodland. This is where my friend remarked that woods don't get better than this.

Enter a corridor lined with ironwood and black birch. You are at John Allen's old farm. Foundations lie on either side in the woods, many marked by barberry thickets. Explore them with care. There's a narrow but deep well that you do not want to fall into. Watch for a magnificent stand of witch hazel *(Hamamelis virginiana)* on your right. These bloom in fall, when all other plants produce seeds. Once you've smelled the autumn-subtle yellow, spiderlike blooms of witch hazel, you can identify its proximity simply by the honey-sweet odor in the air on a sunny day. Oil distilled from the inner bark makes a popular sore-muscle remedy. A rod of witch hazel with a crotch is the original divining rod.

At the dirt road (Sunk Mine Road), turn around and look back the way you came. See the mine cut on the right? That's Hamilton Mine.

Turn right onto Sunk Mine Road to return to your car. Just before duck-weed-covered Mud Pond, you'll pass a house foundation on your left built of dressed, native stone.

Other wood frog pools to visit

The first rainy, steamy night in late March transforms the dead wintry landscape into spring. On that night, the amphibians emerge from their hibernation burrows and make their way en masse to the woodland pools of their birth to spawn the next generation. Hundreds are crushed on roads. Thousands make their way through the nighttime forest. Count about two weeks from that first night when you hear the spring peepers chorusing, for after that the wood frogs are done mating and disperse back to the woods. To view wood frogs in the daytime, stop at any pool where you hear peepers and listen for the wood frog calls, which some people say sound like ducks. Wood frogs usually (but not always) appear in the same pools as peepers. It must be a pool with shallow open water, if interspersed by tussock sedge hummocks all the better. Two parks that have wood frog pools are Manitou Point Preserve, Putnam County (see the chapter) and Whitlock Preserve, Stanford, Dutchess County, which offers the most convenient wood frog viewing. From the Taconic State Parkway, exit onto US 44 east toward Millbrook. In about 1 mile turn left onto NY 82 north toward Stanfordville. Go 4.9 miles to a right onto Knight Road. The preserve is on the corner. In 200 feet is the parking lot entrance. The pool is to the right (not the deeper pond to the left). Beware of the thorny barberry bushes.

Some new walks in Clarence Fahnestock Memorial State Park

Clear Lake Scout Reservation, Canopus Hollow, Appalachian Trail

This lively 4- to 6-hour hike will take you into the heart of the old Fahnestock park, to Sunk Mine Road, and also along new trails through Clear Lake Scout Reservation, previously closed to the public. You'll travel through quintessential highland woods interspersed with wetland openings, rock cliffs, views of lakes, and hills to climb. Be sure to have a trail map with you for this walk (available at the park office). Park opposite the boat rental on Canopus Lake on NY 301. Facing away from the lake, cross the highway and walk to the right along the road onto a side trail that parallels the road. Keep on until you see the blue trail on your left. Follow this past Phillips Mine on your right to a left onto the green trail. You will pass through lovely green woods floored in acres of hay-scented fern, a hallmark of Fahnestock Park. An aggressive species, this fern can hold control of a place for decades, crowding out other plants. Turn right onto a second blue trail that traverses ridges with views of the scout camp lakes (closed to the public). Keep on the blue all the way to its end near one of the scout lakes. Turn right on an old woods road, then right again onto Sunk Mine Road. Follow through gorgeous and wild Canopus Hollow until the white Appalachian Trail on your right. Take the Appalachian Trail all the way back to your car along the old mine railroad.

School Mountain Road

Only got a short time? Park at Hubbard Lodge off US 9, just north of the intersection of US 9 and NY 301. A gate on the right marks old and magical School Mountain Road. Follow gradually uphill along a brook past stone walls and the woods of old farmland. You can walk for about 5 miles deep into the forested hills, and it just keeps getting better the farther you go. Since trails link up with the road several wide loops are possible, even a whole day's rigorous hike.

Wiccopee Pass

A remote area. From the intersection of I-84 and US 9 in Fishkill, drive south on US 9 for 2.7 miles. Just as you cross the county border, slow down for the left turn onto narrow East Mountain Road North. Follow for 0.4 mile and keep straight on Esselborne Road. Take this for 0.9 mile and turn left at the stop sign onto East Mountain Road South (unmarked). Follow this for 1.1 miles. It will become dirt along the way. When East Mountain Road North comes in on your left just keep straight on the dirt East Mountain Road South (still unmarked). Drive 0.6 mile. You'll pass the trailhead for the north end of Schoolhouse Mountain Road (white trail). Keep on to a right turn onto Troutbrook Road. Drive 0.3 mile to a fork. Bear left. In less than a tenth of a mile watch carefully in the woods on your left for a trailhead, just before the fork rejoins. Drive down this dirt track to park at the gate. The yellow trail leads past a recent farm into upland woods interspersed with the familiar hay-scented fern groves, past several historic charcoal pits (oval depressions in the ground). This meets up with the red trail, where shortly there is a view on the left within a scrub oak–ringed opening clear across the hills of Putnam County, especially if you stand on top of the glacial erratic boulder (caution: slippery when wet). A wide loop of perhaps 8.5 miles is possible by following the red trail to a right onto the blue, to a right onto the yellow, and right again on the white of School Mountain Road, and a final right on the blue again. Or you might want to just laze around the lake by the abandoned farm (if headed back to your car, follow the old road from the farm to the right for the lake). Either way, when it's time to leave descend off the plateau via scenic East Mountain Road North.

13 • Other Parks in the Hudson Highlands

Manitoga

Industrial designer Russel Wright made these 80 woodland acres one of his crowning achievements. Four miles of trails along a once hemlock-wooded slope of the Highland hills link up with the Osborne Preserve section of Hudson Highlands State Park and the Appalachian Trail. The grounds are open (donation requested) weekdays all year from 9 AM to 4 PM and on weekends from April to October only, 10 AM to 6 PM. Dragon Rock, Wright's experimental home and studio, is open for guided tours (fee). Call before you go for hours. Manitoga is 2.5 miles north of the Bear Mountain Bridge on NY 9D, or 2 miles south of Putnam County 403. Information: 845-424-3812 or visit www.russelwrightcenter.org.

Manitoga

Millionaires' Row

The aristocratic east bank of the Hudson River is the traditional abode of a landed gentry. With land bought from the Indians, the Livingstons, Van Cortlandts, Beekmans, Schuylers, Ten Broecks, Philipses, and Verplancks were granted their patents by European royalty. These manor lords lived at the expense of their tenants, a feudal serf system that did not end until 1876.

With the onset of the Industrial Revolution, the scenic east bank experienced another infusion of wealthy estates. The Vanderbilts, Morgans, Tiffanys, Wendels, Rockefellers, Goulds, Reids, and Sterns built mansions along the Gold Coast of the Hudson's shore near their financial empires in New York City.

Just before the 20th century, Newport and other places became popular. The owners of Millionaires' Row left and their homes were closed. Property prices dropped. Upkeep was too expensive for many of the mansions to remain in private hands. Knowing a good deal when they saw one, tax-exempt medical and religious institutions bought many of the estates and turned them into monasteries, schools, and hospitals. Others were abandoned. Some were preserved in what today are public parks.

14 · Denning's Point

Location: Beacon
Distance: Less than 1 mile, 1.5 hours
Owner: State of New York

The views from Denning's Point are superb, and the walk around it level and easy. Plans call for an estuarine research facility and museum to be built on this historic peninsula where Fishkill Creek joins the Hudson River and for a 1.7-mile trail to connect the Beacon MetroNorth train station with Denning's Point and Madam Brett Park.

This park is good for bird watching, and you may also see turkey, woodchucks, and cottontail rabbits. Be sure you can identify poison ivy before you visit this park. While there is none on the trail itself, plenty grows on the verge.

Access

From the intersection with I-84 just before the Newburgh-Beacon Bridge, take NY 9D south through the city of Beacon for 1.4 miles. Pass signs for the train station. Pass Hudson Avenue. At the next light, turn left onto South Avenue. Take an immediate right onto Dennings Avenue. Go 0.1 mile to a stop sign. Bear left to continue on Dennings Avenue. Continue to the dead end, bearing right at the wastewater treatment facility to a metal gate. As of this writing, a new parking lot is being created on the other side of the railroad tracks, so if that's been done simply follow the signs. Dogs permitted on leash. Park closes at dusk. Information: 845-225-7207.

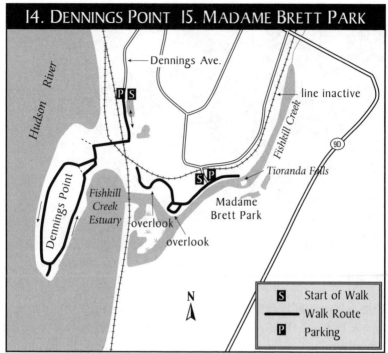

14. DENNINGS POINT 15. MADAME BRETT PARK

Dennings Ave.

Hudson River

line inactive

Fishkill Creek

P S

Dennings Point

Fishkill Creek Estuary

9D

Tioranda Falls

S P

Madame Brett Park

overlook

overlook

N

S	Start of Walk
—	Walk Route
P	Parking

© The Countryman Press, Inc.

Trail

People have lived here for a long time. All over the world, cultures favor settlement at the junctions of major tributaries to large rivers. We don't know exactly how long Native Americans lived at Denning's Point because the archaeological evidence was disturbed during colonial times, when Europeans took up residence on or near previously native village sites. It's probably safe to assume this site was always popular. European colonials noted there was an established Indian trail from the Hudson River at Denning's Point across the county to the Housatonic River in today's Connecticut, via Whaley Lake and Matteawan Stream (today's Fishkill Creek). In the early 20th century, remains of a village with arrowheads and spear points were chronicled near Denning's Point. Peter

View south of Breakneck and Little Sugarloaf, with the lowlands of Dutchess Junction in front.

DuBois leased the point from Madam Brett in the early 1700s. In the early 1800s, William Allen, whose grandfather founded Allentown of Pennsylvania, built a mansion on the point. William Denning bought it just nine years later, enlarged the mansion further and set up a brick works that took advantage of the Hudson's famous clay deposits to make bricks by the millions. Much of Manhattan was built of Denning's Point bricks. As you walk the trail around the point you will find bricks still, stamped DPBW for Denning's Point Brick Works. You will pass the mansion foundations, too.

From the old parking lot, walk around the gate along an old paved road. If the new parking lot has been opened, then you'll be driving in. There's Mount Beacon with its towers and South Beacon Mountain with its fire tower, through the trees off to your left. The road leads over the railroad tracks. On the bridge, framed dead center to the left is Little Sugarloaf with its bald patches. Continue, and at the fork bear left to an abandoned paper clip factory (future home of the museum and research facility). Keep right in front of the building to a view of the 80-acre bay of the confluence of Fishkill Creek with the Hudson. Osprey hunt here often, and you may hear their high, songbirdlike cheep-cheep. This bay is an irreplaceable spawning area for anadromous ocean fishes and includes the tidal portion of Fishkill Creek, from perhaps the railroad bridge you see there on upstream to the first waterfall in Beacon at Madam Brett Park. Straight ahead you see Storm King standing over Polle-pel Island and Bannerman's Castle. To the left rises Crow's Nest, then on the east bank is Little Sugarloaf and the wavy ridge of Breakneck that leads into the Beacons and Lambs Hill.

The path mown through the mugwort curves right into weedy woods. At the fork bear right. Walk the woods of walnut, elm, black locust, box elder, basswood, and the pervasive buckthorn, a Eurasian shrub with blue-black berries. Foundations, holes, excavations, and earthworks can be found throughout the point. The whole peninsula has been worked over many times. But as you continue, the forest contains mature sugar maple, Norway maple, black locust, and black cherry. Soon you see the Hudson's water through the trees and hear the waves. Keep on to the end where herd trails split off to the right to gain the water's edge. The first leads to a sand and pebble beach with views of Newburgh with wide Schunemunk Mountain behind. Beachcombing reveals black caltrops, the "devil" seed heads from the Asiatic water chestnut that clogs our water-ways, reams of them thrown up to the high-water mark; rounded bits of historic bricks; silvery driftwood; and smooth, rounded, gray stones and glass fragments. Return to the main trail and keep on to a second herd path that leads down to the very tip of the point with its view of the North Gate and grown over in dull-leaf indigo bush. Rushes sprout in the shallows. The rocks are the perfect place to sit and watch the waves and the boats, the light and the clouds on the hills. If you visit in late August, you can feast on the warm fruit of a wayward pear.

To return, simply continue on the main trail. Plans are in the works to connect Denning's Point with Madame Brett Park, making it possible to extend your walk up the Fishkill Creek to Tioronda Falls.

15 · Madam Brett Park

Location: Beacon
Distance: 1 mile, 45 minutes to 1 hour
Owner: Scenic Hudson

A new park and a delight. Praise to Scenic Hudson for making public the finest views on the Hudson River and its tributaries, sites previously off-limits for centuries because they were prime locations for industry. This entire area where Fishkill Creek joins the Hudson at Denning's Point was heavily used by Native peoples over millennia for villages, camps, and burial sites. Catharyna Brett, daughter and sole heir of Francis Rombout and his share of the Rombout Patent purchased from the Wappingers, built her home and gristmill at this park that today bears her name. It was the perfect location for settlement and industry, between waterfall and river: on one side, the shipping channel of the Hudson River; on the other, a natural, abrupt change in elevation where water above the falls could be directed to race through pipes into the mill, there to turn the various wheels and cogs of the mill's machinery. Today's NY 52 began as a footpath from the mill to a Wappinger Indian village in today's Fishkill Plains. Madam Brett sympathized with her native customers, including Daniel Ninham. In Fishkill Library you can read about the letters she penned to government officials testifying to the integrity of Chief Ninham and attempting to help Indians with various land and other legal disputes against the colonial Europeans.

As the centuries advanced, the site was used for a cotton factory and then a hat factory. The 12 acres of today's park include a boardwalk and two viewing platforms, one at the millrace at Tioronda Falls, and another over the creek mouth estuary. Future plans call for a bike trail link to Denning's Point and to Beacon Landing.

Access

On I-84 take the last exit just before the Newburgh-Beacon Bridge and go south on NY 9D into Beacon for 2.2 miles. Turn right onto Tioronda Avenue. After 0.7 mile turn left under the railroad overpass to the old factory. The parking lot is on the left. Dogs allowed on leash. Information: 845-473-4440 or www.scenichudson.com for Scenic Hudson, or 845-838-5000 for the city of Beacon. Open dawn to dusk. Note: none of the trails are marked. (See map on page 113.)

Trail

Take a seat on the bench by the information kiosk at the parking area and, through ingenious tapes, the bench describes the history of the site. For your first walk, head to the right to the elevated boardwalk along the 1800s Tioronda Hat Works factory building. Tioronda Falls may not look high, but the height differential harnessed through the millrace (which you'll see later) was more than plenty to power centuries of mills at this site. Falls like Tioronda—where streams thunder over bedrock escarpments just before reaching the Hudson—are the norm for practically all tributaries to the Hudson River in Dutchess and Putnam counties. Those at Wappingers Falls, where Wappinger Creek roars to the Hudson, and near the Poughkeepsie train station, where the Fallkill plummets, are even larger. The green water and stones here are murky with silt below the falls because the Hudson River tides reach all the way to the foot of the last rapid. The fresh water of Fishkill Creek mixes with the brackish water of the Hudson forming an estuary rich in plant and animal species. As with all major East Coast estuaries, the water of Fishkill Estuary is muddy. But watch the water; you'll see schools of Hudson River fish swim past, along with the familiar single sunfish of creek coves.

Fishkill and Wappinger Creeks are two of five major tributaries to the Hudson Estuary. Both form little estuary mouths onto the mother estuary of the Hudson and are irreplaceable spawning spots for adult eels and for anadromous fishes, which spend their adult lives in the ocean and their young larval lives in the Hudson and the small estuaries of its tributaries. Between April and June alewife, blueback herring, white perch, and striped bass come to Fishkill Estuary to spawn. Soon after, they return to the ocean. The eggs hatch within several weeks and the estuary becomes a nursery. Tomcod swim into the estuary to spawn in December and January. Year-round residents include largemouth bass, bluegill, pumpkinseed, redbreasted sunfish, and brown bullhead.

Continue to the end of the boardwalk and along a dirt trail, fragrant around Memorial Day with blooming Japanese honeysuckle and the European multiflora rose. Watch for an old city sewer manhole in the trail. A side path leads left down the bank to the estuary marsh's edge. In late summer you may hear the chirping of American bittern, Virginia rail, and marsh wren. Continue to a wood platform overlook. Fishkill Creek runs at the far left and the estuary marsh of sweet flag, spatterdock, pickerelweed, cattail, phragmites, and other emergent vegetation spreads before you. That's Denning's Point behind the marsh. Listen for the chirp of hunting osprey. In August and early September look for the scarlet blooms of cardinal flower on tall spikes in front of this platform. This is one of our most special native wildflowers, deep red as velvet.

Continue on the side trail to another open spot where you have a view of the Hudson Highlands: Little Sugarloaf and Storm King in the center, to the right the hills of Black Rock Forest, and to the left the rolling ridge of the Beacon hills. The bluff behind you has seen much historic use. All this stone and brick rubble lying about makes for good snake homes. You may see a black rat snake here, our native constrictor.

The return trail leads through riverside woods of the type that grows on old industrial sites where the soil has been disturbed: ailanthus, black locust, elm, and walnut. Throughout this park you will also see the trees of undisturbed major rivers in the Hudson Valley, namely silver maple and basswood. Keep to the main path. This follows along the bluff top and a verge of mugwort, goldenrod, and snakeroot. In spring watch for

Madam Brett Park

yellow-blooming coltsfoot. By the end of the trail you are almost to Denning's Point. Plans call for a trail link here, so once it is built you can extend your walk around the peninsula. Return to the talking benches of the parking lot.

The second walk leads upstream past the benches to Fishkill Falls, the old name of this spot when the creek was called Matteawan Creek. A side path leads to the foot of the falls and then continues to the millrace. You'll come to a spot where water flows across your path. This is a bypass flume. When the millrace was functioning, a vertical wood board was placed in the slots on either side at the head of the fall of water out of the race. You will see such boards still in place farther upstream. If there was a flood, the board was lifted to prevent damage to the mill and the race itself. With the floodgate closed, the bulk of the race water flowed through the grate and shot underground to the mill's machinery. If you don't mind walking atop the millrace cement wall, you can continue upstream. Older stonework from earlier mills stands at the head of the race. And at the top of the falls is a manmade stone dam, the even line of the creek rippling over a remarkable single timber of wood.

Side Trip of Historical Interest

Madam Brett Homestead

The original Dutch home to seven generations of the Brett family, the county's oldest homestead is at 50 Van Nydeck Avenue in Beacon, one block south of Main Street on the east end of town. Owned by the Daughters of the American Revolution, the house can be viewed from the outside anytime. The interior is open 1 PM–4 PM the second Saturday of each month, April through December (fee), or by appointment. Information: 845-831-6533.

16 · Stony Kill Farm Environmental Education Center

Location: Wappingers Falls
Distance: 1 to 4 miles, 1 to 3 hours
Owner: State of New York

Driving through the new suburbia of NY 9D, gain a fresh breath of old country sights preserved at Stony Kill Farm: wide, green fields, sheep and cattle at pasture, and historic houses, along with trails through 756 acres homesteaded and farmed since the late 1600s. This land was part of the original purchase from the Wappinger Indians by Gulian Verplanck and his partner, Francis Rombout. It remained in Verplanck family hands for centuries and today showcases a fabulous stone farmhouse built by tenant farmers in the 1700s, a manor house and barns from the 1800s, and a trail past foundations of what may have been tenant farms that were part of the Underground Railroad that helped protect freed slaves. Some of the fertile bottomland was allowed to grow back into woods, making this the perfect park in which to learn about backyard ecology, since the same pattern of regrowth happened (or is happening) in most of our backyards. Most of the trails contain loops of varying length so that you can shorten or lengthen your walk as needed.

Access

Stony Kill Farm is located between Beacon and Wappingers Falls on NY 9D. From exit 11 (Wappingers Falls/Beacon) off I-84, take NY 9D north for 2.5 miles. There will be two main entrances, both on the left. The first one is at the historic tenant farmer house and barns. The second is

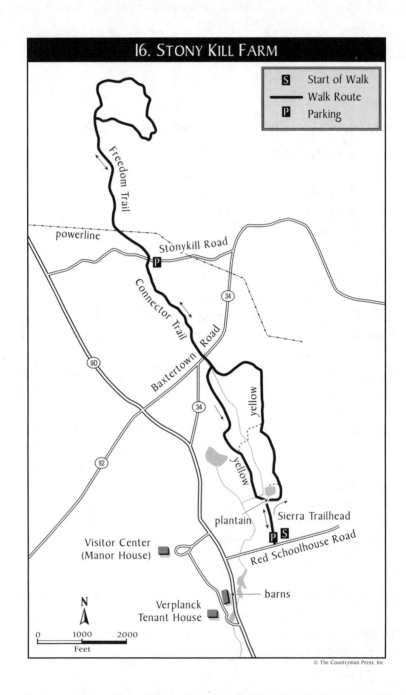

16. STONY KILL FARM

S Start of Walk
— Walk Route
P Parking

Freedom Trail

powerline

Stonykill Road

P

Connector Trail

34

Baxtertown Road

9D

34

yellow

92

yellow

plantain

Sierra Trailhead

Visitor Center
(Manor House)

P **S**

Red Schoolhouse Road

barns

N

Verplanck
Tenant House

0   1000   2000
Feet

© The Countryman Press, Inc.

at the manor house, which houses offices and exhibits (you can also pick up trail leaflets and maps here). Tour the historic buildings and the working farm. For the hiking trail described below, go to the traffic light, which is midway between the two entrances on NY 9D, and turn onto Red Schoolhouse Road. Proceed 0.2 mile, past the sign for the Muller Pond trail on the right, to a dirt driveway on the left signed Sierra Trail. Park in the field. No dogs allowed. Information: 845-831-8780 or visit www .dec.state.ny.us.

Trail

The yellow Sierra Trail, level for nearly all its 2 miles, begins as a dirt road at the end of the meadow. This is an old cow path, which was used for centuries. A short way in, watch for the white trail on your left that leads across NY 9D to the manor house. Thirty feet past this intersection on the left grows a swamp white oak—majestic, tall, and lopsided. There are practically no branches on the left side, but on the right the limbs stretch so far they overhang the trail, and the trunk leans so that you'd swear one good blow would knock it down. Oaks will reach for full sunlight as far as gravity allows. When you see a large old tree with low-slung branches in a forest, you know as a young sapling it grew in a field where it had the sunlight to itself. When it grows lopsided, it grew on the edge of a forest out into the sunlight of an open pasture. You will see such trees throughout Stony Kill's woodlands.

At the T-intersection, the trail is covered with the round leaves and the maroon-tipped stems of plantain *(Plantago major)*. A medicinal plant brought to America by European colonists, plantain escaped the herbal garden and today plagues suburban lawn-owners nationwide. They should be happy they've got it. Plantain is the cure for the kind of shallow skin-scrape kids get when they skid on pavement. Four plantain leaves folded, scrubbed on concrete to extract the juices, and applied to the hurt for ten minutes cures the pain and the swelling. No kidding.

For an old country trick, pluck a plantain with stem intact. Notice how the veins run close to the underside of the leaf, and how this underside looks like the hull of a wooden boat. Hold it in your palm top side up. With a fingernail, cut through the leaf at the base just above the stem, through the green but stopping short of the veins. Carefully, pull the stem from the leaf. With practice, you'll stretch out the veins, and you've got a miniature fiddle.

Take the right fork and follow the trail past the man-made ponds. A side trail on the left leads to the water. Stand on the bridge at the brook and look upstream. See the old-style stone culvert? This was a bridge wide enough for farm wagons. How old do you think it is?

Continue, and shortly enter open woods of red, black, white, and pin oak, red maple, tulip tree, and beech. To your right is a large red maple swamp. Throughout these woods you'll find a tree with a trunk like a muscled arm. This is ironwood *(Carpinus caroliniana)*, and as its name implies, it resists hammer and nails. Pass farmers' rock piles and failing red cedars overmastered by the deciduous trees. As you walk, listen for a high sharp chirp, sometimes repeated incessantly. This is chipmunk, the only ground squirrel of the eastern woodlands. Listen also for the many songbirds that live in these woods, especially the waterfall notes of the veery.

The trail turns left for the return loop of 1 mile. If you wish to continue for the full 2 miles, keep straight. At the footbridge grow jewelweed and royal ferns. You may see an oil slick on the surface of the mud or the water. This is marsh gas, a natural byproduct of bacterial decay in an anaerobic, or nonoxygen, environment. It's smelly but indicative of a healthy swamp. If the water pools over a few inches, you may wish to try another country trick. Look for a jewelweed, the plant with the green translucent stems that resemble glass tubes. The stems swell at the nodes where the leaves sprout, and there is a purple base at the roots. Pluck one jewelweed leaf by the stem, careful not to touch the leaf itself. Hold the leaf underwater. Twirl it. The leaf turns as silver-bright as aluminum foil. Take the leaf out; it will be completely dry. This works even better in a sunny pond, or in a clear glass of water.

Jewelweed is also called touch-me-not. The jewels of yellow *(Impatiens pallida)* or orange *(I. capensis)* flowers ripen into green pods. When

Stony Kill Farm Environmental Education Center

ready, the pod walls turn translucent; you can see the black seeds inside. Touch the fat pod and pop! it explodes. The seeds wing away in all directions, propelled by a coiled green spring.

Yet another old country trick is to pluck a bursting-ripe jewelweed pod without exploding it, take it to a city friend, and tell them to close their eyes and put out their hand.

Up the tree trunks climbs poison ivy, lush and oily with urushiol acid. Should you touch poison ivy and get the toxin on your skin, don't wait until you get home to scrub with brown soap and smear on the calamine. Pick a large jewelweed, slit the glass-tube stem, and apply the ample juice. For most folks, this counteracts the toxin, but only if you use it right away after exposure.

Cross a stone wall and enter a stand of white pine. This was once a nursery, and you may not notice the tall tamarack for the denser spruce that follows. Hear the crickets ahead, toward the green glimmer through the trees? Cross a stone wall and walk out into a field. The trail turns left and follows the field edge.

In summer, many plant stems are globbed with spit. Grasshoppers and snakes get blamed for this, but if you explore inside a glob (not so disgusting as you think), you'll find a spittlebug nymph. Early in the morning, the spittlebug, soft bodied, green, with two red dots for eyes, exudes two chemical secretions that combine to form a liquid waxy soap. Dipping its abdomen tip into the soap, it bubbles the soap up until it is surrounded with a cool foamy nest in which to spend the day. The sweet-smelling spittle attracts small insects. They wade into the spit and into the waiting jaws of the spittlebug.

Follow the field edges with care; the ground is uneven from generations of plowing. Red clover, yarrow, hawkweed, bouncing Bet, buttercup, and milkweed are only a few of the native and alien species that bloom among the many species of grasses. Enter woods. Just before you descend a bank to a boardwalk, there is an obscure trail on your right, flagged but unmarked. This is the connector to the Freedom Trail. If you'd like to extend your walk, you can follow this to Baxtertown Road. Turn left for a few yards until you see the yellow trail resume. Follow to Stonykill Road (where there is parking for the trail). Follow the yellow discs past the power lines (surprisingly good for botanizing and butterflies) through moist woods that border upon the extensive red maple swamplands to a right onto an old farm lane delineated by the stone walls on either side. Here find the foundations and stone-wall enclosures for livestock production of an old farm. Tenant farmers of the Verplancks once homesteaded the land here. It has been suggested that this farm was a member of the Underground Railroad. The trail splits to make a loop that is marked in both yellow and blue blazes, which you should follow carefully past other, unmarked trails. It is interesting to try to mentally reconstruct the farm from the stone-wall patterns.

Return to the Sierra Trail, turning right to continue through woods, fields, and successional areas. Cross a bridge over the pond's outlet and you're back at the plantain spot. Turn right to return to your car.

Side Trip of Historical Interest

Mount Gulian Historic Site

Mount Gulian is the Verplanck family homestead, with restored Dutch house, original Dutch barn, garden, exhibits, and events. It was the Revolutionary War headquarters of General von Steuben and birthplace of the first American war veterans' organization, the Society of the Cincinnati. From the pond entrance on Farmstead Lane at Stony Kill, drive south on NY 9D for 1.4 miles. Turn left into Hudson View Park Apartments and made an immediate left onto Lamplight Street, which becomes Sterling Street. Drive to end. Open (fee) mid-April through October, Wednesdays through Sundays, 1 PM to 5 PM. In November and December, open only on Wednesdays and Sundays from 1 PM to 5 PM. Also open by appointment. Information: 845-831-8172.

17 · Locust Grove,
the Samuel Morse Historic Site

Location: Poughkeepsie
Distance: 3.5 miles, 2 hours
Owner: Locust Grove

Telegraph inventor and portrait painter Samuel F. B. Morse bought Locust Grove, a Livingston (and then a Montgomery) property for many years, in 1847 as a summer home. The site is now a registered National Historic Landmark open to the public.

Graceful and sweet, the romantic grounds and gardens contain 145 acres of woodland and fields historically farmed, pastured, and landscaped for carriage rides. It is a pleasant place to walk in spring or autumn, popular on Sunday afternoons and with Poughkeepsie business people on weekday lunch breaks. Locust Grove is one of the best places on the Hudson's bank to enjoy early spring wildflowers. Be sure to bring mosquito repellent if you visit in summer. The manicured trails, old carriage roads, are marked at all intersections with destination signs, so it is easy to wander along with nary a worry as the fancy takes you.

Access

Locust Grove is located 2 miles south of the Mid-Hudson Bridge, or 11 miles north of I-84, on US 9. The entrance is on the west side of US 9 at a stoplight at the intersection with Beechwood Road, just north of the Hudson and Poughkeepsie Mall plazas, and just south of Poughkeepsie Rural Cemetery. The grounds (free entrance) are open year-round 8 AM to dusk, weather permitting. No dogs allowed. The house and visitor

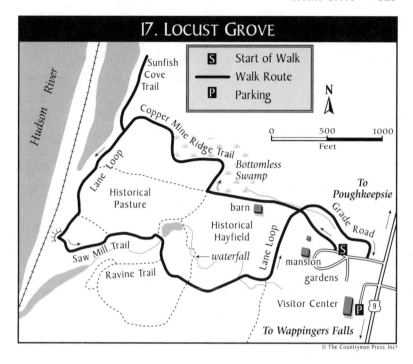

17. LOCUST GROVE

Sunfish Cove Trail

Copper Mine Ridge Trail

S Start of Walk

━ Walk Route

P Parking

N

0   500   1000
Feet

Hudson River

Lane Loop

Bottomless Swamp

To Poughkeepsie

Historical Pasture

barn

Historical Hayfield

Grade Road

Lane Loop

Saw Mill Trail

waterfall

mansion

S

Ravine Trail

gardens

Visitor Center

P

9

To Wappingers Falls

© The Countryman Press, Inc.

center are open May 1 to November, daily 10 AM to 3 PM; call for December hours. Admission to the house: $7.00 adults, $6.00 seniors, $3.00 children 6 to 18 years of age, under 6 years free. Information: 845-454-4500 or visit www.morsehistoricsite.org.

Trail

After a long, cold winter of bleak trees, one yearns for the green leaves of summer. Visit Locust Grove in mid-April where buds break open and woodland flowers bloom weeks before other, more inland sites due to the moderating effect of the Hudson River on local air temperature.

Pick up a trail map at the visitor center if it is open, then walk past the cottage through the gardens to the Tuscan villa–style house. The rows of blue Siberian squill or *Scilla* have escaped over the century into the lawn and spread blue carpets across the new-greening grass, along with the other blue but wider blossom called glory-of-the-snow. It sometimes seems that Hudson Valley houses built in the early 1900s can be dated simply by the sheets of *Scilla*, those old-fashioned bulb favorites, in their lawns. In a few weeks the blue cloud finishes and the plant goes dormant or senescent, drying up and disappearing for the remainder of the growing season. This survival technique is used worldwide by many plants, usually because something is in short supply and they must bloom and produce seed quickly. In the case of most early spring garden bulbs, the something is the shortness of the growing season itself in the north Eurasian native land where they evolved.

You might like to circle the house and admire the view off the bluff before following the carriage road to the right back around the front of the house and toward US 9 for about 80 feet. The trail begins on your left at a kiosk where you can pick up trail maps and leaflets that describe the grounds and paths. Pass pet cemeteries as you head downhill through a mixed deciduous forest of large tulip tree, Norway and sugar maple, black birch, hickory, locust, beech, ash, and witch hazel. In mid-April, the ravine wall is covered in an early, purple variety of corydalis, a native to China, and, happily, a native wildflower called trout lily. Before the non-native bulbs came, the trout lily probably carpeted the bank. By mid-May, both will be dying and soon gone as the bulbs go into senescence. *Erythronium americanum*, our native trout lily, is also known as dogtooth violet or adder's tongue. Look for it especially opposite the second pet cemetery. The single leaves sprouted out of the ground are shiny, leathery green mottled with purple-brown, one leaf per bulb. When this native lily bulb reaches maturity in seven or more years, it grows two leaves and blooms. The flowers are yellow, down-draped bells fringed on the inside with orange and purple-pollened stamens. They last perhaps a week, then wither.

So, what is the *something* that causes a native wildflower to senesce like a garden bulb? It is sunlight, available to the woodland floor in its full radiance only when the forest leaves are down. Trout lily takes advantage of another phenomena, though, and in so doing plays a key role in the overall health of the woodland. The spring rains of April trickling through the soil could leach out the nutrients essential for healthy forest growth. *Erythronium* and a few other spring woodland flowers, such as hepatica and anemone and, at this site, the masses of non-native flowers, are the only plants active at this time. Growing in carpets that blanket the forest floor, *Erythronium* roots absorb quantities of the soil nutrients before they can be leached away and store them in their purple and green leaves. The leaves photosynthesize until the tree buds break out overhead in the tree canopy. Once the full sunlight gets shut out, trout lily's flower and leaves wither and die. As they decay, the stored nutrients are released, just in time for the burst of tree activity and growth that needs them. The *Erythronium* bulbs expand underground, then go dormant in the soil until next April.

I have seldom seen so much trout lily as here at Locust Grove. As you walk you will find it everywhere throughout the entire forest except under the hemlock trees, or where celandine has pushed it aside.

At the fence, push open and close the gate behind you. The banks of the brook are verdant with lesser celandine, the beloved wild spring buttercup of England. Once a Victorian favorite along with *Scilla*, celandine has been mostly forgotten in the modern American garden. Here it grows so thickly that nary a trout lily shows. Wordsworth compared flowers of all of England but concluded

> *There's a flower that shall be mine,*
> *'Tis the little celandine.*

Now you can compare the yellow of the celandine with that of our native marsh marigold (see Franklin D. Roosevelt National Historic Site chapter, or the Black Rock Forest chapter in *Walks & Rambles in the Western Hudson Valley*). You know how I feel about it; which one is more golden in your view?

Take the right fork, which leads downhill and past the barn. The flat-topped, single-stone dry wall that borders the trail is quite unlike the rubble stone walls of the common historic farmer's fences. In late March, snowdrops looking like a drift of snow mass at the edge of the Bottomless

Locust Grove

Swamp on your right, and it is possible in the last week of April to see the one marsh marigold plant in bloom. One winter's day somewhere between 1900 and 1910, some people out for a drive thought they might take their carriage straight across this swamp. The carriage sank in and never was recovered, giving the swamp its name.

At the next intersection, turn right onto Copper Mine Trail. Many horticultural escapees occur in the woods. In mid-April the unfurling leaf buds of Japanese barberry mist the woods with green. Over them stands a yellow mist of blooming native spicebush. Juncos feed in the moist woods in a last farewell to winter as they head north for the summer. Skunk cabbage stands a foot high in the swamps and shadflies circle your head. Fortunately, the mosquitoes are not hatched yet. You might see a deer, still in the gray coat of winter soon to shed to the red-brown coat of summer. Wherever there's water, there is spring.

The trail leads to the oak woods of the river bluff. You can walk Sunfish Cove Trail to the right, coming back the same way. When the leaves are down there is a view through the trees of the river, Sunfish Cove, and the wooded hills. The only sounds are from pileated woodpeckers drumming, peepers chorusing, and the wind in the bare forest limbs, a peace suddenly startled by the passing of a train on the shore.

Take the right fork when you meet up with the Lane, then right again for a view from on top a cliff whose face in May is drenched with blooming columbine. Downriver is the Pirate Canoe Yacht Club, upriver the Mid-Hudson and Cantilever Bridges. You cannot see farther south, because this stretch of river runs straight for so great a distance that Robert Juet, a mate on board Henry Hudson's *Half Moon* named this long, straight stretch Lange Rack, or Long Reach. It runs from about Danskammer Point to the lower end of Crum Elbow. A sailing ship could navigate this impressively long straight sailing course with only one setting of the boom. North of the bridges, you can see the river turning to the left; that is the stretch called Crum Elbow.

The best and easiest view of the entire Long Reach is from the Mid-Hudson Bridge. As you drive across (or walk; there's a pedestrian walkway, see the Other Parks along the Hudson River chapter at the end of this section), you can see straight downriver, down the Long Reach, to Danskammer Point and, if it is a clear day, the Beacon Range on the horizon.

From Vanderbilt Mansion to Bowdoin Park, through Crum Elbow and the Lange Rack, runs the Poughkeepsie Deepwater Habitat, a 14-mile, nearly continuous river-bottom trench 30 to 125 feet deep. Such deepwater estuaries are rare in the eastern United States. The endangered shortnose sturgeon spawns and winters here, along with large numbers of anchovy, silverside, bluefish, weakfish, and hogchoker.

Do not continue past the solitary pitch pine where a herd path leads precipitously down to no purpose at a dead end at the tracks. Rather, return to the bench and find the trail that leads away from the river. In summer in these moist woods you may hear a trilling up in the trees, always a few trees or more away, never very close. These are gray tree frogs, amphibians found throughout the eastern woodlands and alert to your presence. At the ends of their long flexible fingers are tree-climbing pads. Most likely you'll never see one; though large as wood frogs, their skin is patterned like gray and green army camouflage. As soon as you come close to zeroing in on their tree, they clam up. Even should you locate the tree they're in, they blend in so perfectly you might be looking right at one and not notice.

Pass the site of Henry Livingston Jr.'s sawmill where you can see the earthen remains of the dam for the millpond. At the T-intersection turn right and head toward the house. At the pond, go right over the stone dam. To extend your walk, you can follow the ravine and hemlock trails, or visit the cascade trail on the left where purple and yellow early woodland violets lead to a little waterfall that curtains over an outcrop of bedrock. The Lane leads directly back to the house. When opposite the barn but still in the woods, peer into the swamp on your right for another single marsh marigold in bloom in late April.

At the fence and gate, you can vary your return with a left onto the Grade Road. This less steep carriageway leads through a ravine plush with snowdrop, Dutchman's breeches, and other wildflowers.

18 · Franklin D. Roosevelt National Historic Site

Location: Hyde Park
Distance: 3.75 miles, 3 hours
Owner: National Park Service

On the 290 acres of this site, there are the hay fields, the gardens, the lawns, Springwood (the mansion), the presidential library, and the various estate buildings. That's what visitors from all over the nation and the world mostly see. But there are also old carriage roads, now trails, through acres of wild ravines and a hemlock forest so vast you'd think you were in a state forest, the woods where FDR roamed and rode. Two long-range trails link this site with Vanderbilt Mansion to the north and with Val-Kill, Eleanor Roosevelt's estate, to the east. This is a good place to walk any time of year. In summer, the hemlock woods are lush and green. When the leaves are down come the best views of the dramatic rocks and knolls of the woods.

Access

Franklin D. Roosevelt National Historic Site is located 6 miles north of Poughkeepsie on US 9 in Hyde Park. From the entrance, drive to the Wallace Visitor Center, stop in for a look at the exhibits, and ask for a trail map. Then park all the way to the rear of the parking lot. The grounds are open from 9 AM to sunset. Dogs allowed on leash. Information: 845-229-9115 or visit www.nps.gov/hofr.

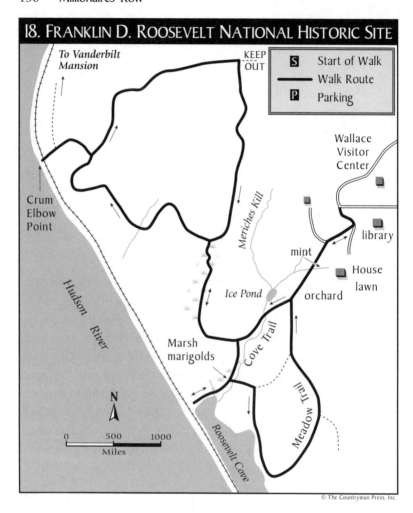

18. FRANKLIN D. ROOSEVELT NATIONAL HISTORIC SITE

S Start of Walk
— Walk Route
P Parking

To Vanderbilt Mansion

KEEP OUT

Wallace Visitor Center

Crum Elbow Point

Meriches Kill

library

mint

House lawn

Ice Pond

orchard

Hudson River

Marsh marigolds

Cove Trail

N

0   500   1000
Miles

Meadow Trail

Roosevelt Cove

© The Countryman Press, Inc.

Trail

Walk to the left-rear corner of the parking lot, where a paved road leads toward a gray, wooden house with delicate millwork, the old gardener's cottage. The road curves to the left in front of this small, historic house, then forks. Bear right downhill under hemlocks following the tulip-tree leaf "Hyde Park Trail" discs and blue "Cove Trail" discs. Take your next left (the paved road goes to a private residence) and pause a moment, if it is summer, to arm yourself with insect repellent. As you walk, listen for the sound of not the first but the second brook that runs through the grasses and bubbles under the road through a culvert. Mint grows on the left side where the brook disappears underground. If they've been mowing, you'll smell it. Feel a stem. Members of the mint family have square stems. These are the sort of mint leaves to float in a pitcher of pink lemonade.

Pass the apple orchard and the view of FDR's house up on the bank. Take the right fork into the woods, still on the Cove and Hyde Park Trail, headed toward the ice pond. In summer, the female deer flies will greet you. Great trail buddies, they follow and circle your head for as long as you walk the woods. While their males are off frequenting flowers, the females patrol for blood. Bodies gold and black, wings striped with brown, they hover over trails where they know from experience a full-blooded creature will come sooner or later. Their bite is painful, and their buzzing and swooping annoying. A hat is about the best you can do; that'll keep them off your scalp. Unfortunately, it won't get rid of them. A small consolation is knowing that it's much worse for the deer than for you.

The microclimate is cool and the ailing hemlocks dark. In a short while pass the ice pond on your right. Throughout the Hudson Valley, ice cutting was once big business, most of the ice being packed and shipped to New York City. Some even went as far as the West Indies. Most estates and larger farms formed their own ice ponds by damming small streams. This also made for good swimming in summer.

Back on the road, the trail follows the stream, known as Meriches Kill. Northern copperheads live in these woods, preferring the sunny rock outcrops at the top of the hills. Unless you go bushwhacking, you're not likely to encounter one. But should you see a snake, copperheads are unmistakable. Pictures and photographs rarely do them justice. Their heads are bright red-copper, like an Irish lass's hair. Their bodies have bright copper, dog-bone patterns against a lighter brown background. Despite this metallic coloration, copperheads are so well camouflaged against brown leaves that they usually go unnoticed.

The head is triangular, the poison glands being located at the base of the triangle. Nonpoisonous snakes that lack such glands have round heads. Get close enough to a copperhead (that is, caged—nature centers often have such exhibits) and you'll see the dark vertical slit for a pupil and, between the nostril and the eye, another hole. This is the pit. The copperhead is a pit viper. With this sensory organ, the snake in the black of night can see its prey by the infrared heat of the prey's body.

Copperhead poison is a blood toxin. A mouse bitten by a copperhead runs. The poison is pumped throughout its body and, shortly, the mouse drops dead. The copperhead follows the mouse's heat trail, locates it by smell (using its forked tongue, which withdraws into the mouth into two holes called Jacobson's organ), and swallows it whole, head first.

A human infant bitten by a copperhead is in mortal danger. An adult bitten by a copperhead is in more danger of nausea from a hospital's antivenin shot. Each year many nonvenomous snakes, thought to be copperheads, are killed. Unfortunate, seeing as how copperheads are mostly gentle, lethargic serpents content to lie motionless and hunt mice.

If you can't resist heading straight for the Hudson, at the fork go left, still on the Cove Trail. Walk out of the hemlocks into sunlight and a swamp. Come in May to see the marsh marigolds *(Caltha palustris)* that glimmer out in the wetland. No flower—neither buttercup nor England's celandine—blooms a petal so glossy gold-yellow as marsh marigold.

At the fork keep right on the Cove Trail. Meriches Kill empties into Roosevelt Cove, an inlet of the Hudson subject to the Hudson's tides. Cattail, arrowhead, wild rice, and spatterdock clog the inlet in warm weather. At the trail end sign and gate, head straight over the railroad tracks for the Hudson. (Be careful! Amtrak comes through here quietly at more than 70 miles per hour.)

Downriver are the Mid-Hudson Bridge and the railroad bridge. And yes, the deer flies are gone! This is a good spot to come in winter to see the ice floes.

As you face the river, on your right grows the tropical-looking dull-leaf indigo bush *(Amorpha fruticosa)*. In June, indigo-purple spikes bloom

Franklin D. Roosevelt National Historic Site

fringed with yellow anthers. Although dull-leaf indigo occurs commonly from Canada to Mexico along the Mississippi River system, it is specific to the Hudson River shore in Dutchess County. To your left grows ninebark *(Physocarpus opulifolius)*. Clustered white flowers in early June mature into green and salmon-pink dry bladders.

Return back across the tracks and up the trail. Pass the Meadow Trail on your right, and keep on to the next left onto the Forest Trail. This winds through hemlocks, steep ravines, outcrops of bedrock, brooks, and hollows. Soon you'll pass standing water in a swamp. Red ash *(Fraxinus pennsylvanica)* is the slim, straight tree that grows in the water with the swollen trunk base and a compound leaf of seven leaflets. Although extensive draining was attempted in the past, still, at the bottom of every hollow lies a black pool of water. Some keep their water all year. Others fill only in spring. These vernal woodland pools are the breeding centers for wood frogs, toads, spring peepers, spotted and Jefferson salamanders, and fairy shrimp. Come June, the amphibian larvae have either matured and fled or died, and the fairy shrimp larvae have matured and burrowed for the remainder of the year into the pool mud. Slowly, the pool dries, until all that is left is a black mat of dried dead leaves.

Next spring, rains refill the pool. The first steamy, warm rainy night of spring brings a mass movement of amphibians back to the pools of their birth. So also did their parents return to the same pool, and their parents before them, on down the ancestral line. Returning all on one night, in the mist and the rain, they lie in writhing mats of mass mating orgies.

At the fork you can go either way for the Forest Loop, which is about 1 mile long. The woods through here are stunning. The left fork is the Hyde Park Trail that, in 2 miles along the Hudson River woods and on paved roads, brings you to the Vanderbilt estate, but if you jog down it for just a few hundred yards, a left-hand spur will take you out over the railroad tracks to Crum Elbow Point smack on the river with a great view, a good resting spot. "Crum Elbow" comes from *kromme hoek*, "rounded corner" in Dutch, which later became *krom elleboge*, "crooked elbow," the name given by Dutch homesteaders to the point and to the bend in the Hudson River and to the creek that joins the Hudson at today's Vanderbilt Mansion. As you return, first turn right, then left to resume the Forest Loop. If you are walking here in April, watch for early spring woodland wildflowers such as Dutchman's breeches among the rocky outcrops.

Return to the Cove Trail. Turn right again and then take the next left for the Meadow Trail which will lead you back to your car. The deer flies will accompany you until you hit pavement.

19 · Val-Kill National Historic Site

Location: Hyde Park
Distance: About 1 mile, 1 hour
Owner: National Park Service

These 250 acres of woods, streams, and fields are seldom visited, and the wildlife and birds plentiful. The trail is just long enough, and the hill it climbs just steep enough, to provide a pleasurable outing on a Sunday afternoon, especially when paired with a tour of the estate. The loop trail leads through a beautiful hemlock and mixed-deciduous woodland interspersed with wetlands among knolls and hollows. Here you will see most of our regional trees, shrubs, wildflowers, and nearly all the main animals that earmark the eastern woodland biome: deer, beaver, turkey, and gray squirrel, pileated woodpecker, wood frogs and peepers, and painted turtles. All that seems missing is the black bear.

Access

From the intersection of US 9 and NY 9D just south of Hyde Park village, turn east onto Dutchess County 40A. Go 1.1 miles to a left onto NY 9G. The park entrance is 0.4 mile on the right. Park in the lot before the pond. Dogs allowed on leash. Trail open sunrise to sunset, every day all year. House open every day all year 9 AM–5 PM except Thanksgiving, Christmas, and New Year's Day. Information: 845-229-9422 or visit www.nps.gov/elro.

Trail

Walk toward the house past a row of northern white cedar on the right, tall and straight-trunked. These are identical to the riverside species you see growing twisted and rugged out of the sides of cliffs at Mills–Norrie

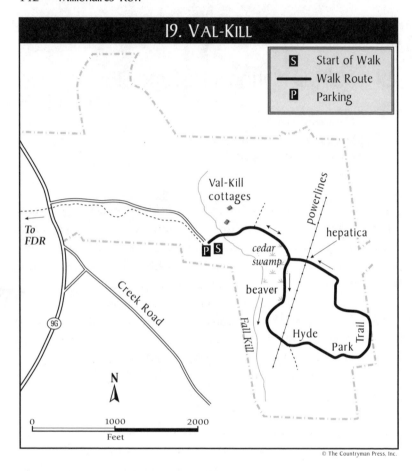

19. VAL-KILL

Legend:
- **S** Start of Walk
- ▬ Walk Route
- **P** Parking

Val-Kill cottages

To FDR

Creek Road

9G

Powerlines

hepatica

cedar swamp

beaver

Fall Kill

Hyde Park Trail

N

0   1000   2000
Feet

© The Countryman Press, Inc.

State Park, Tivoli Bays, and Manitou Point. These particular individuals, however, were planted, and in conditions of higher nutrient availability, better protection from storms, and—let's just say it as it is: they're growing in soil rather than scrabbling for a roothold in some crack in a rock face battered by Hudson River waves and ice. No wonder they're straight and tall. I point them out because if you watch, you'll see them elsewhere in your travels, usually planted in a row around old graveyards, and in one other place which we'll talk about shortly.

Val-Kill National Historic Site

Cross Fallkill Creek, whose name the Roosevelts borrowed for Eleanor's retreat estate, and stop in at Stone Cottage, Eleanor's old home before she moved into the larger Val-Kill Cottage, by the visitor center. Stone Cottage was designed by President Roosevelt in the old Dutch style of the Hudson Valley and is faced with local fieldstone. Entry is free into this charming and quiet home.

Walk toward the back parking lot past conifers—a good place to learn the common native and commonly planted non-native species (such as red pine, old-growth red cedar, white pine, Scotch pine, hemlock, and white spruce). You'll see the Hyde Park Trail discs ahead, the tulip-tree leaf markers, at a road blocked by a chain prohibiting mountain bikes. Notice how the conifers appear to have escaped their planting restriction and have seeded into the woods. At the fork, bear right. Watch for flocks of turkey lounging beside the red-osier dogwood swampside; you'll likely first hear them padding swiftly away through the leaves. At the next fork bear right again.

Here grows a stand of northern white cedar, in the swamp. It looks as though they escaped from Eleanor's plantings, but, whatever their origin, they are in their other typical habitat of the cedar swamp of the north woods. Other than secret cedar swamps in Putnam County, we don't get to see this sort of growth often in the Hudson Valley.

The path comes close to the Fallkill, where beaver keep trying to dam the flow. You'll find plenty of old chew marks on stumps, and signs of human attempts to disrupt the dam. Cross the power lines, surprisingly a good place for botanizing. At the fork go left uphill into a hemlock-mixed deciduous forest. A large woodland pool on the right hosts rows of painted turtles sunning on logs. Watch for mallard and wood ducks throughout the rest of the loop anytime you approach a quiet woodland pool. You will pass many other woods roads, all of which lead onto private property. Simply follow the tulip-tree leaf discs. As you return across the power lines, in early April look a few yards across the ground on your left for blooming hepatica. As you rejoin the loop, turn right to return to your car.

20 · Vanderbilt Mansion National Historic Site

Location: Hyde Park
Distance: 2.5 miles, 2 hours
Owner: National Park Service

Through the stone arches of the main gate, over the formal White Bridge topped with urns of flowers, past the waterfall, and up the long grassy lawn past the walled rose gardens, the mansion looms ahead. Built of gray-white Indiana limestone in the classic European style at a cost of $660,000, the 1898 palace of Frederick W. Vanderbilt sits in the center of a 212-acre sculpted and natural estate.

Access

Vanderbilt Mansion is north of the village of Hyde Park on US 9. Grounds open daily all year round 9 AM to sunset. Mansion (fee) open 9 AM to 5 PM daily except Thanksgiving, Christmas, and New Year's Day. Dogs allowed on leash. Information: 845-229-7770 or visit www.nps .gov/vama.

Trail

Park in the visitor center lot. The planting of exotics was begun on the grounds in 1828 by the previous owner, Dr. David Hosack, whose landscaping won the property international renown. It's worth a trip to Vanderbilt's just to explore the lawns and the many strange and ancient trees. After you come out of the visitor center, turn left on the paved North Drive walking beneath sugar maples, basswood, oak, white pine, and imported firs, being careful of occasional traffic.

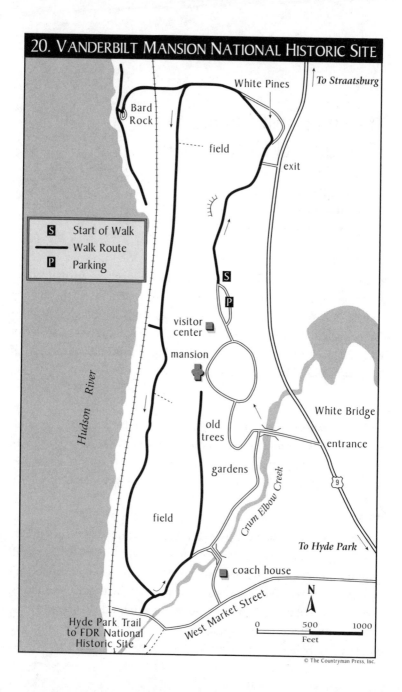

20. VANDERBILT MANSION NATIONAL HISTORIC SITE

White Pines

To Straatsburg

Bard
Rock

field

exit

S Start of Walk
━━━ Walk Route
P Parking

S

P

visitor
center

mansion

White Bridge

old
trees

entrance

Hudson River

gardens

Crum Elbow Creek

9

To Hyde Park

field

coach house

N

Hyde Park Trail
to FDR National
Historic Site

West Market Street

0   500   1000
Feet

© The Countryman Press, Inc.

Crickets sing in the grasses as you walk the east bluff of the Hudson River. The view is a famous one: grass slopes away to woods, the blue Hudson River, on the opposite shore the blunt-drop profile of Shaupeneak topped with communications towers (a Scenic Hudson park property; see *Walks & Rambles in the Western Hudson Valley*), and the Catskills obscured in a summer haze or sharply defined when there is a wind. Head toward Bard Rock. Before the road curves downhill toward the river, there will be a plantation of white pine on your left. Walk in under the first trees and find the path that follows along the bluff edge.

Curve down the slope with the pines and rejoin the paved road. Follow past the meadows and locust trees over the railroad to Bard Rock for a view of the river. An unmarked path leads along the rocky shore to both right and left. The vegetation of northern white cedars, red cedars, white pine, pitch pine, and ailing hemlocks looks nearly identical to that at Manitou Point many miles south in the Hudson Highlands, except here there is more pitch pine. As you walk south (left) the dramatic cliff-rock shoreline and coves of shale beach look nearly identical to those on the white trail at nearby Mills-Norrie State Park just north in Staatsburg. Bard Rock is a good place to sit with binoculars to observe lines of white snow geese, solitary loons, and other waterfowl migrating along the river in spring and fall.

Return over the railroad and turn right onto a dirt road blocked by a chain and a sign that prohibits mountain bikes. This is the Hyde Park Trail, marked with tulip-tree leaf discs. Walk a bit. Where the Norway spruce stand ends, the straightest, tallest, highest trees are tulip tree *(Liriodendron tulipifera)*, a tree once prized for ship masts and dugout canoes. Tulip-tree leaves are distinctive. On younger saplings they're often as large as plates.

In June, tulip trees bear flowers that look exactly like green and yellow tulips with orange centers, but the blooms are high up, visible from the ground only as bright vases. Should you find one fallen, you'll see the many long male stamens that bear the pollen. In their center sits the fat female pistil. Pollen from the male stamens falls onto the female pistil and fertilizes her eggs. Functions completed, the petals and the stamens fade and fall to the ground. The eggs mature into seeds.

In autumn, you'll see the candelabra seed heads high up where the flowers bloomed. On a windy, winter day, the seeds blow down and can be found on the snow. Native Americans cooked the fat sticky green buds of spring into a salve for burns and scalds. The inner bark of tulip is white, and so strong it can be twisted into cordage.

Walking when the leaves are down, you gain a view of the river and the hills along this entire route. Just before the lawn, a small trail breaks through the iron-rail fence that separates the estate from the railroad. Go through it and you have a cliff-top view of the river, the railroad, Bard Rock, and the opposite hills. Lowbush blueberries grow here. Visit in July and enjoy—maybe! They can prove tart! Bracken fern and sassafras indicate a well-drained soil. Bracken fern can be gathered dry in autumn, and stuffed into cloths to make mattresses. Sassafras bears three leaf shapes on one plant: round, mitten, and three-lobed hand.

The majestic mansion sits up on the hill. Half the fun of this walk is seeing the columned house from different angles and settings. At the fork keep right. Beyond the evergreen groundcover of planted vinca (blue flowers in early spring), watch on the left for bladdernut bushes. The inflated seedpods hang like balloons, green in June, brown and rattling by August. Beyond the bladdernuts comes another break in the iron-rail fence with another view from a cliff top.

As you come out to the paved road, you'll hear the waterfall ahead. Turn right onto the paved road for a view of the falls over a dam and rapids beyond that. For those who would like to extend their hike, you can continue straight on the road following the tulip-tree leaf discs of the Hyde Park Trail all the way to the Franklin D. Roosevelt National Historic Site. First you'll walk along the paved road for over .75 mile, then through the woods on an old carriage path for another mile to link up with the Roosevelt trail system near Crum Elbow Point (a good resting spot on the river). Return is back the same way, unless you left a second car at the FDR site.

Vanderbilt Mansion National Historic Site

To continue at the Vanderbilt site, return to walk on the paved road uphill following Crum Elbow Creek upstream. Near the top of the rise, watch for a left turn onto the Hyde Park Trail (tulip-tree leaf discs). This leads you to the formal gardens and onto the lawns headed toward the mansion. Marvel at the strange Norway spruce and white fir trees with limbs so old and low they lie on the ground and sprout trunks. Enjoy the gigantic weeping beech (be sure to duck beneath its limbs and go inside to see its snaking trunks) and the odd ginkgo. Rest behind the mansion upon a bench and admire the view.

At the northwest corner of the mansion on the bank edge grows a tulip tree with branches so low that in June you get a chance to see, smell, and feel, within reach, a tulip-tree tulip.

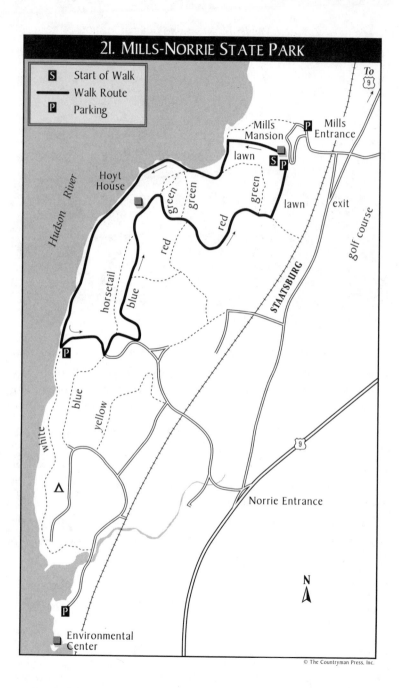

21. MILLS-NORRIE STATE PARK

S Start of Walk
— Walk Route
P Parking

To
9

Mills Mansion
Mills Entrance

Hoyt House

lawn
green
green
green
red
lawn
exit

Hudson River

horsetail
red
blue

STAATSBURG
golf course

blue
yellow
white

9

△

Norrie Entrance

N

P
Environmental Center

© The Countryman Press, Inc.

21 · Mills-Norrie State Park

Location: Staatsburg
Distance: 4 miles, 3 hours
Owner: State of New York

Two Hudson River estates gifted to the people in the 1930s make for a precious park because of this rare occurrence: the railroad travels inland. The walker has direct access to the Hudson River on the wild and dramatic white trail for about a mile (wear good hiking shoes). There are more than 1,000 acres, large parts of which are a golf course and a "Great Lawn." On the Norrie side, there are cabins to rent and a public campground, marina, and environmental museum. At Mills, there's Staatsburgh, the Mills's mansion.

Access

Park on the Mills side. Staatsburgh State Historic Site at Mills Memorial State Park is located just north of the hamlet of Staatsburg, which is midway between Hyde Park and Rhinebeck. The entrance is off Old Post Road, which can be accessed from US 9. The grounds are open daily all year from dawn to dusk. Dogs allowed on leash. Staatsburgh Mansion hours vary, so it's best to call before you go if you want a tour of the inside: 845-889-8851. Other numbers: restaurant 845-889-8864; Dinsmore golf course 845-889-3126; marina 845-889-4200; campground reservations 1-800-456-CAMP; park office 845-889-4646.

Trail

Staatsburgh, previously called Mills Mansion, is New York's single largest state-owned historic building. It's immense, with 65 rooms and 14 baths in a 70- by 170-foot Beaux Arts extravaganza remodeled by the same architects who dreamed up the Vanderbilt Mansion and the White House of Washington, D.C. The land was owned by the Livingston family beginning in 1844. The house and grounds, built in 1895, are an example of the gilded, European taste of the wealthiest class in America before the turn of the century.

The urge to walk down the Great Lawn to the river is not to be resisted. If you prefer a paved road, Gardener's House Lane borders the length of the lawn on the right. Magnificent European copper beeches on the Great Lawn in summer look cloaked in deep purple-black fur. When you get to the river, turn left and proceed along Gardener's House Lane until you come to a large and stately brick building (that's the Gardener's House). Keep right on the paved road, now the blue trail, which curves right, downhill to the water's edge.

Ah, the Hudson. What a view! And from a natural sand beach, no less, flanked by sweet mulberries (ripe in late June) and basswood. There stands isolated Esopus Meadows Lighthouse out there in the middle of what looks like an inland sea, the blue misty Catskills beyond. This was one of the last manned lighthouses on the Hudson. Built in 1839 and rebuilt in 1872, it was one of nine Hudson River "family stations" under the jurisdiction of the U.S. Lighthouse Service. The various keepers and their families cleaned and tended the lens, living for years in isolation out on the water in the white clapboard house built on a granite pier. Their logs report several large barges jammed against the house in storms. One winter, great ice sheets dislodged the structure from its foundation. Keeper John Kerr lived in the lighthouse with his wife, two pet skunks, a bantam rooster, and a dog. In 1939, the lighthouse came under the control of the U.S. Coast Guard. In 1965, Esopus Meadows Lighthouse was closed and automated. A citizens' group, Save Esopus Lighthouse Commission, is working to open the structure to the public. For information, visit www.esopusmeadowslighthouse.org.

The lighthouse sits on the east edge of Esopus Meadows, a stretch of Hudson River 3 feet at its deepest. At low tide, you can see grass, actually

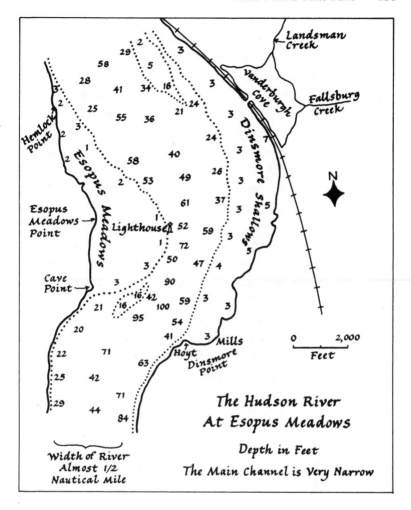

The Hudson River
At Esopus Meadows

Depth in Feet
The Main Channel is Very Narrow

Width of River
Almost 1/2
Nautical Mile

water celery, and Eurasian water milfoil. Just east of the lighthouse, the river bottom drops to 52 feet. Nearly all the Hudson River's shortnose sturgeon spend their winters in this narrow channel. Come spring, they swim north to Troy to spawn. Just east of where The Point (the peninsula to your left) juts out, the bottom rises again to the Dinsmore Shallows. This ecosystem, 3 to 5 feet deep, grows more "grass," providing an important feeding and resting habitat for waterfowl and a spawning ground and nursery for large numbers of anadromous fishes (those who spend their adult lives in the ocean but return to fresh water to spawn, such as herring, alewives, striped bass, and shad).

Follow the road. When it enters the woods, the white trail peels off on your right, also marked with a tulip-tree leaf disc. This trail will lead you along a unique section of the Hudson River, along the steep-sided, natural, stony bank. Deciduous trees, dying hemlocks, and northern white cedar scrabble among the shale ledge and cliff. Northern white cedar *(Thuja occidentalis)*, sometimes misidentified as the coastal Atlantic white cedar, attracted legion European sailors and financiers to North America during the colonial era. Straight, tall, strong, northern white cedar could be cut into superb masts, especially valued by admirals for their navies. The scales of the leaves are flattened, unlike the rounder, stiffer red cedar of sunny fields. Other than on the Hudson River shore, there are only three places in Putnam and Dutchess where northern white cedar is found today: secret cedar swamps in Putnam County, a small swamp at Val-Kill in Hyde Park, and the planted rows of old graveyards everywhere. In two of these locations the trees attain the straight height so coveted by seamen. Here on the rocky Hudson, the cedars grow gnarled and stunted.

Continue on to the first shale beach with 1920s graffiti carved into bedrock exposed at low tide. *Mahicanituk* is one of the Hudson's original names, which in all Wappinger, Lenape, and Mahikan dialects means "Tidal River of the Mahican People." Watch the water. Which way is the tide going? Can you spot where the main channel flows? Why is the water so dirty?

Polluted is the better word for the treated sewage, pesticides, and vastly assorted chemicals in the waters and bottom silt. But the dirt? The Hudson has probably always looked a dirty green-brown. Twice a day the tides stir up sediments that never get a chance to settle. Turbid, ecologists call such murky water, and perfectly natural: a soup of organic and inorganic debris that is the basis for the food chain of the rich Hudson River estuary.

Mills-Norrie State Park

Swedish naturalist Peter Kalm reported in 1749 that the residents of Albany drew their drinking water directly from the Hudson, but the water was so muddy they had to store it in their cellars so the sediment could settle to the bottom.

As you walk you may notice brick buildings through the trees on your left. Those are the stables and barns of the old Hoyt estate called The Point, which you are now rounding. At one spot you'll pass the stone remnants of what was once The Point's dock. After a bit, if you watch carefully up the hill you will see Hoyt House itself, which we'll visit later; the soft Gothic browns of the mansion camouflage it well, so you really have to look. In its heyday, The Point was kept cleared of trees, and the view up and down river from the mansion was unrivaled.

Continue beneath chestnut oak and hemlocks. Be careful of crumbling cliff edges and loose shale, where rue anemone and polypody ferns take root. Tree roots twist and struggle for a hold in the rock faces, many of these exposed by wave, storm, and erosion. Already stressed by natural dangers, the river bank is susceptible to soil compaction and resultant erosion caused by human use. The big gray building across the river is the Mount St. Alphonsus retreat center.

Soon you'll encounter signs of past estates. First there is a pumphouse, which pumped water to a huge well house still standing in the woods uphill. This supplied water to a number of estate houses. Then come stairs, stone foundations, perennial flowers, and lawns. The deepest foundations were commercial ice houses, tall things that housed blocks of ice cut from the Hudson. "On both sides of the river one sees great numbers of monolithic icehouses which border, during the wintertime, those fields of ice that furnish such an abundant harvest," wrote Emile de Damseaux, a French traveler in 1877. The blocks were kept insulated with a covering of sawdust.

From here you can walk various paved roads through Norrie Park. In winter, a visit to the environmental center with its many glass windows looking out on the river may reward you with the sight of bald eagles. Or begin to loop back home to Mills by heading up the stairs and then uphill on the road. Take the first left turn you encounter, and keep choosing left turns (the blue trail is ideal) to arrive at the front yard of Hoyt House. Even though this is the front door, the house was designed to be seen first from the right, the side with two *H*'s carved high up on the wall. This abandoned mansion is a Calvert Vaux original, one of the last in the nation. (For more information, see the Poets' Walk chapter, especially the endbar.) Follow the road, the original romantic entranceway, back to Staatsburgh Mansion. Any left turn will lead you to the Great Lawn, but this entrance carriageway can be followed in its entirety as it winds through deciduous woods past many intersections. First it starts out marked in green, then becomes red. If you go all the way you'll end up crossing the railroad onto Old Post Road, where a left turn will bring you back.

Or, for fun, follow the entrance carriage road *almost* all the way to the railroad. Just before that, you'll come to an intersection with a trail on your right and a dirt road on your left that leads to some sheds. Keep on straight for one sweet detail. The estate stone wall on your left parallels the entrance road. Off to your left, lawns come into view; that's the old greenhouse site of Mills's mansion. The stone wall goes up and over a small knoll. As it comes down the other side, watch oh so carefully for a rare stone stile made of flat coping stones, original stepping stones built into the wall for the walker to scale it. Go ahead. Cross up and over, meander through the greenhouse site and back to the big house. Or simply keep on straight on the road a bit farther to two cement pillars for easier access.

22 · Poets' Walk Romantic Landscape Park

Location: Red Hook
Distance: 1 to 2 miles, 1 to 3 hours
Owner: Scenic Hudson

Exquisite. Relaxing. At once spacious and intimate. Sublime. If this is your first visit to Poets' Walk, it is overwhelmingly best to come in summer or any season when there are leaves on the trees, in order to experience the full effect. This is one of the few parks where having the perspective of other people on the path enhances the picturesque design. Do not hesitate to visit on the popular weekends.

Access

From the stoplight at NY 9G and NY 199 north of Rhinebeck, go east toward the Kingston–Rhinecliff Bridge on NY 199 for 0.7 mile. At the stoplight, turn right onto Dutchess County 103 north/River Road. Go another 0.7 mile. Entrance on the left. Open 9 AM to dusk daily. Locked gate after hours. Dogs allowed on leash. Information: Scenic Hudson, 845-473-4440 or visit www.scenichudson.org.

Trail

Sign in at the cedar arbor information exhibits, then embark with no expectation. Leave the mind open. Relax. Stroll the wide gravel and dirt path, and look about. First walk past a series of meadows and wood lots. White cabbage butterflies and copper skippers flit over numerous wildflowers that people the fields: purple tufts of Japanese knotweed, tall

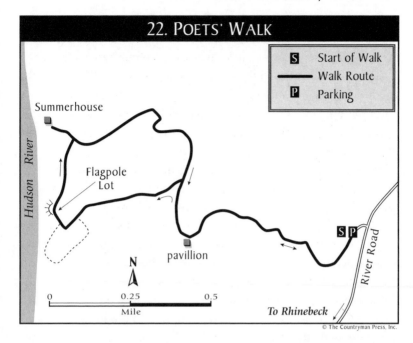

22. POETS' WALK

S Start of Walk
— Walk Route
P Parking

Summerhouse

Hudson River

Flagpole Lot

pavillion

N

0   0.25   0.5
Mile

S P

River Road

To Rhinebeck

© The Countryman Press, Inc.

native milkweed, flat-topped white yarrow, black-eyed Susan, and oxeye daisy. Even the grasses bloom, which of course they do everywhere they grow, but at Poets' Walk they add to the savor. Pass a grove of hemlock and pastoral cedar benches, gradually headed downhill.

Emerge from the trees to a view of a rustic house amidst the fields with the Catskills behind. The trail gradually winds toward the house. If you are carrying this book with you, reading as you go, close it now and do not read further until you come to the house.

At what point did you recognize the illusion? Because the trail winds, it gives the appearance of greater distance than is really there. Turns out the "house" is only a pavilion. The steep-slanted roof made it seem a country cottage on a far hill, the illusion further enhanced because the cottage is tucked against a copse of tall trees, with another copse of woods before it, increasing the illusion of distance. Had it been out in the field with open horizon behind it, the effect would not have been as pronounced. All this conspires to lull the walker into imagination, perhaps pulling images from some storybook European folktale. For me, in the distance there was what I took to be a hand pump beside the cottage. It gave me the impression the house was inhabited. I half expected the goodwife to step out with the washbasin at any moment to use the well. The simple act of walking toward this pavilion and experiencing that illusion, letting the mind run as it will, relaxes you. That is the success of this landscape design.

The Romantic Era, a national movement of landscape appreciation fueled by the arts, included Newburgh's own Andrew Jackson Downing, America's first landscape gardener and creator of America's first unique style of architecture. By "garden" I do not mean pansies and posies, but a total lifestyle experience. Downing has been called the tastemaker of his era, nationally famous in his day. From Newburgh, Downing laid out the original grounds (now gone) for the Capitol in Washington, D.C., the White House, and the Smithsonian (he also designed the building). His "moonlight and roses" career was cut short when the steamship *Henry Clay* blew up on the Hudson River; Downing was on board. His partner, Calvert Vaux (who later persuaded Frederick Law Olmsted to join him in designing Manhattan's Central Park and Brooklyn's Prospect Park) continued to popularize country homes situated within serene landscapes. These men and others, such as Alexander Jackson Davis, believed that American families would live happily in homes designed to be in harmony with their landscape, proposing an architectural basis for a national civilization uniquely American. At the time, Americans were still measuring their civilization by how closely they mimicked European styles. Sadly, few of Downing's or Vaux's works remain intact. Happily, here at Poets' Walk is the Romantic Era revived! Originally designed in 1849 by Hans Jacob Ehlers, Poets' Walk preserves some of what developed in America into the urban parks movement, the creation of national and state parks, and, ultimately, the environmental movement. It all began in the Hudson Valley, the concept of giving value to aesthetics in landscape.

Poets' Walk Romantic Landscape Park

Rest a while in the pavilion cloaked in bittersweet, trumpet vine, and clematis, favored vines of the romantic designer. Follow down the path from the pavilion and you gain your first view of the Hudson River and the Kingston–Rhinecliff Bridge. Somehow, the bridge takes on a graceful form within this view. Little sound of traffic impinges on the birdsong. Continue. The trail turns into a grassy mown swathe through meadow. At the fork go left to the Flagpole Lot and keep on. The first bench you encounter is wrapped around a white mulberry tree. When the luscious berries are ripe this spot is busy with squirrels and birds.

Bluebirds perch atop the houses offered to them out on poles in the fields. Bright goldfinches flame over the grasses. Continue down rolling mounds of the grassy bluff to the end at benches made especially deep and comfortable. From this vantage point you can visualize down the center of the Hudson River from Barrytown to Kingston for 4.5 miles, underwater, a ridge called The Flats. In depths as shallow as 2 feet, The Flats contain mud bars and beds of wild celery and Eurasian water milfoil. It is the largest flat in the Hudson.

In mid-March the shad run from the Atlantic Ocean up the Hudson River. One of their primary destinations is The Flats. On The Flats' shoals and sandbars the silverbacks spawn, and during that time gill nets are forbidden on The Flats. The adults return by June to the Atlantic, leaving the young to hatch and mature into what once was one of the largest commercial fisheries in the United States. Unfortunately, shad have declined for several reasons, one being the changes wrought by the alien zebra mussel.

Other fish spawn here, among them striped bass and white perch. Shortnose and Atlantic sturgeon feed and rest in the adjacent deeper channels. From the flagpole lookout, if you use strong binoculars, you might see large flocks of waterfowl that feed on the wild celery of The Flats: scaups, redhead, canvasback, common goldeneye, mergansers, mallard, black duck, and blue-winged teal.

The trail bends downhill into cool woods of hemlock and mixed deciduous trees. Skirt a tidal river marsh. At the Summerhouse a cedar gazebo perches on the edge of the sweet flag wetland with a view of the river. Sweet flag *(Acorus calamus)*, the long, swordlike leaves that resemble irises, is known to native folks as singer's root. A lozenge of the root held in the mouth allows a singer to accompany the drum for hours without getting hoarse. Powdered calamus root was used by Europeans and romantics to stabilize scented oils in potpourri. But don't think to dig up these sweet flags for use. You know how you've heard that the Hudson River has cleaned itself, that marshes act as great filters and hold pollutants, including PCBs and toxic heavy metals, releasing purified water. Where do the pollutants get held? In the marsh muck and in the marsh plant roots, leaves, and stems: good for the river but bad for plant harvesters. (Of course it is also illegal to disturb plants in this park.)

Begin the return route via Poets' Walk Path as male chipmunks serenade you with territorial *chirp chirp*. Pass over a stone bridge at the head of the ravine, past hog peanut and wood asters as you climb with lovely woodland views of the forested ravine. Cross the cedar bridge past the art area and uphill into fields. By the pavilion turn left to return to your car.

Other Romantic Parks: Wilderstein

Other Romantic Parks

The Wilderstein and Hoyt House romantic landscapes work best in summer when the leaves are out. Springside is best before the leaves are out, in spring and autumn.

Wilderstein

Thomas Holy Suckley built romantic Wilderstein in a unique Queen Anne style in 1852. Perhaps because of its lived-in feeling, Wilderstein may well be the most exquisite historical house in the Hudson Valley. Sitting on the vine-draped porch verandas that frame the blue air of summer and the view of the misty Hudson alone is worth the trip. A combination of woodland trails and original garden roads loop through the grounds designed by Calvert Vaux, with river views of Esopus Meadows Lighthouse. From Wilderstein you can sight the length of Vanderburgh Cove to Hoyt Point, and downriver. The grounds are open year-round from dawn until dusk and are free of charge. Call for hours for when the house itself is open (fee). Information: 845-876-4818, trail map at

www.wilderstein.org/trail.html. Access: From US 9 just south of the village of Rhinebeck turn west onto Mill Road and drive its length (2.3
miles) to Dutchess County 85/Morton Road. Turn right. At 0.3 mile, you
will pass the main entrance on the left. The free trail parking is another
0.2 mile beyond that, also on the left, at Wilderstein's Gate Lodge.

Hoyt House at Mills-Norrie State Park

One of the most notable Romantic Era gardens in the nation is now
almost in ruins. Designed by Calvert Vaux and built around 1855, the sta-
bilized mansion, bereft of its vine-cloaked verandas (in storage), stands in
the woods at The Point, far away from noisy trains on perhaps the most
valuable piece of real estate on the Hudson River. The public can view
the house from the outside only. Vaux and Downing abhored the glaring
white popular with country cottages, and advocated soft earth tones such
as used here with natural warm brown stones, cleverly scored for texture
and appeal. Vaux's landscape is grown up and the wide river and pastoral
views gone, but the original entrance road is intact. It winds and curves
with the landscape, creating an illusion of distance from hurried civilization without any formal or grandly scaled manipulation of the land. Park
at Staatsburgh State Historic Site (formerly Mills Mansion, the gilded
Beaux Arts antithesis of The Point) and walk to the end of the south parking lot. Walk south down the lawn, keeping the river at your right shoulder,
to a trail that leads to the old greenhouse site. Keep heading south on any
road you see and you will intersect the Hoyt entrance road headed toward
the river. Tip: at the southernmost end of the greenhouse site are two
cement pillars in the trees. Walk between them and there is the Hoyt drive.
Turn right and follow past all intersections to Hoyt House. (For more information, see the Mills-Norrie State Park chapter.) Information: 845-889-
4646. Staatsburgh State Historic Site is located off US 9 in Staatsburg.

Springside National Historic Site

One of the secrets of Poughkeepsie, this jewel is located in the north side
of the city at 181 Academy Street. It's the last surviving landscape of

Andrew Jackson Downing in the nation, yet concerned citizens have had to fight for its preservation. Twenty acres contain the romantic landscape remains of what was a larger *ferme ornee* ("ornamental farm") Downing designed for Mathew Vassar. Downing's charming gatehouse, closed to the public since people still live in it, is in great shape and can be viewed from the outside. Excellent brochures and signposts lead the visitor on a tour of the carriage paths and transport you back to a gentle era. Despite decades of neglect, the site retains the design and magic of the master and all the stamp of a great park. I look forward to its complete restoration. Guided tours are available by calling 845-471-0183. Open dawn to dusk. From the Taconic State Parkway, take US 44 or NY 55 east to Poughkeepsie. Go through the city until just before the Mid-Hudson Bridge. Stay in the right lane for US 9 south toward Wappingers Falls. Proceed for 1 mile to the Academy Street exit. At the bottom of the ramp, turn left and drive to the first entrance on the right. Park in lot behind the gatehouse.

23 · Burger Hill Park

Location: Rhinebeck
Distance: about 0.3 mile, 1 hour or less
Owner: Scenic Hudson, managed by Winnakee Land Trust

Looking for a short outing to take in a summer's windy view? Fly a kite or picnic on a hill top? Sled a *real* hill in winter? See bobolinks and hear their entrancing song? Come to Burger Hill.

Access

From the intersection of US 9 and NY 9G just northeast of the village of Rhinebeck, go 2.6 miles south on NY 9G. The park entrance will be on your right shortly after Violet Hill Road. Dogs allowed on leash. Park open 9 AM to 8 PM or dusk. Gate locked after hours. Information: Scenic Hudson, 845-473-4440 or visit www.scenichudson.org.

Trail

Pasturage and farmland for centuries, this 550-foot-high clay hill was rounded by the last glacier. It was named after a Palatine named Burkhardt, a tenant farmer of Henry Beekman, the land- and patent owner in the early 1700s. Over the generations, the tenant's family name evolved into Burger, and the family obtained ownership of the land they farmed. This hill has been under continuous agricultural use since those times, and it looks it: grassland, well established. As I climbed the mown trail up Burger Hill for the first time in summer, I found it reminiscent of the grassy chalk hills and open sky of Wiltshire, England, land also used as farmland for centuries. The only difference was that the grasses here are long, not sheep-cropped. There are field flowers here. And bobolinks. And larks.

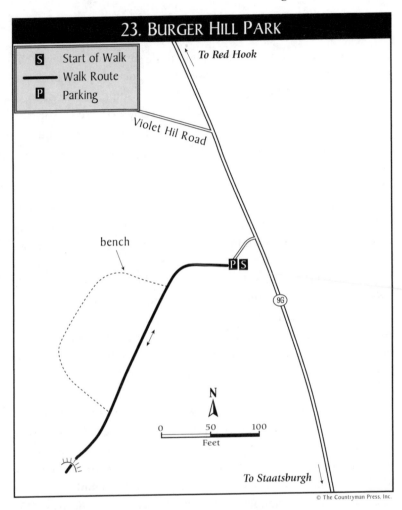

23. BURGER HILL PARK

S Start of Walk
— Walk Route
P Parking

To Red Hook

Violet Hil Road

bench

P **S**

9G

N

0   50   100
Feet

To Staatsburgh

© The Countryman Press, Inc.

All our farms would be home to nesting bobolinks and meadowlarks were it not for the hay mowing. If the first haying is left for after mid-July, these birds can rear their broods in time. But the first haying usually comes before that, and so there are few ears in the Hudson Valley that hear the musical calls of the bobolink or the meadowlark, the pastoral songs of summer. As it is, the first field you pass through from the parking lot is mowed more regularly, and barren of bobolinks. It is only on the hill itself that the wonders fly and sing.

In a field of territorial breeding bobolinks and larks, the vivacious males fly about just above the grasses singing, perching, fighting, and feeding the young. The air is full with song and sunlight. There, atop a post, perches a meadowlark, his breast butter-yellow, crossed by a black V, singing full-throated long whistles clearer than the daylight. If you startle him, he spreads his chunky brown wings and skims the field, spreading wide his tail with the outer white feathers, then tilts and drops into the grass.

Atop a slender stem of grass perches a bobolink male in full breeding plumage. He seems like just an ordinary black bird, until he flies and you see he is black only on the breast. On the back of his head shines bright gold, and silver-white crescents deck his back and shoulders. As he flies, he sings, and there is no way to describe it. Imagine two people holding a stretch of sheet metal between them, bending it so it twangs as it warps. Now imagine that with a musical, metallic quality to it, and you've approximated a bobolink. Let's be realistic. There is no approximation that does justice. You've got to hear the real thing while you stand knee-deep in the summer's warm grasses.

Both meadowlarks and bobolinks build flimsy grass cups of nests in slight hollows in the ground within the thick cover of the grasses and weeds. During the summer, they pluck insects off the grass stems. Come fall, their diet changes to grass seeds, and they turn into plainer brown birds. The meadowlark flies south to winter in the southern United States, Mexico, Central America, and the West Indies. The bobolink undertakes one of the longest migrations of a New World passerine: as much as 5,000 miles south to northern Argentina.

When they reach their winter grounds, they often find their habitat bulldozed and changed. If they survive to return to us, they often find their breeding grounds mown. Partly because of this ongoing habitat loss, some years find even our unhayed fields silent and unvisited by larks and bobolinks. Some years they appear here at Burger Hill, in the fields of

Burger Hill Park

Buttercup Sanctuary in Pine Plains, and in the fields of Boyce Park in Dover. And some years they don't.

From the top of the hill gain vast views of the Hudson Valley. From the tree line to your left, the closest hills are the Marlborough Hills on the west bank of the Hudson River. The river itself is hidden in a trough at their feet; you can trace its route from there northward past the Ulster County lowlands of the Rondout Valley. See the Devil's Path of the east escarpment of the Catskill Mountains, with a view of the Catskill high peaks far in the distance midway between the Marlborough Hills and the Devil's Path. The Shawangunk Ridge is just visible as it forms in the Rondout Valley and lifts behind the Marlborough Hills. To the right, the Taconics stretch far north beyond the Dutchess County hills. There is a flank of Stissing Mountain and a peek at the tall South Taconics on the county border. What a place to come to for sunsets! Bring a folding chair or a blanket and picnic and watch that changing light and glow that inspired the Hudson River School of painters. Even on the hottest day, there always seems to be a breeze on Burger Hill.

In winter, snow on the Catksills shows up their horizontal, river deposit lines, and the high peaks region is easier to see. The best time to come is before noon while the sun is at your back and the light casts full onto the Catskills, showing up every stark ridge and slope. The peaks above 3,500 feet are shadowed on top by spruce and fir boreal forest.

On the way down, take the left fork for a short loop. This will lead you down the hill to a stone bench in the shade of a lone white pine. In summer, sit quietly and still, and you'll be rewarded with a close-up view of the lively bobolinks.

24 · Montgomery Place

Location: Annandale-on-Hudson
Distance: Less than 1 mile, 1 to 2 hours
Owner: Historic Hudson Valley

I magine yourself in white evening clothes stepping out onto the veranda. Beyond the lawn and a meadow of wildflowers, the Saw Kill meanders through the still, green marsh of Tivoli South Bay. The Catskills stand high and blue against the sky. A breeze riffles up from the Hudson, blowing the feathery locust tree limbs overhead. It is summer.

As you explore the Hudson Valley, you find certain family names appearing over and over, names of people who held America's purse strings and kept mansions on the Hudson's famous bluffs. Perhaps no name recurs more often than Livingston, whose family members inter-married with other Hudson Valley families to such a degree that Livingston became *the* name of the valley. Montgomery Place was a Livingston home, first built in 1804 but completely redesigned during the Romantic Era. It is the quintessential summer country estate.

Access

Traveling north on 9G in the town of Red Hook, turn west (left) onto Annandale Road/Dutchess County 103. Turn left at the triangle, still Annandale Road. The park's entrance is 0.25 mile on the left.

Montgomery Place is open April 1 to October 31, except for Tuesdays, 10 AM to 5 PM and until sunset on summer weekends; weekends in November and the first two weekends in December. The grounds are open only on the weekends for the remainder of December and in March. Since hours may change, it's best to call first. Admission to the grounds costs $4. Include

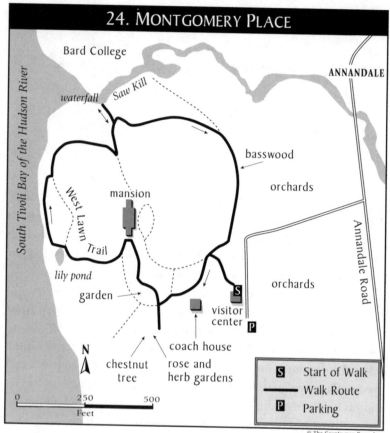

24. MONTGOMERY PLACE

Bard College

ANNANDALE

South Tivoli Bay of the Hudson River

waterfall *Saw Kill*

basswood

orchards

West Lawn Trail

mansion

Annandale Road

lily pond

garden

orchards

S

visitor center

P

chestnut tree

coach house

rose and herb gardens

N

S	Start of Walk
—	Walk Route
P	Parking

0   250   500
Feet

© The Countryman Press, Inc.

a house tour, and admission comes to $7 adults, $6 seniors, $3 children, under six years of age free. Bring a picnic and plan to spend the day. Dogs are not allowed. Information: 845-758-5461 or visit www.hudsonvalley.org.

Trail

Ask for a trail guide at the visitor center. Take the trail to the mansion through grounds designed in part from advice given by Andrew Jackson Downing. The trail leads to a carriage road and past an English park lawn. Take the left road, past Alexander Jackson Davis's coach house.

Go into the herb garden for a look at the size of the trunks on the native trumpet vines in front of the garden house to the left of the door. If you sit patiently, you may see a ruby-throated hummingbird come to sip from the gorgeous red blooms. Walk the garden rows and paths. On the right side of the greenhouse and the herb garden proper stands a Eurasian chestnut tree. When it blooms in early July the tree looks draped in white lace. Imagine how the landscape looked before the chestnut blight took the American counterpart of this tree from the ecosystem it once dominated: an entire landscape of chestnut forest abloom in spring. A walk in the woods then must have smelled sweet (although in the herbal sort of way) and your ears would have been abuzz with the droning of pollinating wasps and flies. Instead of the dark green of oaks, a view from a hilltop in July must have been of silvery white-green hills cloaked in blooming chestnut.

Come back out under the arched trellis gateway, go straight across the road past the Ellipse reflecting pool and onto stone paths through the Rough Garden and Wild Garden. Rejoin the road at the mansion. A double avenue of black locusts ushers the way. Go to the front and proceed to circle the house to the right—such peace and beauty! There are views of the Hudson and the Catskills, and another impressive double row of locusts at the rear. Richard Montgomery never lived here, never saw this estate. He died in the American Revolution during an ill-fated assault on Quebec, where Benedict Arnold also played a heroic role in the unsuccessful American siege. In 1818, Janet Livingston Montgomery, fifty years a widow, stood alone on this portico as her husband's bones were carried by steamship at long last down the Hudson for burial in New York City. "*Richmond* halted before the mansion; the band played the 'Dead March,' and a salute was fired."

Continue around the house, or backtrack around the front, to the southeast corner where there is a sign for the West Lawn Trail. Pass a root cellar on your right. It's getting harder to find root cellars nowadays, once so numerous in the woods where agriculture once flourished. You will see a mown path through the field; follow that. It leads past the pond.

Montgomery Place

Just after that find the trail into the woods on the left (do not go up other side of the lawn). This path leads along the bank of South Tivoli Bay through hemlock and mixed deciduous woods. Briefly cross the edge of the field, then climb uphill. Watch on the left for post #7, which marks the old quarry for the estate's building needs. If there's been rain, you will soon hear the cataract of the Saw Kill thundering in the distance.

At the intersection, take the left fork of the Saw Kill Trail, downhill through North Woods' ailing hemlocks. There is also spicebush, which grows more densely as you descend, indicating increasing soil moisture. *Lindera benzoin* is the bush with brown twigs, green at the tips, and the raised dots on the bark. Taste a young leaf. Yum! Next time you're baking fish or chicken, wrap the meat in spicebush leaves (they must be fresh, not dried). Nip off a small bit of twig. Smell. More lemons? Chew. Oooof! Strong stuff. What can I say, some folks like it. European colonists dried and pulverized the bark and berries for a spice.

Continue down to the Saw Kill and a series of fast cataracts and falls. Tivoli South Bay is visible through the trees. The opposite bank is owned by Bard College, which you can visit (see Tivoli Bays chapter). Please do not leave the trail; you can see the damage done by those climbing the fragile slope. Go back up the path, and uphill just a bit, to a little-used footpath on the right that leads along the Saw Kill bank downstream to a point on the edge of South Tivoli Bay. Water chestnut clogs the water in a green carpet. Watch for kingfisher, a pigeon-sized, steel-blue bird that perches on limbs overlooking the water or flies by with a rattling call. They dive beak first in the bay and creek pools to catch fish.

Return back up the bank toward the house. The trail continues to the left past the shell of the mansion's powerhouse and up to the lawn. There are many European specimen trees planted around the lawn; those familiar with European parks will recognize copper beech and London plane trees. As the Saw Kill path meets the dirt road you are beneath the shade of lindens. If you visit in July you will hear the humming, even from a distance, of the multitude of bees sucking from the linden flowers, and the air will smell fragrant with linden blooms. Pass the orchards of heirloom fruit trees and vines, and you are headed back toward the visitor center.

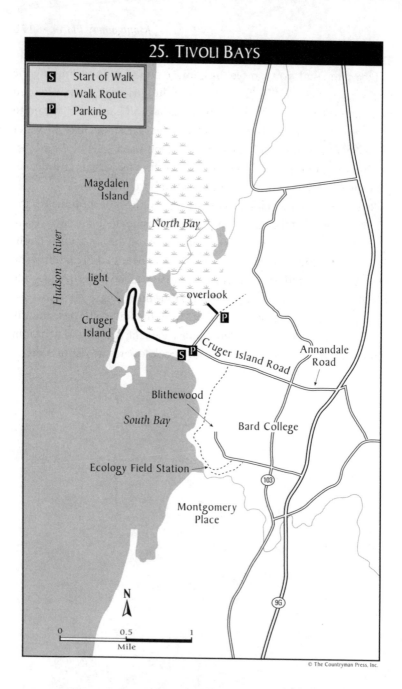

25. TIVOLI BAYS

S Start of Walk
— Walk Route
P Parking

Hudson River

Magdalen Island

North Bay

light

overlook **P**

Cruger Island

S **P** Cruger Island Road

Annandale Road

Blithewood

South Bay

Bard College

Ecology Field Station

103

Montgomery Place

N

0   0.5   1
Mile

9G

© The Countryman Press, Inc.

25 · Tivoli Bays

Location: Annandale
Distance: 1 to 4 miles, 2 to 3 hours
Owner: State of New York and Bard College

Here is something for almost everyone: the Hudson River, woods, waterfalls, gardens, and historic houses. Time it right, and you can enjoy a world-class concert at the Fisher Center for the Performing Arts at Bard College (for information phone 845-758-6822 or visit www .bard.edu). The main attraction, the marshes of the bays themselves, are of course difficult for the walker to explore. Cruger Island is your main destination. Alternatives are suggested at the end of this chapter.

From Troy north to Lake Tear of the Clouds, the Hudson is a river. From Troy south to New York City, it is an estuary. An estuary is a place where fresh water meets salt, and since seas flow inland on the tides, estuaries can be found miles upriver of an ocean. The mixing of salinities, sediments, and organic detritus in an estuary supports an incredibly rich and complex community of plants and animals. Estuaries are special places. But they, along with wetlands, have been considered good dumping grounds for garbage. They have been filled in and used as building sites. Such practices continue today. The National Estuarine Research Reserve System was finally established in the 1960s to study and preserve these invaluable natural areas.

New York is blessed with an estuary that reaches through the Appalachian Mountains and inland—the lower Hudson River. The Hudson River is one of 26 protected areas designated nationwide as part of the National Estuarine Research Reserve System and consists of 4,838 acres in four sites. Tivoli Bays, 1,468 acres, is one of them. Part of the land and the marshes are also owned by New York State as the Tivoli Bays Wildlife Management Area.

The glacial gorge of the Hudson riverbed lies below sea level for 152 upstream miles. Tides are felt all the way to Troy, but brackish water reaches only as far north as Poughkeepsie due to the Hudson's tremendous freshwater flow. Therefore, Tivoli Bays are freshwater marshes, the largest undeveloped tidal freshwater wetland complex on the Hudson River. Tivoli North Bay contains an intertidal cattail marsh, tidal creeks, and pools. Shallower South Bay fluxes in a successional stage of mud flat, European water chestnut, spatterdock, arrowhead, and pickerelweed.

Both bays are important feeding, spawning, and nursery areas for Hudson River striped bass, alewife, and blueback herring, especially at the mouths of Stony Creek and the Saw Kill. Along with the usual largemouth and smallmouth bass, white perch, and various minnows, the bays also support the regionally rare American brook lamprey, central minnow, and northern hogsucker. There is an extremely large population of snapping turtles in North Tivoli Bay. Many birds breed in the bays, including least and American bitterns, Virginia rail, marsh wren, sora rail, common moorhen, and king rail. Many species of waterfowl use the wetlands during migration times. There are also rare species of plants, such as goldenclub, heartleaf plantain, and Eaton's bur marigold.

Access

From the intersection of NY 199 and NY 9G just north of Rhinebeck, go north on NY 9G for 1.8 miles, passing the main entrance to Bard College. Turn left onto Dutchess County 103/Annandale Road. Go 0.3 mile. Annandale Road will turn sharply left. You keep straight ahead onto a dirt road called Cruger Island Road. In 0.6 mile is parking on the left for the trail along South Bay. At 0.7 mile is the gate with parking for Cruger Island. At 0.8 mile is the end of the road and parking for North Bay. You may wish to start here with the short walk to the marsh overlook, then park back at the gate for the walk to Cruger Island. In summer, bring a hat to keep the deer flies off your head. Once you're out on the river's shore, the breeze will keep them away. Dogs allowed on leash. Information: Bard College Ecology Field Station, 845-758-7053, and New York State Department of Environmental Conservation, Bureau of Wildlife in New Paltz, 845-256-3090.

Trail

For a view of the marsh before you head out to Cruger Island, from the end of the road take the short path on the left. Swamps have trees. Marshes don't. Before you stretches Tivoli North Bay, a marsh of acres of pickerelweed, cattail, and arrowhead. Until the late 19th century, these bays were open water. The building of the railroad causeways in 1850 cutoff the bays from the main channel and allowed the Hudson to flood the new still-water coves twice a day, bringing in sediment and laying it down. Marshes formed, and plants died and decayed. The muck is as deep as 25 feet, yet extremely variable. Here it's sand, there it's mud. Should you step into it, you might sink in only 6 to 8 inches—or 2 to 3 feet.

Between muck particles are spaces filled with water. The muck is a sponge and holds enormous quantities of fresh water, filtering and purifying it. A 10-acre marsh can hold 3 million gallons of water. Flood and drinking water protection are two of the special qualities of marsh-fringed estuaries (and all marshes).

Return to the bend in Cruger Road, and walk through the gate and along the man-made causeway built upon what may be a glacial sandspit, or tombolo. There is excellent botanizing along the way. If it has been raining, the potholes and ruts in the road will be brimming with water. Search for opossum tracks. The hind foot has a toe dexterous as our thumb, so the footprint resembles a human hand. Swallowtail butterflies sit in pools (that's what you call a collection of butterflies sitting on the ground in the sunlight beside a puddle: a pool).

At one point, the high tide floods from South Bay across into North Bay. It's fun to slosh through, scaring the killifish, but if you don't care to get wet feet, time yourself for low tide. Black, pointed, hard cases, or caltrops, of European water chestnut from South Bay bob on the current.

Spatterdock on South Tivoli Bay

Watch for herons, ducks, and other marsh birds. Like Constitution Marsh in Cold Spring, this is a spectacular birding spot, heavily used during fall migration. When you arrive at Amtrak's tracks, check for trains and walk north and south along the railroad for a view of North and South Bays.

Return to Cruger Causeway and walk directly across the tracks for the trail to Cruger Island. Watch out for trains and don't play chicken. People get killed underestimating the 70 miles per hour speed of an Amtrak cruiser. Approaching trains are surprisingly quiet.

Vinca groundcover is a remnant of the 1835 estate of John Cruger. Follow the unmarked trail that looks most traveled; it tends to keep straight and right past intersections of lesser paths and leads into a native oak, sugar maple, and hemlock woods on resistant sandstone bedrock knolls. Come to a small pebble beach and a view of the Hudson. There's Magdalen Island, part of the reserve, and one of the red railroad bridges that lets water into North Bay.

The trail continues up a slope to the bluff and the view and the waves of the Hudson's main and mighty current, 50 feet deep, ripping past the rocks. Come in winter when the ice is dramatic (if the causeway isn't blocked with floes). The current in the Hudson rarely exceeds 3 miles per hour. Yet there is a 4-foot rise and fall in the tides, and the flow of the tides dwarfs the river's freshwater output. These tidal fluctuations and currents, plus ship wakes and the frequency of sudden storms, present hazards to small craft and swimmers.

The plants here grow in xeric conditions, including pitch pine, oak, low-bush blueberry, polypody ferns, and mosses. Northern white cedar, dull-leaf indigo bush, and ninebark grow at the shoreline. The trail follows south along the edge of the island. Wave erosion has undercut banks and exposed tree roots. When you reach the shale and sandstone beach and have explored the flotsam, you'll be close to the navigational light and the first view downriver of the Rhinecliff Bridge. There are deep eroded coves here.

The trail keeps on for about half a mile atop the mossy bank of cliff edge and rocky shoreline similar to the white trail at Mills–Norrie State Park just downriver. Watch the water for diving birds and paddling ducks. The trail ends at a view of South Cruger Island, where John Cruger built ruins to house Yucatan relics (gone now). This came during the height of the public craze for sublime scenery and the Romanticism of Hudson River School painting.

To return, come back to the shale beach and watch for the right turnoff through the vinca. Turn right at the next trail and you're on your way home.

Other Trails at Tivoli Bays

Please note, that due to past criminal activity, women are advised to walk in these areas in larger groups of more than two and/or with male friends.

There is a parking lot and a kiosk with trail information on NY 9G north of Annandale Road. Further parking is available north of this off Kidd Lane. From either of these you have access to the North Bay trails.

Another very pleasant walk runs along the Saw Kill. Enter the Bard College campus by motoring along Annandale Road. Turn onto Blithewood

Avenue and park in the lot on the left just past the community vegetable gardens opposite Ravine Road. Walk left toward the stream (the Saw Kill), following it downhill to the Ecological Field Station, past the falls, then up to Blithewood Mansion.

26 · Clermont State Historic Site

Location: Germantown
Distance: 1.5 miles, 2 hours
Owner: State of New York

Well, yes, Germantown is in Columbia County. But thirty-two acres of Clermont State Park do lie in Red Hook, and the place is so close, straddling the county border. So, here it is, another Livingston home.

Robert Livingston, a Scot, acquired 160,000 acres from the Indians. In 1686, Governor Dongan designated it Livingston Manor with Robert Livingston as the lord. The patent extended for 12 miles along the Hudson and east to Massachusetts. In 1728, Livingston's young son, Robert, captured an Indian by the feet as the native squirmed down the chimney into Robert's bedroom. Impressed, Livingston gave young Robert 13,000 acres of his estate on which to build his home, Clermont.

The Livingstons were a politically important and patriotic family. The British didn't care for them and, in 1777, after sailing through the Great Chain at Anthony's Nose and torching Kingston, they burned Clermont to the ground. Mrs. Margaret Beekman Livingston, wife of Robert Robert Livingston (this one the son of our Robert of Clermont) and mother of another Robert (later called the Chancellor, one of the five who drafted the Declaration of Independence), immediately rebuilt it. Clermont became state property in 1962.

There are many carriage roads and trails at Clermont, in addition to the house and formal gardens. Offered here is a short walk.

Access

Travel north on NY 9G. Just after crossing into Columbia County, turn left at a sign for Clermont and follow the signs to the main entrance. Park by

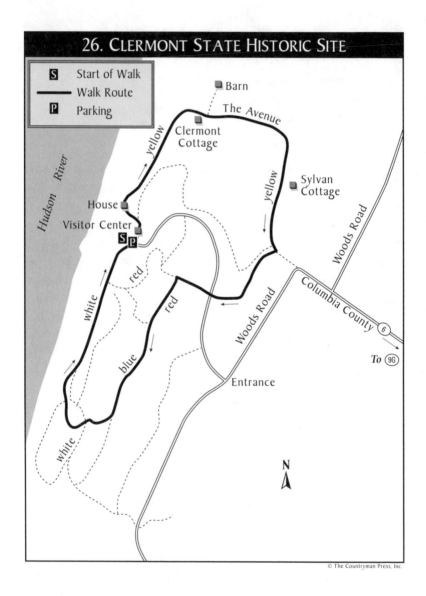

26. CLERMONT STATE HISTORIC SITE

S Start of Walk
— Walk Route
P Parking

Barn

The *Avenue*

yellow

Clermont
Cottage

Sylvan
Cottage

yellow

Hudson River

House

Visitor Center

S **P**

red

red

white

blue

white

Woods Road

Columbia County (6)

To (9G)

Entrance

Woods Road

N

© The Countryman Press, Inc.

Clermont State Historic Site

the house. The grounds are open year-round, sunrise to sunset; there may be an entrance fee in summer. The visitor center and house are open April 1 to October 31: Tuesday to Sunday, and Monday holidays, 11 AM to 5 PM. From November 1 to December 15 hours are on weekends only from 11 AM to 4 PM. Last house tour always begins half an hour before closing time. The visitor center only is open January 1 to March 31 and only on weekends 11 AM to 4 PM. Admission is charged. Dogs allowed on leash. Information: 518-537-4240.

Trail

Spend some time at the visitor center, then ask for a trail map and go to the house. Stand behind the house on the bluff. Across the Hudson is Saugerties and Malden-on-Hudson. Behind these towns stand those blue mountains for which Clermont ("Clear Mountain" in French) is named. Katzberg, the Dutch called them, which roughly translates as "The Mountains of Lynx and Bobcat." Somehow Katzkill, the Dutch name for the stream (*kil* being Dutch for "stream") that flows through the Katzberg, got

The Catskills From Clermont

applied to the entire mountain range. Actually, the Catskills are not mountains, in the sense of having been shoved up by plate tectonics, as were the Hudson Highlands. They are stream deposits. When the air is clear, you can see the horizontal stripes on some of the Catskill slopes. These were once layers of mud and silt deposited in a sea by rivers that eroded the once incredibly high mountains to the east. Consolidated into shales and sandstones, streams eroded valleys to form what we today call the Catskill Mountains.

Following the ridgeline from south to north, there looms Meads Mountain, Overlook Mountain, Indian Head, Plattekill Clove (that's the name of the valley), High Top, Black Dome, Kaaterskill Clove, South Mountain, North Mountain, and Windham High Peak. Masters at acquiring land, the Livingstons came to own all the mountains you are looking at.

Just north, in the middle of the river at low tide can be seen Green Flats, a shallow spot of mud and silt that stretches north for a mile. Flats are unstable things, changing year to year from storms, ice movement, shipping, and blind building (for duck hunters). The green stuff of Green Flats is wild celery (native, important for ducks) and Eurasian water milfoil (an alien pest that displaces wild celery). Flats like this are important feeding and resting habitats for fish (including shad and perhaps sturgeon), turtles, osprey, and waterfowl. Green Flats particularly is a very important resting spot for black and mallard ducks, who may lounge here

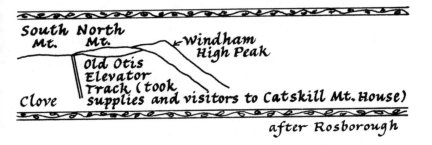

South Mt. North Mt. ← Windham High Peak

Old Otis Elevator Track (took

Clove supplies and visitors to Catskill Mt. House)

after Rosborough

during the day and fly to Tivoli North Bay to feed at night. All midriver flats on the Hudson are owned by New York State. In autumn, you'll often see the temporary blinds of duck hunters.

From the knoll to the left of the house you can see downriver. What's that on the other side, sticking out into the river ... are those houses? The closest one looks like some kind of grain elevator. That's Saugerties Lighthouse, the oldest lighthouse still standing on the Hudson River. Originally built in 1835, the lightkeeper's house was replaced with a handsome period home in 1869. Starting salary for keepers was $500 a year. They kept their houses spic and span, tended the cut-glass lenses, rescued boats and people, and raised their families in isolation. Saugerties Lighthouse was closed in 1954, but today is open to the public (see *Walks & Rambles in the Western Hudson Valley*).

South of Saugerties Lighthouse is a long causeway that ends midriver with a private home. This causeway was the steamship stop Saugerties Landing. Up and down the Hudson River were many landings of the flourishing steamship business. Landing, however, is hardly an appropriate word. On approach, a steamship would cut its engines, slowing enough to allow the captain to throw his passengers and their bags into a rowboat, sprint for the landing, hand them off, throw the next load of passengers and bags in, and row hard for the steamer just as it was coasting out of reach and about to kick its boilers back into full power. Since

Chancellor Livingston backed Robert Fulton's first commercially success-ful steamship (the *Clermont*), Clermont had its own steamship landing.

There's a lot of history in this view from Clermont, but we are going for a walk.

Meander into the gardens, then head for the dirt road that leads north from the back of the house; it is easily reached from the upper gardens by heading toward the river. This is Clermont's original entrance. Old trees line the route. Impressive are the Avenue's tall white pines and Nor-way spruce. Pass the 1830 Clermont Cottage and the cow barn, watching for bluebirds in the pastoral fields and woods. Pass Sylvan Cottage, built in the early 1900s, and follow all the way to the entrance gate, but don't go through it. Instead, take a right through another gate. This will loop you back to the house. It also links up with other trails and carriageways, so you can extend your walk if you wish.

Keep straight on the woods road, once a tree-lined carriageway past fields. Go straight over the paved road. On your left a woodland pool swims alive with tadpoles. Here grow witchlike pin oak trees, twisted limbs black over the black water. Turn left onto the red trail, another car-riageway. Keep straight on this as it becomes the blue trail. This will loop around back to the parking lot.

27 · Other Parks along the Hudson River

Bowdoin Park

Been shopping at the malls and want a breath of fresh air? Try nearby Bowdoin Park, or a walk along Wappinger Creek at Reese Sanctuary and at Reese Park.

Many trails run through the 301-acre county Bowdoin Park beside the Hudson River. Basically, there are two sections, along the wooded bluffs and in the low-lying fields. A map stands at the main trailhead on the lawn above the four-way paved intersection and first stop sign. Several loops of varying length are possible along marked trails. Although located adjacent to the Hudson, for the most part the visitor is cutoff from the river by railroad tracks and fence. Driving down the hill or standing

Other Parks along the Hudson River: Bowdoin

behind the nature museum you can see the power plant atop Danskammer, a level jut of bedrock noted by early explorers and colonists as a ceremonial native site. So important was this site to regional natives that they continued to gather and dance here for over two centuries despite war, disease, and strife. Several cliff faces at the park were used historically as rock shelters. Amenities include a museum (hours vary), animal barn, playing fields, picnic pavilions, and playground. Dogs allowed on leash. Open 9 AM to 8 PM. Access: From US 9 there are several ways to get onto Sheafe Road. One way is from the north end of the Galleria Mall. Turn left onto Spring Road and go downhill to the stop sign. Turn left onto Sheafe Road. Bowdoin is 2.3 miles down Sheafe Road, on the right. Information: 845-298-4600.

Reese Sanctuary and Reese Park

Reese Sanctuary is a 98-acre woodland corridor on top of the west bluff of Wappinger Estuary in New Hamburg. It has been closed due to dangerous conditions but is due to reopen spring of 2005. Trails link to Bowdoin Park. Managed by National Audubon Society. Information: 845-485-3628. Access: From the light at the intersection of US 9 and Dutchess County 28 (just south of the village of Wappingers Falls), turn west onto Dutchess County 28. Drive 1 mile to the light at Hughsonville. Go straight through, still on Dutchess County 28/New Hamburg Road. Drive 1.2 miles. You will cross over the mouth of the Wappinger Estuary, with a view of the Hudson River and Central Hudson's plant at Danskammer Point, arguably the most sacred, traditional Native American site in the entire Hudson Valley. Upstream, you can see the creek's west bluff; that is Reese Sanctuary. At the next four-way intersection, you will be in the hamlet of New Hamburg. Turn right onto Main Street. Go 0.1 mile to New Hamburg Playground on your right. Park in the paved lot.

Directly opposite the bluff of the Wappinger Estuary is the town of Wappinger's Reese Park where pretty Hunter's Brook tumbles through a deciduous ravine to join Wappinger Creek. This is the perfect place for a short walk in the woods. From the Galleria, take US 9 south for a few hundred yards, getting in the right lane. Turn right onto NY 9D. Drive for 1.3 miles, through the village of Wappingers Falls (where the road turns sharply left in the village, park on the street to view the falls for which the village is named), to a right turn onto Market Street. In one block, bear right and downhill as the road becomes Creek Road. Wind along for 0.4 mile. The park will be on your left. It doesn't look like much at first, but park at the gate, walk in, and take the first trail on the left. This leads down to Hunter's Brook and then follows upstream through the ravine. You can loop back by bearing right at the head of the ravine and return on the dirt road. Information: 845-297-7026.

Ferncliff Forest Game Refuge and Forest Preserve

Once part of John Jacob Astor's estate, Ferncliff is a 192-acre forest in Rhinebeck with woods charming in summer; the mixed deciduous and hemlock stands grow on a folded ravine and knoll landscape. There is a well-developed trail system, and the birding is excellent. Church Trail contains foundations from the late 1800s when Thomas Suckley of Wilderstein provided homes, farm buildings, and a chapel for retired Methodist ministers. Access: From the village of Rhinebeck, drive north on US 9. Just before Northern Dutchess Hospital, turn left onto Montgomery Street. Drive 0.6 mile. Take the left fork, Mount Rutsen Road. Drive 1.1 miles. The park entrance will be on the left. Information: 845-876-3196.

Hudson River Bridges

These are wonderful places to observe the awesome current of the Hudson River ripping past channel buoys and feel the wind in your hair. You will see grand colors in autumn, ice floes in winter. The bridges are an excellent alternative if you cannot climb mountains; the spaciousness feels similar. Note: there is no pedestrian walkway on the Kingston-Rhinecliff Bridge.

Bear Mountain Bridge

Walkways pass along both sides of the bridge. There are invigorating, high and windy, large views. See Anthony's Nose chapter for a description. Parking is available in pull-offs along NY 9D just north of the bridge.

Mid-Hudson Bridge

Great views are found along the pedestrian walkway, but parking is only on the west bank at Johnson-Iorio Memorial Park, reached by crossing the bridge and going north on US 9W to the first right turn. Follow to the end, bearing right at forks. This bridge is not for those afraid of heights. You gain windy views of Poughkeepsie and Kaal Rock, upriver to the railroad bridge and Crum Elbow, downriver to the Beacon Range in clear weather. Open dawn to dusk.

Newburgh-Beacon Bridge

Park on town roads on the Newburgh end and walk up to the pedestrian walkway. Do not park on the Dutchess County side. Best views of Newburgh Bay and the North Gate of the Hudson Highlands.

The Harlem Valley
and the South Taconics

Driving north from Brewster on NY 22 the visitor enters the Harlem Valley, a narrow, agricultural trough that runs for miles along the Connecticut border. The hills to either side mount higher and higher until, in the northeasternmost section of Dutchess County, you reach the South Taconic Range and the highest mountains in the county. Northward the valley continues along the Massachusetts border and into Vermont. South of Pawling this valley is largely flooded in what is known as the Great Swamp, at 6,768 acres one of the largest freshwater wetlands in the state and a supplier of drinking water to over a million people. You can continue to follow the valley, somewhat, all the way to Harlem in New York City.

It is said the Harlem Valley was named for its railroad. The Harlem Valley division of the New York Central Railroad was completed in 1850. It was one of the first railroads in the country, and the oldest that leads to Manhattan.

It was the Harlem Valley Railroad that put an end to the livestock drives. Farmers in Vermont and the northern states drove thousands of cattle, sheep, and other livestock south to New York City for slaughter via the Harlem Valley. Monday was market day in the city, and as many as two thousand head of cattle could be seen on the road between Dover and Pawling at the end of most weeks. With so much livestock moving through, taverns for the thirsty drovers flourished. Old Drover's Inn in Dover is all that remains. After a walk up Boyce's high escarpment, you may want to visit the inn to look at the historic painting of a cattle drive on their barn. The inn is located a short jog east of NY 22 driving north from Wingdale.

What makes the Harlem Valley special is based on its special geology. The Harlem Valley walls are composed of a gray granite-schist gneiss studded with garnets, common enough. But the valley floor is pure carbonate;

a gleaming white marble, overlaid by deep layers of glacial sand and gravel. Rainwater percolates through the sand and gravel at a high rate into the groundwater, creating a valuable aquifer, a place where groundwater is recharged and purified—not a place to seal with blacktop or dump full of toxins. It is a fact that Dover has the purest water in New York State. So pure is it that, as a public drinking supply, it need not be chlorinated.

While lime belts are common in sections of Dutchess County, the public has little if any access to the regionally unusual lime-spawned forests, the gleaming white quarries, and the marshes of rare plants. Here are the places you can go to see these unusual things. And here are some of the best hill hikes, including Brace Mountain, the highest hill in either Putnam or Dutchess counties.

28 · Pawling Nature Reserve

Location: Pawling
Distance: 1 mile, 1 to 2 hours
Owner: The Nature Conservancy

The Pawling Reserve spans Hammersley Ridge, part of the west wall of the Harlem Valley. It is a large place, 1,015 acres, and there are many trails to walk besides the short loop described in this chapter. Pawling Reserve contains a diverse cross section of natural habitats characteristic of eastern New York. Rare, threatened, and endangered species of plants and animals live here, including a large number of songbird species. My favorite part of the reserve is the brook gorge.

Access

From the village of Pawling, take NY 22 north about 2 miles. Turn east onto Dutchess County 68/North Quaker Hill Road. In 0.3 mile, continue as this road forks off to the right. Set your odometer at zero, and from this point drive 1.1 miles to the top of the ridge. Turn left onto Quaker Lake Road. Go 1.3 miles. Quaker Lake Road turns to dirt at the lake, sometimes very muddy in spring. Continue past the lake for 0.75 mile. Trailhead parking on the left. No dogs allowed. To prevent overgrazing, there is a limited deer-hunting season that lasts for about three weeks in autumn. Information: 914-244-3271.

Trail

Follow the trail to the sound of rushing water for a view of the gorge, reminiscent of Stone Church in Dover Plains, shadowed by hemlocks that still appear healthy. In the channel below this cool hemlock ravine nests the

28. PAWLING NATURE RESERVE

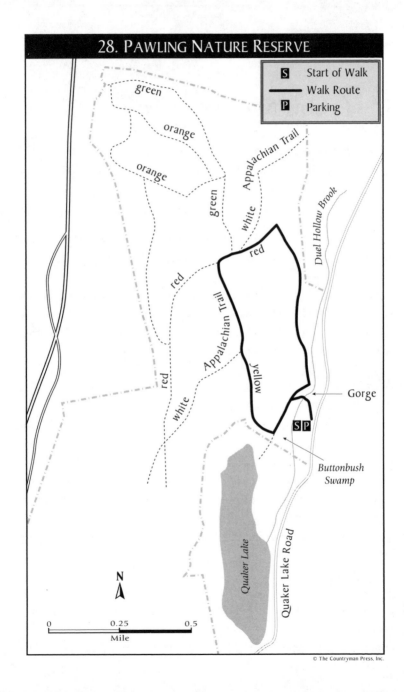

Legend:
- **S** Start of Walk
- Walk Route
- **P** Parking

green

orange

orange

green

white

Appalachian Trail

Duel Hollow Brook

red

red

red

Appalachian Trail

yellow

white

Gorge

S **P**

Buttonbush Swamp

Quaker Lake

Quaker Lake Road

N

0   0.25   0.5
Mile

© The Countryman Press, Inc.

Acadian flycatcher, the Louisiana waterthrush, and the winter wren. The winter wren is a northern bird. Pawling Reserve lies near the southern border of its summer range at this elevation. It is also one of only a few places in Dutchess County where the Acadian flycatcher breeds.

The ravine bedrock is a micaceous, or mica-bearing, schist veined with marble. The limestone that weathers from the marble into the soil and the cool, moist microclimate of the ravine combine to support a unique fern community among the rocks: bladder fern, bulblet fern, fragile fern, walking fern, maidenhair spleenwort, and silvery spleenwort. The soil bank of the stream is cloaked with liverworts. Back on the trail, stop on the footbridge and take a look at the Duell Hollow Brook. Shiny flakes of mica sparkle in the sand and gravel of the brook bed. Whole slabs of mica-schist gleam under the water.

Cross the stone wall and go straight on the yellow trail. You may notice the red trail on your right; that is your return. Climb the ravine wall under hemlocks and white pines. Some of the hemlocks are giants. This species can live for up to six centuries, but in one generation we may see it wiped off the face of the ecosystem. Up until the end of the 20th century, hemlocks grew and tended to persist on slopes in southern New York where it is cool and moist year-round. Various adaptations to shade made hemlock a dominant species no other tree could compete against in the cool, moist ravines. In traditional ecological terms, such a growth was called a climax forest: self-perpetuating and stable unless some catastrophe occurred. Well, catastrophe has occurred. Only time will tell what will become of the slopes vacated by the hemlock.

While you can still hear the falls of the gorge, watch on your right for a mica-schist overhang large enough to just walk beneath. This was a rock shelter used by archaic and woodland Indians during hunting expeditions thousands of years ago. Several species of lichens and mosses coat the rock.

The trail levels off and the hemlocks end. Slight differences in annual mean temperature, water availability, and soil composition caused a different association of tree species to develop. The soil here is thicker and

Pawling Nature Reserve

warmer and the slope no longer so steep. Here grow oaks and sugar maples in a mesic, or medium moist, soil environment.

And here lies the buttonbush swamp. Buttonbushes *(Cephalanthus occidentalis)* grow in the standing water. Few plants have round flower clusters, but buttonbush blooms are perfect spheres, clusters of cream flowers so sweet smelling the shrub's old country name is honey balls. The fruits develop from the globe, and these balls hang from the twigs far into the winter.

Continue on the yellow trail through mountain laurel until it ends at the white-blazed Appalachian Trail. Turn right. The AT travels the crest of Hammersley Ridge, although there are no views. Wood boards (which may be slippery) span wet spots. Japanese barberry and buckthorn, both alien shrubs, have established themselves atop Hammersley Ridge, in what many decades ago was field. See the stone walls? This land was farmed for over two hundred years. Once these aggressive, alien species dominate a site, it is difficult to eradicate them. You can see buckthorn elsewhere in Dutchess County where the soil was disturbed by human use and forest clearing, such as at Denning's Point in Beacon. Barberry grows just about everywhere nowadays, but it seems to do especially well in the bottomlands and on the slopes of the Harlem Valley, crowding out all other shrubs and even herbaceous plants.

If you want to extend your walk, at the red trail turn left. Climb slightly, then turn right on the green trail. This leads along the ridge slope and then downhill to a left turn on the orange trail. Follow along the slope to a view of the Harlem Valley and its Great Swamp. Retrace your steps back to the AT, or, if you're feeling like a workout, you can make a loop by climbing down the ridge and then back up again. To do this, continue steeply downhill on the orange to a right turn, still the orange (orange also goes left at this intersection), climbing until you meet the green. Turn right, still climbing, until you meet the white Appalachian Trail. Turn left.

Whether you have extended your walk or not, turn right onto the red trail to begin the return to your car. Where the boards begin again you pass through a wet area of red maple, ash, spicebush, and sensitive fern, all native plants. Bedrock lies close to the surface at this site. Even though you are on top of the ridge, the water has nowhere to go and simply stays put. The trees, shrubs, and ferns can tolerate such wet soil that disfavors other plants, such as the aggressive barberry and buckthorn.

Continue for the descent off the ridge. As with the ascent, you traverse a mesic slope of red oak, tulip tree, black cherry, and sugar maple. Should you walk this route when the leaves are down, you get a view of the opposite ridge and the steep valley wall.

Cross a brook and start up a knoll. Bedrock outcrops appear, covered with lichens and mosses. The soil layer thins to mere millimeters and the air smells of pine resin. The sugar maple and the red oak end, to be replaced by scrub and chestnut oak, white pine, mountain laurel, and lowbush blueberry.

This is a dry, or xeric, upland soil site where the bedrock is close to and at the soil surface. In the red maple site, the bedrock formed a sort of dishpan that trapped and held the water. But here, even though you are at a lower elevation, the bedrock is shaped as a peak, and the water runs right off. All year round, the soil stays dry. A xeric-condition-adapted scrub oak or chestnut oak can outcompete any sugar maple or red oak in this spot. One pitch pine stands in the path with a trail blaze painted on it. This pine has three needles per cluster, whereas white pine has five. Pitch pine is adapted to growing in near-desert conditions, although it also grows in bogs (where all the water actually inhibits the ability of roots to take up water, mimicking xeric conditions!).

Watch along the ground for a small evergreen plant that looks like infant mountain laurel. This is wintergreen *(Gaultheria procumbens)*, which makes red berries in autumn. The trail winds downhill along the ravine wall. The soil becomes moist and the microclimate cool, and you're back in the hemlocks. Rejoin the yellow trail just above the gorge for the return to your car.

29 · Thomas J. Boyce Park

Location: Wingdale
Distance: Almost 3 miles, 2 to 3 hours
Owner: Town of Dover

The town of Dover consists of two long north-south ridges and a valley: West Mountain, East Mountain (which separates New York from Connecticut), and the Harlem Valley in between. This corridor continues north into Columbia County.

Boyce Park lies just south of East Mountain proper. It is a 199-acre municipal recreational facility with the added bonus of a hill that forms part of the Harlem Valley wall—a 1,126-foot escarpment with a windy view of the valley.

Access

Boyce Park is on the east side of NY 55 just north of the intersection with NY 22 and Dutchess County 21 in Wingdale. Park by the playground. Dogs allowed on leash. Information: Town of Dover Recreation Department, 845-832-9168.

Trail

Walk the dirt road to the fields out back. Stand a moment and look around. The road heads up and over the hay field. An escarpment rises behind. What's that on top, that cleared area? A platform within the cleared area? The hang gliders' platform: our destination.

Once in the fields, the road may expose sand, gravel, and cobbles. The Harlem Valley is choked with such glacial outwash. If you drive around the area, you will see many mining operations digging up what the last

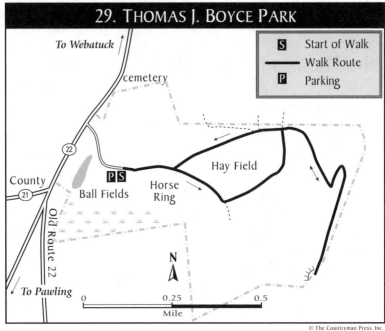

29. THOMAS J. BOYCE PARK

To Webatuck

S Start of Walk
— Walk Route
P Parking

cemetery

22

County

21

P S

Ball Fields

Horse
Ring

Hay Field

Old Route 22

To Pawling

N

0   0.25   0.5
Mile

© The Countryman Press, Inc.

glacier dumped. Follow the road to the top of the fields. Swallows swoop over the grasses in summer. This field gets hayed for horse fodder twice each summer, which keeps the natural process of succession halted so the field stays a field and does not proceed to woodland. If the field is totally mown and there is no trace of any road, just cut straight through and head to the field's extreme left, rear corner.

A view of the escarpment when the leaves are down shows a stratification of tree species. The dark green evergreens toward the top are hemlock (ailing, sad to say). The midsection of the slope grows bone-white paper birch. They look like giant nerve endings. Across the base grow brown-tipped tulip trees. The brown tips are the dried seed heads.

The road forks. Follow the fork of your choice. At the top of the field you feel a big breeze and see a big view: the Harlem Valley from Wingdale north into Dover. The Ten Mile River flows through a gap between the hill you are about to climb and the next closest hill to the northeast, Schaghti-coke Mountain in Kent, Connecticut. This mountain was allotted to the Schaghticoke Indians in the 1700s, part of a larger reservation parceled off from original vast homeland that got whittled down to the mountain alone, all ledge and rocky slope. Even from this distance you can see it is rocky. The Appalachian Trail passes through the reservation.

Go to the field's northeasternmost corner, where the road enters the woods and begins its ascent. At the fork bear right. See the huge old white oak in the woods on the left? The low, wide arms of branches that grew in full sunlight with no other tree around? These woods were once a field. All-terrain vehicles are forming new, illegal trails. Just keep on the main road, the one most traveled. The climb is steep.

The hang gliders' platform is not the summit but close enough. What a view! It's a long way down to that hay field, especially if you're flinging yourself off the platform with a giant kite. If it felt breezy below, the wind's terrific up here. The tops of hills bear the brunt of storms, and to such storms the hilltop flora and fauna must be adapted.

Thomas J. Boyce Park

There spreads the Harlem Valley aquifer, a calcite and dolomite marble trough deep in alkaline soils and glacial outwash. The fields of Boyce below look flat as a pancake. There is Wingdale and the growing housing developments. Straight ahead is Sharparoon, south of the power line. The Catskills peek behind West Mountain. The Swamp River meanders below. To the north it joins the Ten Mile River.

The high spots in the valley floor are marble bedrock outcrops or, plainly put, marble hills, where rare plants grow. These hills are what gave Dover its name, after the white cliffs of Dover in England. The ridge walls of East and West Mountain are made mostly of more resistant schists with some phyllites where rare timber rattlesnakes live.

Return the way you came. You can vary the walk through the hay field by taking a different road fork.

30 · Sharparoon

Location: Dover
Distance: 2 miles, 2 hours
Owner: New York City Mission Society

A visit here is like a walk back in time. After decades of farming and a lively iron mining and smelting history, Sharparoon Pond and its nearby, intact 1800s iron furnace, iron mines, and charcoal pits were purchased directly from the mining company in 1922 by the New York City Mission Society as a summer camp for New York City boys. What this means for walkers is that you can view a historic landscape largely unchanged, other than for the growth of trees, since the date of sale. Land purchases continued, so that today the society owns nearly 2,000 acres of forests, streams, and ponds in the Harlem Valley and along the Swamp River and West Mountain. The hiker can visit land left wild for almost 80 years. There are few parcels in the Hudson Valley that can boast such a history of preservation, especially one in a fertile valley ripe for development. Presently, there are two camps on the property: Camp Green Acres and Camp Minisink. Both are in full session during the summer and are used for various programs throughout the year.

Since 1957, Sharparoon has been closed to the public. However, the director has kindly given permission for the inclusion of Sharparoon in this book. For the first time in a long time, strictly *by appointment only*, and only during fall, winter, and spring, Sharparoon is open to the general public.

There are many trails at Sharparoon. If you'd like to extend your walk as described at the end of the chapter, check first at the office on trail conditions.

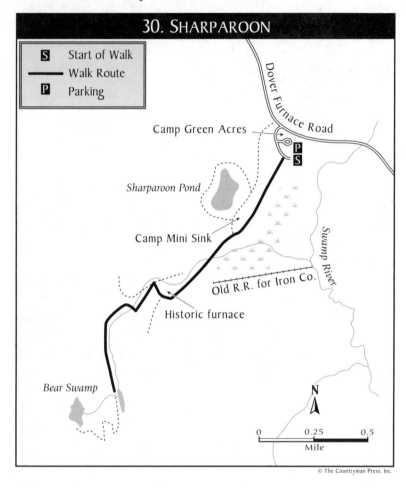

30. SHARPAROON

S	Start of Walk
▬	Walk Route
P	Parking

Dover Furnace Road

Camp Green Acres

Sharparoon Pond

Camp Mini Sink

Swamp River

Old R.R. for Iron Co.

Historic furnace

Bear Swamp

N

0   0.25   0.5
Mile

© The Countryman Press, Inc.

Access

Call before you go. From the Wingdale traffic light at the intersection of
NY 22 with Dutchess County 21, head north on NY 22, 2.5 miles, to a
left turn onto Dutchess County 26 west/Dover Furnace Road. Drive 0.5
mile, over two bridges. Watch on the left for a newer building called Zaccara Center. If you come to Camp Green Acres, you've gone one driveway too far. Park at Zaccara Center and register at the office.

Sharparoon is open to the public from Labor Day to Memorial Day by appointment only. The grounds are closed in summer when the camps are in full operation. No dogs allowed. Information: 845-832-6151.

Trail

From the parking lot at Zaccara Center, walk back to the main road and turn left. Turn left at Ore Bed Road and follow this straight through Camp Green Acres and on as it turns to dirt. After a bit of walking, you may notice that the ground falls away from the road verge rather steeply into swamp-filled hollows. These are pit mines. The Hudson Highlands, the Fishkill Range, and the South Taconic Range were famous for their iron ore, present in varying purities. (Historically, the name Fishkill Range was applied to the mountains that began at the Hudson River with Breakneck Ridge and ran inland and then north to end with the Harlem Valley's West Mountain.) Mines begun in colonial times reached their peak operation in the 1880s. Iron companies employed thousands of men as ore diggers, coal-men, colliers, smelters, teamsters, and limestone diggers, creating many of the county's hamlets and towns. When the mines were no longer operating, many of the pits filled with water to become lakes. Sharparoon Pond is such a lake.

Once you reach the next camp keep left along the left side of Camp Minisink. The road continues from the rear left corner of the camp complex. This is the original road that connected the furnace with the hamlet of Dover Furnace in the 1800s. Pass another steep-sided mine pit on your right. When the woods open into a field, bear right to the furnace stack, a registered national landmark.

Built in 1881 at the height of the iron mining industry, the Sharparoon hot blast charcoal furnace smelted bog iron or limonite ore dug from the foss ore bed, just up the hill. "Bog iron" is created when water dissolves iron from ore-bearing rock and carries it downhill to collect in small hollows and creases in the land, creating a new deposit of bog iron. After the ore was washed and crushed, it was stored in warehouses whose foundations you see behind and above the furnace.

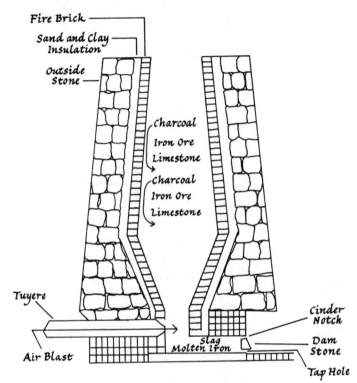

Fire Brick

Sand and Clay Insulation

Outside Stone

Charcoal
Iron Ore
Limestone
Charcoal
Iron Ore
Limestone

Tuyere

Cinder Notch

Air Blast

Slag
Molten Iron

Dam Stone

Tap Hole

Cross-section of a Hot Blast Furnace
(After Jose Alvira)

The furnace itself is built of perfectly fitted white Harlem Valley marble. Its innards are lined with layers of a special fire brick, called "bosh," which is more porous than ordinary brick for greater heat retention. Much of this brick has turned back into sand and clay. (The bricks lining the arch are newer supports to help stabilize the structure.) On top of this furnace stack sat a tall wooden building, where people worked and where coal and ore were stored, with more buildings all around.

From the warehouses, charcoal was hauled across a bridge to the furnace and dumped directly into the top of the furnace stack. The charcoal was lit, and on top of it was layered limestone, as a flux, and the iron ore.

What is charcoal? Cut down a forest. Dig a pit. Stack 25 cords of logs just right. Cover with soil and leaves. Set on fire and let smoulder for about a month, watching like a hawk. Too hot, and the wood burns to ash. Just the right temperature, and the wood carbonizes into what feels like a crumbly rock: charcoal.

Who would do such work? Colliers. Charcoal makers. Men willing to spend days without sleep and months away from the human race, watching their charcoal pits.

Twenty-five cords of wood, or one pit, yielded up to two thousand bushels of charcoal. The Sharparoon furnace used one thousand bushels of charcoal per *day*. In 1843, within 12 miles of Amenia 10 furnaces burned, and more were built later. The appetite for charcoal quickly clear-cut the second- and third-growth forests of the region. Furnaces for years imported charcoal from Vermont, contributing to the clear-cutting of that state.

With the "charge" of charcoal, limestone, and ore lit and burning in the stack under blasts of hot air, which were funneled through iron pipes up and down the stack, the temperature rose to 2,450 degrees Fahrenheit, the melting point of iron. Carbon from the charcoal combined with oxygen in the iron oxide ore, giving off carbon monoxide, carbon dioxide, and pure molten iron. Impurities melted and combined with the molten limestone to form slag. The charge slowly descended the hearth to the bottom, the slag floating on top of the iron. The slag was drawn out through the hearth's upper cinder notch. The molten iron was drawn out through the tap hole on the bottom and allowed to run onto the floor of a casting shed at the front of the furnace. This floor was lined with a special sand molded into long ditches called "sows" and, off the sows, little ditches called "pigs." This tough but soft pig iron was of a high quality. It was used to make anchors, musket and pistol barrels, wire, car wheels, cannon, and steel.

After walking around the base of the furnace, avoid the obvious dirt road to the right of the stack (as you face it) and instead head to its left on a dirt road. Take the first, immediate right. If the way is blocked by thorny barberry just push through for a short bit until you are behind the furnace. If the trail has been cleared, then it's no matter. You are at the warehouse foundations. They are built of both alkaline, lowland, white Harlem Valley marble and acidic, upland, gray West Mountain mica-schist gneiss. The gray schist contains numerous red garnets, though not of gem quality. The iron industry died out at the beginning of the 1900s for several reasons: the discovery of purer iron ore in the Mesabi Range in Minnesota, the lack of wood for charcoal, and the failure of the companies to invest in the newer and more efficient Bessemer smelting process.

Join that obvious dirt road you avoided as it comes up the bank from the furnace. As the road turns left, take a jog right to see the waterfall. Water from the waterfall was piped to cool the working iron parts of the furnace. Return to the road and continue. Look for green, glass-like slag in the road. Excellent landfill, slag from furnaces was carted away for decades, first in wagons, then in trucks, and underlies driveways, roads, houses, and churches, nearly all the older properties in the surrounding towns. At forks, choose trails on the left that parallel the stream as it passes through the hemlock-mixed deciduous ravine. Part of the road may be washed out. Just keep following until you reach Ore Pond. This is the flooded foss ore pit, a pit mine of cloudy green water of great depth.

A footpath skirts to the right of the pond over rocks on top of a waterfall where the iron companies built a dam to hold back Bear Swamp's stream, come from uphill. At the pond's south end, under late-morning sunlight, the water glows an incredible luminous green. Near the end of the ravine, look across to see the rusted bedrock cliffs and the squared-off cuttings of where they took out the entire valley. The pond below is simply where the water table intersects the hole of a deep and narrow mine.

The return is back the same way. For the adventurous, the trail keeps going uphill to Bear Swamp, a beaver pond, marked by old tin can tops. The path is rough and may be overgrown, and there are many old logging roads in poor condition, likewise overgrown, that lead onto private property. You could get quite lost in this large tract of woods. Explore

Sharparoon

this area only if you are an experienced woodsman and willing to bush-whack through difficult terrain. A wide trail loop of 8 miles is possible along the ridge to the power line at the northern end of the Sharparoon property, looping back to the ravine, but check at the office on its condition before you go.

31 · Roger Perry Memorial Preserve at Dover White Sands

Location: Dover
Distance: 1 mile, 1 hour or less
Owner: The Nature Conservancy

The Nature Conservancy has preserved 117 acres of the White Sands of Dover, a strange place of open stretches of white sand, fens, and juniper forest. Those who enjoy odd plants rare to the area will have a field day here. The single trail offers only a short walk, but one that is unique to the Harlem Valley.

Access

From Wingdale, take NY 22 north several miles almost to Dover Plains. If coming from the north, take NY 22 to just south of Dover Plains village. Turn east onto Dutchess County 6 opposite the Andren warehouse (at Oniontown, for old-timers). Drive 1.1 miles to a fork with a bench. Turn left onto Lime Kiln Road. Drive 1.3 miles, crossing the Ten Mile River, past homes with lime cliffs in their backyards, to a sharp right onto Sand Hill Road. Drive almost 0.2 mile to the park's small entrance on the right. No dogs allowed. Information: 914-244-3271 or visit www.nature.org.

Trail

Sign in at the register and pick up a brochure with trail map (check for wasps in the box). There is only the one trail, blazed in red, so directions are simple. Right off you see this place is different. It looks like a beach dune, the stretches of white and gray sand, but this is just the product of

31. ROGER PERRY MEMORIAL PRESERVE

Sand Hill Road

S Start of Walk
— Walk Route
P Parking

sand

sand

sand

sand

sand

wetlands

sand

sand

sand

N

© The Countryman Press, Inc.

Roger Perry Memorial Preserve at Dover White Sands

the weathering of the limestone bedrock. Historic uses of the park include grazing, agriculture, and limestone quarrying. Alkaline lime was used by farmers to sweeten the acidic soil of the fields. Limestone was layered into local iron furnaces along with charcoal and raw ore to smelt iron.

The exposed bedrock is gray and strangely fibrous, sometimes looking like gray folds of silk because rainfall has rounded away all the edges. Some are so rounded they look as though a stream flowed over them. It didn't. All the weathering has been done just by raindrops dissolving the calcium and magnesium of this Lake Ellis limestone molecule by molecule. Bits of the rock in the hand are easily crushed into sand. Pick up a handful of sand from the trail. It is very fine, powderlike, not like the coarse quartz sand of the ocean beach. With so much pure limestone, it is not surprising to find the preserve populated by the plants of lime soils, such as red cedars or junipers and, in late May to early June, lyre-leaf rock cress. Although the cedars did grow in the land after agricultural use was abandoned, this is not the red cedar forest of an old hay field like those commonly encountered throughout the Hudson Valley. No deciduous trees are growing to overtop these cedars. They are remaining, rather than fading away as they usually do elsewhere. Succession will undoubtedly occur as the soil profile matures, but at a greatly slowed pace.

Knolls of silken gray bedrock amidst white sand give views over the black juniper canopy to the Harlem Valley wall of deciduous forest. Large cottonwoods grow in the preserve, too, their seeds clumping together in cottony mats that blow about the ground and through the air by June. The sand makes for good tracking of wildlife.

When the trail bends left for the return, watch for a spur on the right to a fen, a groundwater-fed marsh of grasses, sedges, cattail, skunk cabbage, and a lot of shrubby cinquefoil. There are native medicinals such as boneset and joe-pye weed, and invaders from Eurasia, such as purple loosestrife and yarrow. One of my favorite sedges, cottongrass, grows here, a worldwide species of the northern tundra, along with one of my favorite native wildflowers, the fringed gentian, which blooms at the end of summer. As with the white sands area, this little fen is not your normal Dutchess County marsh. There is no sphagnum moss, and barely any peat, but lime sand muck, instead. On the opposite bank can be seen the seepage that feeds the fen. Marsh gas, a blue oil of methane, slicks the mud surface, a natural byproduct from anaerobic bacteria in the soil.

32 · Nellie Hill Nature Preserve

Location: Dover
Distance: 1.25 miles, 1 hour
Owner: The Nature Conservancy

The perfect park to study old field ecology. Botany students can visit and search for rare plants. The rest of us can admire the pastoral views while knee-deep in blue harebells, black-eyed Susans, and purple field mint.

Access

From Wingdale, drive north on NY 22 almost to Dover village. You will pass Dutchess County 6. Go another 0.25 mile to a small parking area pull-off on NY 22. There is a sign for the preserve, but it is set back from the road. Open dawn to dusk. No dogs allowed. Information: 914-244-3271 or visit www.nature.org.

Trail

Follow the trail to the right of the preserve sign, uphill to the park entrance. See the rounded cobbles of glacial outwash in the road? Even though the same limestone that is seen so readily at Roger Perry Preserve also underlies most of the Harlem Valley, it is usually buried beneath outwash. If you watch carefully as you walk, you'll see gray limestone poking up out of the ground as bedrock outcrops at Nellie Hill. Underground, the entire hill itself is all limestone.

Sign in at the gate (open register box slowly and check for wasps nesting inside under the lip). A bit farther on is an information kiosk with a trail map. Take the trail to the left, an old farm road through old farmland

32. NELLIE HILL NATURE PRESERVE

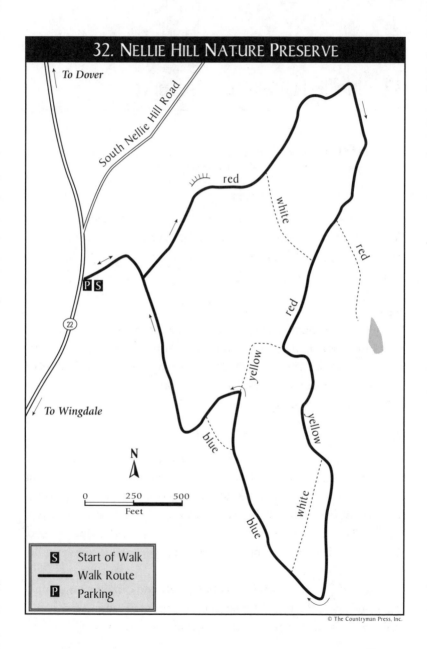

To Dover

South Nellie Hill Road

red

white

red

red

P S

22

yellow

yellow

To Wingdale

N

blue

white

0   250   500
Feet

blue

S   Start of Walk

▬   Walk Route

P   Parking

© The Countryman Press, Inc.

Nellie Hill Nature Preserve

of field species interspersed with the familiar dark silhouettes of tall red cedars. But take a closer look at the cedars as you approach the view. Taller than normal, wide of girth with far-flung and majestic limbs. They have attained the full maturity a cedar is capable of but seldom gets to attain in a field since the normal order of succession is for deciduous trees to over-top them, as you learned at Baird Park. Nellie Hill's junipers look more like something from the tree line of the Rocky Mountains. Now it is true that as you drive throughout Dutchess County you can find such old-growth red cedars everywhere. But here they are preserved.

Goldfinches and warblers sing among the European and native wild-flowers. Keep straight on the red trail for a view of the village of Dover Plains within the Harlem Valley floor, East Mountain on the valley's east side, and West Mountain on the west. Remember this view; you will learn more about it later. The red trail loops around, with a left spur going to a dead end at a pond. Keep on to a left turn on the yellow trail. Successive left turns following the yellow trail will tour the perimeter of the park. Anytime you wish to cut short your walk, just take any trail on the right.

The yellow meets the blue trail. Take the blue past a wooded slope grown up in hog peanut and Christmas fern. Catbirds sing from shrub thickets as you reenter old fields. At the fork bear right and then right again for a short jaunt on the yellow trail through the red cedars interspersed with field, shrub, and deciduous species. Keeping straight, or right, at the next fork returns you to the entrance.

If you are visiting on a weekday between 7:30 AM and 3:30 PM, next drive south on NY 22. Just before you reach Wingdale, turn left into Dover Middle-High School. Park in visitor parking, enter the main entrance, and sign in at the attendance office. Ask for directions to the high school library. I already asked the school if folks reading this book can do this, and permission was given, so go ahead, because this is a special opportunity. Hung on the walls of their library, this school houses a permanent collection of historic oils of the Harlem Valley. Compare the view you saw from Nellie Hill with the oldest painting in the collection, "Dover Plains Village" by Charles Chemmen, painted in 1874 in the Hudson River School style. Here you see what most living no longer know: how the landscape looked under old-style cultivation. You see the double row of stone walls lining a farm road past fields and cows (in how many parks have you walked such a lane, but in the woods?), how a single stone wall such as we see in every park did not necessarily stand alone but was topped by a wood fence, the landscape under haying, the Dover furnace puffing smoke, the woods being cleared uphill for charcoal. The Chemmen painting shows the Harlem Valley wall with fields only halfway up the slope, and the rest wooded. But the valley floor itself is nearly all under agriculture. You saw it from Nellie Hill practically all wooded, a canopy interrupted only by the solitary white steeple of the church and the commercial zone of stores and parking.

The rest of the paintings are impressionistic works of the local landscape from the 1930s and 1940s. There is a portrait of Stone Church, and fifteen other historic paintings.

33 · Wassaic State Forest

Location: Wassaic
Distance: 3 miles, 2.5 hours
Owner: State of New York

Located halfway between Amenia and Dover Plains in the Harlem Valley, Wassaic Multiple Use Area's 488 acres come in two parcels: up in the hills, and down in the valley along the Ten Mile River. There are two possible interpretations of the Native American name Wassaic. He Who Stands Firm, my childhood teacher who studied with native speakers, reports it could mean either "rocky country" (*qussuk* rock, *ick* locality) or "the light (or bright) waters" (*wassa* light, *ick* stream). Well named, either way.

Since this is a state forest, you can leave the trail and wander where the fancy suits you. Trails for timber cutting and hunters give straightforward access to the woods, so there are no hiker's loops. The way in is the same way out.

Whether in the midst of the high hills or down by the river, there are no wide views. Instead, you can lazily chomp a wintergreen-flavored black birch twig and while away a summer afternoon among the ferns and forest, or sit beside the glittering river watching the butterflies. This is a good place to visit when you want quiet time alone with your sketch pad or plant identification books.

Access

Upland parcel: north on NY 22 from Dover Plains to a left onto Tower Hill Road. Drive up a gorgeous hemlock ravine along waterfalls (best in spring or after heavy rain) for 0.9 mile. Parking on the right. Dogs are allowed.

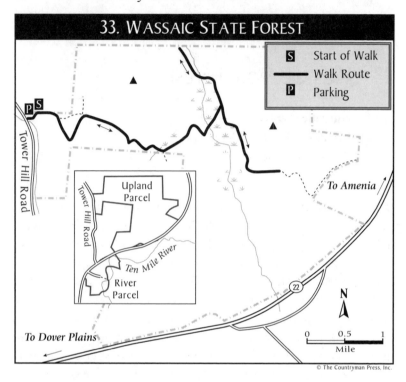

33. WASSAIC STATE FOREST

S Start of Walk
— Walk Route
P Parking

Tower Hill Road

Upland Parcel

Tower Hill Road

Ten Mile River

River Parcel

22

To Amenia

To Dover Plains

N

0   0.5   1
Mile

© The Countryman Press, Inc.

River parcel: from Tower Hill Road, turn right onto NY 22 south. Go for about 100 yards; sign for park is on left. Drive on the dirt road through fields. Keep straight on the main track to parking near the river.

Trail

Walk the dirt road behind the metal gate steeply uphill past side roads. As with most state forests, the trails are unmarked and can change from season to season. This main track, however, is quite old and not likely to disappear for many a decade. It levels off through pleasant mixed deciduous woods with now and then the cool shading of hemlocks. At the fork, keep left around the tussock sedge swamp (the right goes onto private land). Tussock-hop out into the deeper open pools of the swamp in spring for wood frogs (see Clarence Fahnestock chapter) and peepers (see Bog Brook).

As you walk the woods, you will encounter dense stands of saplings. Selective, periodic timber cutting is ongoing in most state forests. The saplings indicate where a tree was lumbered (or possibly where a tree blew down in a storm). You may even find the old, sawn stump. This allowed light to penetrate the forest canopy, which in turn allowed young trees to sprout, the kind that feed deer. Selective timber cutting is considered good wildlife management. Most of these gap closure species are black birch and witch hazel.

Cross a brook. At the next fork at a small clearing keep straight on an old hill road to see the ash trees. In late spring and early summer, after you pass the swamp grown up in skunk cabbage, watch the trail bed for ash seeds. They look like miniature butter spreaders. The leaves come in grouped leaflets of five or more. In autumn, you'll see the purple and gold foliage high up on very straight trunks. No other tree has such regular bark. Some people see diamond shapes. When I stand at the trunk and look straight up I see a pattern like that of a sheet of water running down a wall of faceted grooves.

The road seems to end at a muddy pool; actually it continues on past what looks like an old mine cut onto private land where you cannot follow. Backtrack to the intersection and turn left. Continue onto a sunny opening overgrown with vines, shrubs, and thorns. Immediately after the opening, watch on the left for a hillside of bedrock and the dark opening of a rock shelter. How intriguing! It's large enough to lie down inside, and dry. You could cover the floor with a mattress of evergreen or black birch branchlets, cover the whole with a deerskin or two, to make a cozy overnight camp for a hunter. Ah, but there's no water, so it's not the best of campsites. Yet rest assured historic Native folks knew of this spot and used it for millennia. Why not? Contemporary Native people find it amusing that few people today realize they knew every nook of their land inside and out. Maybe this was used in the past for vision quests. The overhang used to be even larger; you can see where it has fallen. There is another overhang in the rocks above this cave. Look closely at the rock. See the small, raised bumps? Those are garnets. The rock is encrusted with

Wassaic State Forest

jewels (although not of gem quality). They are easiest to see on edges of slabs that fell off most recently; elsewhere the West Mountain schist rock is too weathered.

Beyond this the road continues, then dips downslope into the Harlem Valley toward NY 22. Return the way you came. Stop again at the tangle of vines and thorns at the foot of the cave. Look around carefully. Any time you see brambles and bittersweet, vines and thorns tangled all about a sunny opening in the middle of the woods, on an old road, look for the stone foundations of a house—*if* you can figure out how to get through the overgrowth. Sure enough, there are foundations, on both sides of this old road that led from the hills to the Harlem Valley. Probably the house was on one side and the barn on the other: a farmstead. And those caves, why, what a *perfect* place for cold storage of grain, just as farmers did in old Europe. One large, old, white oak stands at the end of the clearing with a spread of horizontal, dead, lower limbs. It was probably the only tree in the farmyard. And the surrounding woods? Once all fields.

As you return on the road, measure the distance to the swampy woods and brook on the left. Here would have been the nearest natural water supply for the rock shelter. Not far for the occasional, historic hunter. The farmer would have needed a more constant, everyday supply. If you search you might discover it. (I didn't search.) The options of the day were to dig a shallow well or, better, to sink a cistern in the swamp.

Once back at your car, motor down to the Ten Mile River parcel (see Access, above). Park as close to the river as you can get. From here, a path leads to the water's edge and along the bank. Find a grassy spot and enjoy a rustic picnic. Here in July, milkweed is already in full bloom while the sap in its sisters elsewhere in Dutchess County is only swelling the buds. The fabulous pale mauve blooms smell heady with sweetness.

34 · Brace Mountain

Location: Millerton
Distance: About 4 miles, 3 to 5 hours
Owner: State of New York (part of Taconic State Park)

Brace Mountain stands 2,311 feet above sea level, the highest mountain in Dutchess County. Known locally as Monument Mountain because of the cairn on its peak top, Brace is part of the South Taconic Mountains, which continue north through Connecticut, western Massachusetts, and eastern New York into Vermont where they are called the Taconics. Much of this land is protected, so the acreage is large enough to support populations of bobcat and coyote, along with snowshoe hare and occasional visits of black bear. The entire range is actually a klippe, as is older Stissing Mountain, islands of rock that slid into their present locations 450 million years ago during the Taconic Orogeny when North America collided with another continent.

Brace Mountain rises where three states join and is the divide between the Hudson and Housatonic watersheds. From Brace you have access to Alander Mountain and Bash Bish Falls, with connections to trails in the tristate area.

The views from the top of Brace Mountain are spectacular, and the vegetation typical of acidic crest tops. The South Taconic Trail in Dutchess County provides short but precipitous access where hiking shoes are recommended as there is some rock scrambling on the ascent. Expect snow and ice on the trail until the end of March. The trail is not advisable in winter due to ice. At any time of year expect colder weather.

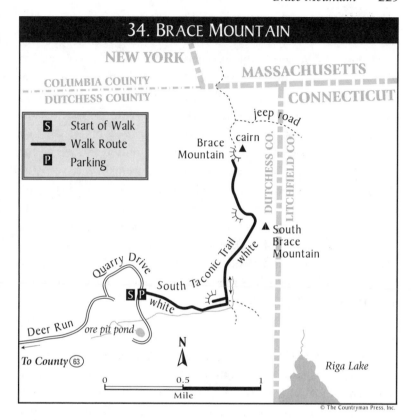

34. BRACE MOUNTAIN

Access

Take NY 22 north from the traffic light at Millerton for 5.5 miles through the Harlem Valley. Turn right onto Whitehouse Crossing Road. Turn left onto Dutchess County 63/Boston Corners Road. Go 0.25 mile and make a right turn onto Deer Run, into the development, then left onto Quarry Drive. There is South Brace Mountain straight ahead, the hemlock-studded notch to the south your trail. Curve around until you are under the shadow of the hills, where you will see a parking area large enough for two cars on your left. Dogs allowed on leash. No area use from dusk to 8 AM. Information: Taconic State Park office at Copake Falls, 518-329-3993 or visit www.nysparks.com.

(If you wanted, you could drive north into Massachusetts, then back into Connecticut on little dirt roads to the far east side of Brace Mountain on the Riga Plateau, and hike to the summit of the mountain without the big climb, but that would be cheating. Directions for how to cheat: continue north on NY 22 to Copake Falls. Turn right on Columbia County 344. In 1.4 miles you'll enter Massachusetts, where the road's name changes to Falls Road. Keep straight on for another 1.8 miles, past Bash Bish Falls, up onto the plateau. Turn right (south) onto West Street and go for 2 miles, where East Street comes in on your left and the road you're on changes to Garrett Farms Road. In a few hundred feet, bear right (still going south) onto East Street and proceed for 2.7 miles into Connecticut. The name of the road now changes to Mt. Washington Road. Shortly, you'll pass several pull-off parking areas for trailheads. You may need to park in one of these and continue down the dirt road on foot. You're looking for an unmarked, old jeep track that comes in on a sharp diagonal on your right. That leads up Brace.)

Trail

The white-blazed South Taconic trailheads east along the edge of a field and into mixed deciduous woods. At the brook, we start to climb. Steep, talus-choked hemlock, paper birch, and striped maple ravines mixed with sugar maple, ash, basswood, and oak are common along the South Taconic escarpment.

Paper birch *(Betula papyrifera)*, the chalk-white tree with the horizontal lenticel lines, can be stripped of its bark in spring when the rising sap makes it slip from the wood with ease, and it is used for many Native American things. (Of course, stripping any tree of its bark kills the tree.) Pliable, it can be sewn with spruce root into various waterproof household containers. The tannin in the bark makes it an excellent bacteria- and fungus-proof wrap for cakes of stored maple sugar, the salt of native cooking. Buoyant, it can be tied on the ends of fishnets. Canoes, moose-calls, games, toys, and water- and rot-proof wigwam shingles are all made from paper-birch bark. To the Dutchess County rambler, paper birch means the

North Country. The middle of Dutchess County is roughly paper birch's southern range limit, a range that extends north to the Arctic. Note how most of the paper birches and hemlocks cluster mainly on the opposite side of the ravine on the cooler north-facing slope. This will change with the demise of the hemlocks, ailing from the woolly adelgid infestation.

The climb is extremely steep. Watch for trillium in late May and early June. The mountain laurel blooms in late June. Take a look at the talus blocks. Rather than the familiar Precambrian Hudson Highlands granite seen on every major hill you've climbed in Dutchess and Putnam counties, here are wavy bands of a Cambrian green-blue metamorphic jumble of schist and phyllite.

The trail climbs straight up. At the waterfall the path angles left along bedrock outcrops where, suddenly, the vegetation abruptly changes to scrub oak and you gain our first wide view. The *entire range* of the Catskills and the Harlem Valley lie before you. You can see Stissing Mountain, with its fire tower on the northern slope. The South Taconics are one of the few places where you can view, in its proper perspective, the true summit of Stissing Mountain. Behind Stissing Mountain are the flat-topped Shawangunks. East and north, the rolling Taconic hills (a separate range with the same name) of Columbia County.

The vegetation is typical South Taconic highland, xerophytic crestline woodland: stunted chestnut oak, red oak, pitch pine, scrub oak, mountain laurel, lowbush blueberry, spirea, reindeer lichens, and sedges. In late June you will also see corydalis blooming. About 2 feet tall at the most, it has finely cut foliage similar to its cousin the bleeding heart, and a whitish powder on the stems. The flowers look like pink trumpets with yellow lips. By July the seeds have set in the upright pods. The plant appears to die and disappears. Only the roots remain alive underground, as the plant goes into senescence until the next spring.

Continue until you reach the top of the notch. The white trail turns sharply left, and water tinkles off to your right. Follow the sound of the water and you'll discover a great resting place: a small, emerald pool of colorful gravel and a cool slide of water down the mossy bedrock amidst dark hemlocks. Be careful to preserve this unspoiled place by not trampling plants or scraping the moss off the rocks. Return to the white trail and begin the second leg up the slope of Brace.

Eastern towhee calls from the bushes, just as it does along the entire length of the Appalachians, from here south to the range's foot in the Atlantic coastal ridge of Florida. In the iron mining days, these hills were crossed by many roads and trails. With time most of these trails have been left unmaintained to be reclaimed into forest. Just as well: this plateau needs protection. You are about to enter a special area, a heath baldy with both southern and northern Appalachian characteristics.

At first, nothing looks different. As the trail keeps to bedrock ledge to give out views onto valley and hills, you pass the South Taconic crest woodland of stunted red oak. In bald openings around the rocks find scrub oak, paper birch, spirea, corydalis, stunted serviceberry, blueberries, grasses, mosses, lichens, and, in the cracks, three-toothed cinquefoil *(Potentilla tridentata)*, an alpine plant familiar to those who hike the higher peaks of the North and South Appalachians. Three-toothed cinquefoil has long been typical of the Taconics as a crevice plant that initiates terrestrial succession on rock.

Everything grows stunted on the ledge, attaining height only in more sheltered areas of deeper soil. In these pockets of protection and greater water and nutrient retention grow diverse species of a mixed deciduous woodland, oak, red maple, and mountain laurel not so different in appearance to the woods of the Hudson Highlands, the Beacons, and Fahnestock State Park. Luxuriant sphagnum moss covers bedrock where depressions pool rainwater. But where there is ledge, there is the scrub or bear oak. The vegetation gets more stunted the higher you climb. Follow the white markers carefully, especially over bedrock where piles of stones (small cairns) also help point the way.

At one ledge, if you glance back the way you came, you'll see you are on a vast upland plateau. Riga Lake sparkles to the left. Climb on, and you'll think you've arrived at the top, but it isn't. Keep on, the scrub oak and stunted paper birch no taller than yourself. Paper birch appears like this

Brace Mountain

on the higher peaks of the southern Appalachians. Follow the Appalachians north of Brace and scrub oak steadily becomes less important as paper birch increases until, walking the arctic-alpine habitats of the end of the Appalachian chain in the Long Range of Newfoundland, you find only this stunted paper birch before the upright trees give way to mats of alpine vegetation. Here at Brace Mountain you see paper birch as it grows in the higher and more northerly Appalachians. Oddly, sapling and the upper limbs of mature paper birch grow deep orange bark with white lenticel lines. With age the bark peels to white with deep red, almost black, lines.

In autumn these paper birches turn bright yellow. The lowbush blueberry leaves turn red. With the sun behind them as it sets over the Catskills, they look on fire, and it is gorgeous up here. As you walk, take care to keep on the trail. These short stubby bushes cannot survive much trampling.

Follow past cairns, then downhill into a notch. Don't be discouraged! You're almost there! Deeper, moister soil grows a taller forest in the saddle, but soon you're climbing the opposite side and are back up in the stunted trees and heath (that means the blueberries and related species). The mountain's history as pasturage, combined with periodic fires, the harsh climate, and the poor acidic soil favored a heathlike appearance, although the heaths themselves have largely disappeared due to trampling. This is why the plateau needs protection even from hikers. In areas where people do not walk the plants are dense and vigorous, the blueberries bigger, forming thickets, the tender, rare plants healthy and numerous, the bedrock richly encrusted with thick lichens.

Go all the way to the baldy and the big stone cairn. There is always a breeze up here ruffling the short grasses (actually a mix of sedges and grasses). Oaks and pin cherry are closing in the view and, if left uncut and if fire is suppressed, the baldy will disappear in time. You view a vast panorama. To the east, the closest hill is Mount Frissell, then, to the right, Round Mountain. To the right of that, the large, bare hill is Bear Mountain, the highest peak in Connecticut. Still to the right but closer is Gridley Mountain. To the north, you can see the long Alander and all the hills of Massachusetts, including the distant but distinctive two-hump profile of 3,491-foot Mount Greylock, one of the highest in the Taconic Range and the highest point in Massachusetts. Herman Melville likened its shape to that of a whale, and it is said that Melville could see Mount Greylock from his window where he wrote *Moby Dick*. Down in the Harlem Valley is the town of Copake Falls, Columbia County. The South Taconic Trail continues for some 14 miles north into Massachusetts to end near Bash Bish Falls. And see another baldy just north.

The return is back the same way. As you descend, compare the red oak and paper birch at the bottom with what you saw at the top. They are the same species, so different in appearance, yet perhaps even the same age.

35 · Other Parks in the Harlem Valley

Rudd Pond

Here is a great 2-mile hike complete with swimming. Rudd Pond is one of the parcels of Taconic State Park, located north of Millerton on Dutchess County 62/Rudd Pond Road. If you want to use the main entrance, you must pay a $7.00 per car fee from Memorial Day to Labor Day. Off-season, the park is free. For free parking in the summer, use Shagroy Road at the south end of the park. The trail is marked in orange discs, passes Iron Mine Pond and its beaver, then climbs up and along the ridge. The only drawback is that nearly half the route uses the paved road through the park. There is swimming in the lake, lifeguard, camping, cabin rentals, picnicking, boating. If you walk in from Shagroy Road it is permissible to use the restrooms and to swim in the lake. Dogs must be on leash and attended at all times. Trails open sunrise to sunset. Information: 518-789-3059, or www.nysparks.com. Access: NY 22 north to Millerton. Take US 44 east, then on the other side of town turn left onto Dutchess County 62/Rudd Pond Road. You'll pass Shagroy Road first on the right. Take Shagroy for 0.1 mile to the free parking lot on the left. The main entrance to Rudd Pond is a bit beyond the Shagroy turnoff, also on the right.

Stone Church

Famous in the Victorian era, this natural wonder of the town of Dover in the Harlem Valley, along with nearby Seven Wells, once drew droves of tourists from New York City. Soon it may again. The town is planning to purchase the property and open it to the public. A stream and waterfall have eroded a cathedral-like arch within a narrow ravine. Watch for the

West Mountain State Forest

opening of this special place, where the Pequot chief Sassacus hid from the wrath of Narraganset chief King Phillip. For information phone Dover town clerk 845-832-6111.

Harlem Valley Rail Trail

A very popular bike path in summer, this paved rail trail runs through the Harlem Valley floor for 8.2 miles from Amenia to Millerton past fabulous views of the surrounding hills. Marked parking is available at Mechanic Street in Amenia (From NY 343, take the first right) or Main Street in Millerton. Another 8 miles are planned to open soon from Millerton to Ancram, and eventually even more miles from Amenia to Wassaic. This new section travels past breathtaking views of the South Taconics, Dutchess County's highest mountains. Always keep to the right and allow room for speedier humans to pass. Biking, walking, hiking, skating. Dogs allowed; keep leash short when others pass. Information: 518-789-9591 or visit www.hvrt.org.

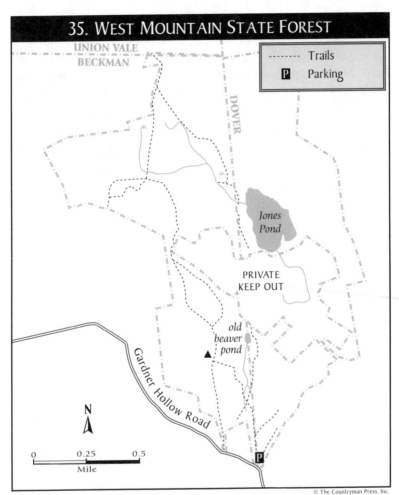

35. WEST MOUNTAIN STATE FOREST

UNION VALE
BECKMAN

DOVER

------- Trails

P Parking

Jones Pond

PRIVATE
KEEP OUT

old beaver pond

Gardner Hollow Road

N

0   0.25   0.5
Mile

© The Countryman Press, Inc.

West Mountain State Forest

This new 802-acre property is fabulous. Located where the Fishkill Range blends into and becomes West Mountain, the western ridge wall of the Harlem Valley, this forest actually spans three towns: Beekman, Union-vale, and Dover. It wraps around a large, private, housing development called West Mountain. This vast tract of upland forest interspersed with perched wetlands and brooks was under agriculture and timber production for centuries, then allowed to grow back into a forest dominated by oak and birch, perfect for exploration along the old woods roads and skid paths and for primitive camping, bushwhacking, and great hill walking. When the leaves are down the hiker gets wide views through the trees. From NY 55 near Poughquag in Beekman, drive to the very end of Gardner Hollow Road. The last few hundred feet to the parking area may be a bit rugged. To avoid the housing development, from the parking area choose the left fork at each intersection (except for hard lefts that obviously lead back in the direction in which you came) for the first mile.

The Inland Hills

MICHAEL TURCO

"I'm suffocating!" cried Maryanne, who had recently moved from the Midwest to the eastern woodlands. "I can't see anything. It's claustrophobic, all these leaves!"

One hundred and fifty years ago, Maryanne would have had little to complain about. Even before Europeans came, the Native peoples had thinned the forests with fire to encourage game and food plants, improve travel and warfare conditions, and ease the harvesting of wild plant foods. Of course, their fires were nothing compared to what the Europeans did.

To Europeans, certain trees were commodities. For instance, large old white pines, tulip trees, and northern white cedars were used in shipbuilding, and sassafras was considered a cure-all. These were scoured from what was originally a forest association of oak, white pine, chestnut, hickory, and hemlock. Hemlocks were stripped of their bark for the tanning industry and left to die. In the 1700s forests were clear-cut near sawmills along major streams. Extensive clearing made space for crops, pasture, and estate grounds, and provided fuel for the charcoal industry, the steamboats, and the railroads.

Almost all the forests of the Hudson Valley have been cut at least once. Some have been cut six, seven, or more times. After each cutting, the woods have grown back, although with each cutting, the soil has been further eroded.

Agriculture peaked in Dutchess and Putnam counties in the decade around 1875, when 85 to 90 percent of the land was under crops and pasture. Since then, farmland has declined steadily. The woods have grown back. Hudson Valley residents today catch glimpses through the leaves of a young-forested landscape.

But these young woods are different from the old. New species have been added, and original ones are gone or leaving. And, as housing and commercial development burgeon, the forested landscape seems slowly but steadily to be shrinking to islands of forest amid suburbia dotted with fortresses of parks that preserve what once was.

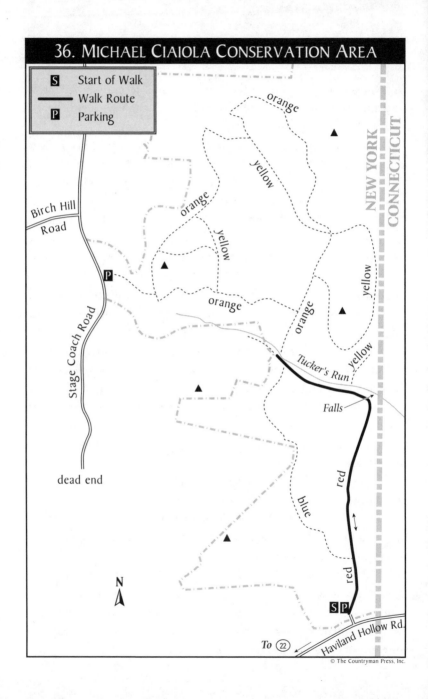

36. MICHAEL CIAIOLA CONSERVATION AREA

S Start of Walk
— Walk Route
P Parking

orange
yellow
orange
yellow
orange
yellow
yellow
orange

Birch Hill Road

Stage Coach Road

dead end

Tucker's Run

Falls

red

red

blue

NEW YORK
CONNECTICUT

N

S P

To 22

Haviland Hollow Rd.

© The Countryman Press, Inc.

36 · Michael Ciaiola Conservation Area

Location: Haviland Hollow
Distance: 1 mile, 1.5 hours
Owner: County of Putnam

This park is open only to Putnam County residents and their guests. A network of trails is accessed from three trailheads, one off Stage Coach Road and another on Haviland Hollow Road. Another is planned off Tower Hill Road, accessible from Dutchess County. Maps are available at the Stage Coach Road kiosk. In this section of the park, several loops travel up, over, and around the wooded hills. The walk described below to the scenic gorge of Tucker's Run off Haviland Hollow is the same way in and out and is mostly level. This park is open to hunters in autumn, at which time visitors should wear bright orange clothing and exercise extreme caution.

Access

For Haviland Hollow Road trailhead: from NY 22, turn east onto Haviland Hollow Road/Putnam County 68 and drive 2.3 miles. Parking is on the left just before a small bridge as you enter a valley.

For Stage Coach Road trailhead: this is north of Haviland Hollow and can be reached from NY 22. If you are coming from the north, drive 0.3 mile south of the intersection of NY 311 and NY 22 and turn east onto Birch Hill Road. If you are coming from the south, take Thunder Ridge Road to Birch Hill Road. Drive behind Birch Hill Inn, go past Thunder Ridge/Big Birch ski area, and proceed for 2.6 miles to the T-intersection. Turn right onto Stage Coach Road. Go 0.4 mile. The park entrance is on your left. Dogs are allowed on leash.

For Tower Hill Road, from NY 22 in Pawling go east on South Quaker Hill Road to a left on Tower Hill Road, which leads south into Putnam County. This is a small dirt road. A path ties into the George C. Cain trail.

Information: County Parks, 845-225-3650.

Trail

This description begins from the Haviland Hollow Road parking lot. The red Great Gorge Trail begins along an old road. In April, the delicious white bulbs of wild leek *(Allium tricoccum)* push up smooth green leaves on purple stems just when the shadflies appear. (Should the flies bother you, munch on a leaf or two of the wild leek. Out from your pores will exude a natural insect repellent.) Sensitive to the heat of summer, the leaves of wild leek die by June. The white flower umbels bloom in June and July. Soon after that, the flowers die, and all that remains are the cloves of the bulbs barely sticking up out of the ground.

The trail veers left uphill alongside the stone walls of old farmland, passing the blue trail on the left, which travels steeply up and over the hill and can be used as your return route if you have the energy for it. Keep on the red, which follows the ridge slope through a mixed deciduous forest of sugar maple, shagbark and pignut hickory, ash, and tulip tree. In the wet areas of intermittent streams grows spicebush, which blooms in late April at the same time that Japanese barberry is just leafing out.

In late April, the spear-long buds of beech trees swell, loosening the gold scales that protected the embryonic leaves and flowers during the winter. The scales are pushed open and fall to the ground. As May progresses, an entire new branch of leaves grows out from that bud. I am always amazed by how fast this happens, how rapidly the tree buds break open and the trees leaf out. In a week's time, the landscape changes from gray, open branches and trunks to a green wall of softness. In autumn, yellow witch hazel blooms, and by early October the woodland is colored by yellow leaves above and yellow leaves fallen below.

The trail brings you to the sound of water. A stone cabin at the Walter G. Merrit campsite has a view of the gorge. Please respect posted private property as you peer at the hemlock and deciduous woodland gorge of Tucker's Run, similar to the gorge at Pawling Preserve, but larger, and full of falls and cataracts. Hemlock ravines such as this were once characteristic of cool, moist slopes throughout the Hudson Valley, until just recently. Some people even say that hemlock ravines are (or were) the jewels in our woodland landscape. The imported woolly adelgid insect has started to attack the Tucker's Run hemlocks, but so far the trees are still healthy and standing tall.

The red trail follows an old farm road headed upstream. Sharp eyes will reward you with signs of the past. When at the head of the ravine, watch on the right for the yellow trail (don't take it; it leads onto private property). Simple stone foundations on either side of the brook are the remains of a farm road bridge foundation, still intact, laid stone on stone without mortar. Continue on the red trail past pools and cascades emerald green in summer. As autumn chills the water, the water turns transparent.

Fine stonework borders what becomes an old road as we continue upstream alongside the cascading brook. If you keep a lookout, you'll notice yet another stone bridge foundation above which Tucker's Run rushes over a sill of bedrock into a small pool, afloat in October with fallen yellow sugar maple leaves. The left turnoff for the blue trail (a possible return route) occurs within the darkness of the shadowed hemlocks at a point where your sight is naturally led yet onward along the red trail by successive heights of cascades falling over rocks. Therefore it is easy to miss this turnoff. If you continue, you will shortly come to an old farm post and fence and will cross an intermittent brook on stepping stones.

County property ends above the waterfalls, so even though a trail continues upstream it is on private property. If you would like to continue, cross the brook for the orange George C. Cain Trail (on the map, but unmarked at this spot). This links up with numerous loops, and you can hike the hills for hours. Or you can return via either the blue trail or simply retrace your steps on the red trail. While you try to decide, you may instead be lulled to sit in a nearby pleasant spot beside the stream and gaze upon the mosses and liverworts among the shiny yellow birches (in this case a species name for a riverside birch with silvery bark, whose leaves do happen to turn yellow in fall).

I myself usually choose to return on the red trail as the gorge is gorgeous both coming and going. As you exit the gorge headed for your car, it is easier to notice from this direction the stone foundations off to the left of a farmhouse and barn.

37 · Bog Brook State Unique Area

Location: Patterson
Distance: Less than 1 mile, 1 hour
Owner: State of New York

Here 131 acres of valuable marsh habitat, crucial to wetland species, have been preserved from the pressures of the adjoining housing development. A narrow, sometimes obscure, path travels along the west side of the marsh, so the walker does not have far to go. The rewards at Bog Brook State Unique Area are a chance to see wildlife, to learn about marshes, and to learn about nature, all compressed into one small place.

Access

From Brewster, go north on NY 22 about 3.7 miles. At a traffic light, turn left onto Old Doansburgh Road. Or, if you are coming from the north, drive south on NY 22 for 0.4 mile from Putnam County 312 and turn right onto Old Doansburgh Road. Drive 0.2 mile and turn left onto Foggintown Road. Proceed 0.5 mile to the parking area. Pass by the water control structure that maintains the marsh habitat. You'll see the state sign for the parking lot at an old sugar maple tree. Dogs are allowed. Information: New York State Department of Environmental Conservation, Fish and Wildlife Division, 845-256-3111.

Trail

Walk back toward NY 22 along Foggintown Road to the water control structure, where you gain an open view of the water and the marsh. Beaver are forever making trouble with the drains, here. In fact, it was beaver that originally formed the wetland; the present-day water control structure

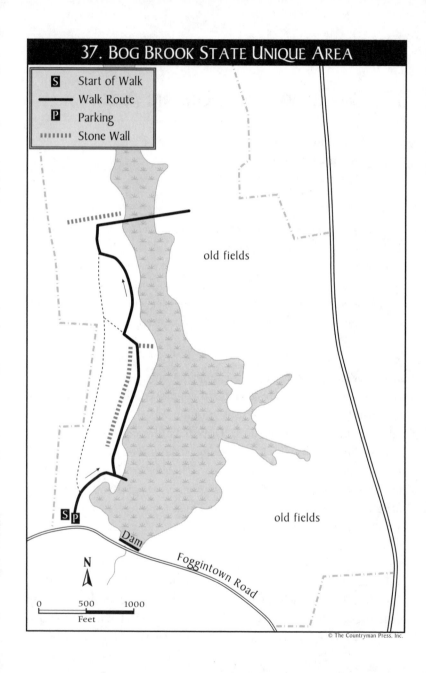

37. Bog Brook State Unique Area

S Start of Walk
— Walk Route
P Parking
••••••• Stone Wall

old fields

old fields

Dam

Foggintown Road

N

0   500   1000
Feet

© The Countryman Press, Inc.

replaces an old beaver dam. The sound of water falling is what triggers beaver damming behavior. Perhaps for as long as beaver wander Putnam County they will be attracted to Bog Brook and the dam will be built in the same spot. In fact, many road bridges cross over sites of ancient beaver dams. The rodents use an area until the food supply of tender, deciduous saplings is depleted, then abandon the pond to go find another spot. Lacking maintenance, the dam is eventually breached by a flood, the pond drains, and new tender, deciduous saplings sprout in the fertile silt, beckoning to another generation of wandering beaver to come, settle down, and build that dam in the same spot where the brook loudly tinkles as it flows through a naturally narrow neck of land. They, in turn, use the pond they form until the food sources are depleted, in turn abandon the site, and the cycle simply repeats itself.

Can you tell if beaver presently reside at Bog Brook? Look out into the marsh to see if you spy a lodge. If it is active, it will look like a mound of sticks plastered with fresh mud. No beaver allows weeds or young trees to sprout on top its lodge, so if you see such things then you know the beaver are gone. Look around at nearby bushes for fresh gnaw marks. Or, even better, come at dusk any season but winter to see if there are any beaver themselves swimming around. Only their heads and hindquarters breach the water as they swim. When they spot you, which they will since you are silhouetted against the sky, they'll give an alarm: raise their tail and smack it loudly against the water as they dive. It happens almost too quickly to see, and the splash is big. But beaver *are* big, large as Labrador retrievers, without the height.

After an alarm tail-smack, the beaver may swim off into the marsh to cut saplings or feed. As I sat on the dam one April evening, waiting, a beaver returned with a sapling in its mouth, swam right up to the dam at my feet, dove, affixed the sapling underwater, and resurfaced. With what greater ease can one observe wildlife?

Of course, it's also possible that the beaver may get trapped out (especially if they flood the road) and you won't see any even for years. All signs of them will gradually disappear, until more wander into the area,

Japanese barberry

following the brooks and marshes that web the landscape, and plug up the drains again. Whether or not you see beaver, there's plenty of other animals to watch. Swallows swoop over the marsh feeding, flying with their mouths wide open and swallowing any insect they encounter. Red-winged blackbirds and grackles smack and trill. Showy wood ducks and Canada geese wing overhead, land, take off. Turtles sun on the banks. Diving beetles and crayfish swim in the water. The marsh bustles and teems.

Return to the parking lot and find the path into the woods past Japanese barberry *(Berberis thunbergii)*. Brush against the ornamental import gone wild, and the thin sharp thorns penetrate even the thickest of jeans. Throughout autumn and winter, you'll find the bright red berries. Scratch a twig and you'll see the bright yellow berberin-containing wood. Barberry roots were used for centuries in Eurasia to dye leather yellow. At the split, take the right, lower fork that leads through a stone wall to an observation platform. Wetland shrubs are closing in the view, but you can still see that the marsh is made up mostly of phragmites reeds, which have outcompeted and supplanted the native cattails. Either one suits the hordes of spring peepers who begin to sing in April. No larger than a man's fingernail, the male tree frogs inflate their throat pouches and force air over their vocal cords in an ear-piercing whistle. I am always amazed that such tiny throats can cause such clamor. You can hear a pond of them a half mile or more away. There can be hundreds of them going at it, all spring long, all day and night, screeching from practically every unpolluted wetland pool and swamp, each male identifying his territory and shrieking for a mate. As spring progresses, the peepers are joined by the quacking of the wood frog, then the trilling of the American toad, and then the bleating of the Fowler's toad.

Return to the trail. Backtrack a few yards and watch carefully for the right turn that leads north as the footpath continues. The trail follows a stone wall along the marsh edge. (In a few more years, we'll be able to say *swamp* edge, since the marsh is succeeding to swamp as the trees grow.) Stone walls were a common technique used by early farmers to keep their livestock out of the marsh mud while at the same time clearing the land of glacial cobbles. Nearly every marsh and swamp in Putnam and Dutchess counties has a stone wall that separates it from what was once field and is now new forest. This shows you how extensively the area was farmed. These stone walls follow the narrow ecotone line between the two habitats.

There are good glimpses of the marsh. In autumn and winter, you can see right through the young trees to open water. In August, the bright purple loosestrife blooms, beloved by bees. Joe-pye weed is the shaggier, pinker bloom. *Eupatorium purpureum* belongs to a genus with members throughout the world renowned for their medicinal virtues, especially for curing cholera, typhus, typhoid, smallpox, and various fevers, and as an antidote to the poisonous bites and stings of reptiles and insects. In New England, the story is told of Joe-Pye, or Jopi, a Native American healer who traveled the land curing whites and Indians alike of the terrible and much-feared typhus fever through the use of this plant that now bears his name.

Perhaps the most prevalent plant in the marsh, besides phragmites, is purple loosestrife *(Lythrum salicaria)*. This alien plant outcompetes native cattails, sedges, and bulrushes, yet has also become an important food source for cecropia moth caterpillars. Undeniably, loosestrife is pretty, and so familiar to Americans that in Peterson's wildflower guide it rates a color plate.

Pass clumps of muscled ironwood trees. The trail leads through the corner of a stone wall system. See how the two ends of the wall on either side of this gap are evenly dressed? Wood was once fitted against these trim stones and a gate hung here. All of Bog Brook was once a dairy farm. The path continues through more barberry, becomes narrower, and strikes away from the marsh.

At either of the next T-intersections, turn right and follow until the trail ends at a stone wall. From this point you can turn right and take a path across the head of the marsh past tussock sedge hummocks and giant cinnamon ferns beneath woody shrubs and young trees. Cross the stream channel on stepping stones (the way may be muddy). Anywhere along the swamp edge where you hear them in spring, search for peepers. They'll know you're coming, and will fall silent. Walk up to the water's edge and stand absolutely still. In minutes, they'll resume their chorus. Most peepers sing from beneath the shelter of an overhang of sedge and are invisible. But every so often, one swims in the open water. Should you catch one (a difficult thing), you'll see a tiny brown tree frog with a "suction cup" on the end of each toe and a brown X across its back, which gives the peeper its scientific name: *Hyla crucifer,* or "cross-bearer." You would need a microscope to see the bristles on the toe pads that allow the frog to climb trees and even walk up glass. Release the peeper back to the swamp. Come early summer, the peepers disperse into the woods and meadows and are rarely seen.

The path leads out into fields. If you are feeling adventurous, you can bushwhack and wend your way back to your car keeping to higher ground to skirt the marsh. There are no trails. The wetland gets wide here, so be sure to choose very high ground by veering left. This part of the park was pasture for dairy cows up until the 1960s. The network of fields has been kept open by the state through periodic mowing around the successional shrub and thorn copses. This is prime deer and bird habitat and is used by hunters in season. You may feel like the beaver who thread their way along the landscape on wetland corridors as you thread your way to Foggintown Road along field corridors. Be prepared for some pushing through of thickets.

If this is too vague and thorny (literally) for you, then return via the trail on the west side of the marsh. Take the upper path back.

38 · Cranberry Mountain State Forest

Location: Patterson
Distance: 3.3 miles, 2 to 3 hours
Owner: State of New York

Cranberry Mountain Wildlife Management Area contains 464 acres of forest, field, and wetland habitats managed to produce wildlife. There are bluebird and wood duck nesting boxes, forest cuttings, plantings, water impoundments, hedgerows, and fields of planted corn; those good things that encourage ecotones and vigorous sapling growth for wildlife cover, food, and reproduction sites. Hunting and fishing are popular pastimes at Cranberry Mountain, along with hiking. This is a good park for when you simply want a walk in the fresh air, or to let the dog run. It is also good for riding the mountain bike or horseback riding (provide your own bike and horse).

Access

Just south (0.3 mile) of the intersesction of NY 311 and NY 22, turn east onto Birch Hill Road. If you are coming north on NY 22, use Thunder Ridge Road to lead you to Birch Hill Road. Drive behind Birch Hill Inn, past Thunder Ridge/Big Birch ski area, and on for 2.6 miles to the T-intersection. Turn right onto Stage Coach Road. Go 0.6 mile (you'll pass the entrance and parking for Michael Ciaiola Conservation Area on the left). The park entrance is on the right. In case the parking lot is full, there is another lot 0.2 mile farther down Stage Coach Road, also on the right. dogs are allowed. Information: New York State Department of Environmental Conservation, Bureau of Wildlife in New Paltz, 845-256-3090.

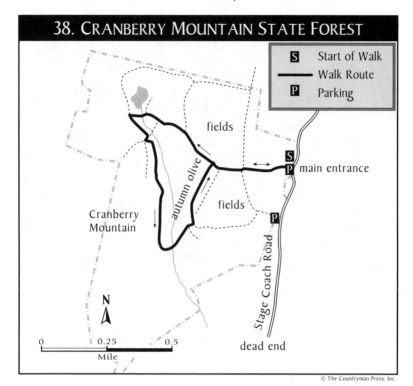

38. CRANBERRY MOUNTAIN STATE FOREST

S   Start of Walk
—   Walk Route
P   Parking

fields

autumn olive

main entrance

fields

Cranberry
Mountain

Stage Coach Road

N

0   0.25   0.5
Mile

dead end

© The Countryman Press, Inc.

Trail

Pick a bright, breezy summer's day; the woods look best then. From the parking area, follow the old paved driveway past a wetland on the left alive with peepers in spring. When the pavement ends, keep straight ahead on an old dirt road through a successional area of old farm fields. Some of the fields are planted in corn. You will pass many trails; some are woods roads, some are game trails, made by deer on their way to the corn. All are unmarked. You can explore these to your heart's content—just don't get lost. Hedgerows of autumn olive (an oriental silverberry planted in the 1960s to provide food and cover for birds and rabbit) and large amounts of Asiatic bittersweet (which invaded on its own) provide flare and color, but it's also good to see our own native goldenrods and milkweed flourishing

Cranberry Mountain State Forest

among the grasses. These fields, kept from succeeding to brush and forest by periodic mowing, are overgrown with native and alien wildflowers. Each species flowers and reproduces at its most advantageous time. Among them, hawkweed and milkweed are early summer blooms. They are followed by campion and oxeye daisy, then Queen Anne's lace, black-eyed Susan, thistle, chicory, and, finally, goldenrod.

Sixty-nine species of goldenrod *(Solidago)* grow in the northeast. Goldenrod pollen is so heavy it cannot be lifted by winds, so none of those sixty-nine species causes hay fever unless you walk right through it. It is the innocuous ragweed, blooming at the same time as the showy goldenrods, that causes the reaction. In August, how many different types of goldenrod can you find here? At first glance, it's all just yellow flowers. Look closer, and here is one with sprays arranged like a trumpet, here's another with stars of blossoms along one central stalk, and another flat as a table top.

All these edges between plant communities—the edge of field against forest, corn against shrubs, hedgerows within fields—are examples of ecotones. An ecotone is any place where two plant communities meet, the species of each intermingling. The border between a field and a forest is an ecotone, as is the border between a marsh and a field, or a tidal cove and a forest. Ecotones are the favorite habitat of much wildlife and many birds, especially since most need a combination of habitats to complete their life histories. Wildlife managers manage for ecotones.

The fields end and you enter mature sugar maple woods. Throughout this park, you may notice old apple trees. One of my favorite girlhood memories of fall is of the many walks that found a bright red apple high up on an old tree in the middle of the woods, the fun and tribulation of getting at it, and then walking on in the crisp, autumn air eating the tart, juicy thing. We used to buff the apples on our sleeves to make them shine before biting into them. This park looks the way most of the Hudson Valley used to look in, say, the 1950s and 1960s, as agricultural use of the land began to decline.

The main road bends left and right and left again. Just keep on the main track as you pass other routes. The sugar maples give way to red maples and mixed deciduous trees with an understory of spicebush jubilant with red berries in fall, indicating increasing soil moisture. There are plenty of private glades for a summer picnic.

Finally, the road brings you to a pretty man-made pond. Peer into the shallows for spotted newts. The tall reeds are phragmites reed, an Asiatic import. You can tell in August how many resident ducks are molting by the amount of feather flotsam on the water. Swallows hunt in the air and ducks preen on the logs. Stocked bass splash in the shallows flailing after smaller fish.

Continue on the road past the pond edge to the left. Have you noticed small frogs leaping out of your way? These are young pickerel frogs. Not all frogs live in ponds. A great number of species forage in the woods where it's moist enough to keep their skins supple.

At the T-intersection, turn left through woods. Pass a path on the left. At the next intersection (three-way) take the left fork that leads gently downhill and parallels the brook that issued from the pond, past more spicebush. After a bit, new plants indicative of dryer conditions appear:

bracken fern, club moss, and lowbush blueberry, along with beech and oak trees. Princess pine (which looks like a miniature tree) and ground pine club mosses produce spores that are flammable. During the Revolutionary War they were collected and used as gunpowder.

Travel the foot of Cranberry Mountain, the bright young woods sunny and scented with groves of woodland ferns, including New York, hay-scented, lowland lady, bracken, and cinnamon ferns. Watch the trail for turkey feathers. Turkey are wary fowl, so you probably won't see the birds themselves. August is a good time to find their large flat-tipped plumes. Turkey used to be one of the most important birds of the eastern woodland biome, part of the chestnut-turkey-oak-deer-hickory-black bear complex. Turkey and deer subsisted off chestnuts, and the American chestnut dominated the upland forests of the Hudson Valley. Can you imagine how it used to be in spring, when an entire chestnut landscape bloomed? The trees would look more white than green, smothered in sprays of creamy flowers and abuzz with pollinating bees, flies, and wasps. Admittedly, it would have smelled more pungent with just an overlay of sweetness. And then the mast crop in fall layered the ground in husks and nuts. Well, those days are gone and the landscape has changed. In 1904, Asiatic chestnuts were planted in New York City. This species had always been the natural host of a fungus disease that did not kill them, but it wiped out the American chestnut. Such habitat destruction, in addition to uncontrolled commercial hunting and the lack of protective laws, also wiped out the turkey and the deer. Over the years, oaks filled the niche that once belonged to chestnut and became the new dominant trees of the region. Some say ruffed grouse partially moved into the turkey's former position. Under heavy legal protection, white-tailed deer were reintroduced from midwestern stock. (Now, can you imagine *that*, our landscape bereft of deer?) When wild turkey wandered back into New York State from Pennsylvania in the 1940s, they were adapted to subsisting on acorns, rather than chestnuts and acorns. With the help of the state's Conservation Department, turkey are now plentiful throughout New York. Those of Dutchess and Putnam counties probably first wandered in from the Taconics where they had been reintroduced. Today, in autumn you can see flocks, even in the hundreds, of hens and their juveniles.

The road finally curves left to cross the brook on a bridge. The red maples of this bottomland bloom in April. Gray squirrel often nip the flowers off to lap the tree sap, or perhaps a strong wind blew, so you might find some fresh blooms on the ground. The stocky deep red flowers with two threadlike pistil parts are females. The red and yellow ones are males, their fuzzy parts the pollen-bearing anthers. Usually, red maple trees are either male or female. Occasionally, they're both, half the tree male, half female. The male pollen fertilizes the female eggs, and from her two pistils grow the twin wings of polynoses, or samaras, a seed inside each.

Climb gently uphill away from the red maples and large cinnamon ferns, past the black birch and spicebush of the brookside to an upland, open, sugar maple stand. In autumn it is easy to see the layout of the old farm fields that were once here by the numerous stone walls running through the woods. At the T-intersection, turn left. This leads out into fields. Follow along the edge of the autumn olive hedgerow. The footpath may be obscure here, so look for the row of tall bushes, silvery gray underside to the foliage, festooned in late summer with salmon, speckled berries. Turn right on the main farm road you entered on. From here you can look back and see the long, low ridge of Cranberry Mountain. Follow the road to return to your car.

39 · Ninham Mountain State Forest

Location: Carmel
Distance: 1.5 miles, 2 hours
Owner: State of New York

The 1,023-acre Ninham Mountain State Forest is bisected by Gypsy Trail Road. The east side, an old farm in the Pine Pond valley, contains two north-south trails that pass through old fields, deciduous woods, a pond, and plantations of Norway spruce, balsam fir, European larch, and red pine. The west side, the mountain itself, also was farmed, mostly by members of the Smalley family, which is why on old maps the mountain is called Smalley's Hill.

These woods are fun to explore, but the main attraction is the 360-degree view from the fire tower of hills forest-cloaked from the Catskills to New York City. To gain a view like this usually takes much effort. The climbs up South Beacon Mountain, Anthony's Nose, Sugarloaf, Brace, or Stissing mountains are strenuous, but most everyone can stroll to the top of Ninham Mountain, Putnam County's highest at 1,426 feet, because the road takes you halfway up before the walking begins.

As of this writing, the 1930s Civilian Conservation Corps (CCC) fire tower is signed as dangerous, but it is open. In previous years, the first flight of stairs was removed to prevent access. Now the stairs are back and the town of Kent Conservation Advisory Committee (CAC) is working to restore the tower.

Access

From the village of Carmel, turn west onto NY 301. Cross the West Branch Reservoir causeway, at the end of which take an immediate sharp right

39. NINHAM MOUNTAIN STATE FOREST

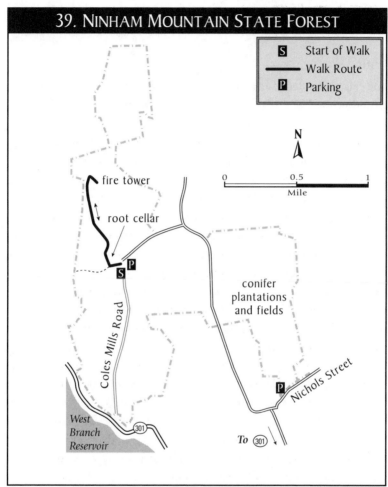

© The Countryman Press, Inc.

onto Gypsy Trail Road/Putnam County 41. Drive 2 miles, past the first two state forest and forest ranger signs to the third sign. Turn left onto Ninham Mountain Road. Drive uphill to the end of the paved road for parking. Do not block the gate or the road when you park, as utility vehicles need regular access to the towers atop the mountain. Bring your binoculars. Dogs allowed. Information: On the forest, New York State

Department of Environmental Conservation, 845-831-8780, and for progress on the fire tower, Kent CAC, 845-225-3942.

Trail

The gate on the left closes off old Coles Mills Road, which you can hike clear down to NY 301. You want the gate on the right, the one that leads uphill.

Already you have a view of the nearest hills. One of the first things you see on the road after the parking area is a large rock outcrop on the right; the road skirts alongside and around it. At the end of the curve, watch on the right for an old root cellar hidden among the grapevines. Opposite this, across the road, runs a double stone wall farm lane.

The road climbs past stone walls, old fields, ancient apple trees, and new stands of sugar maple, ash, black birch, and oak. You can botanize as you go: milkweed, goldenrods, woodland ferns, lowbush blueberry, sweetfern, and spirea. It's a pleasant climb past all our common native trees. There are black cherry, tulip tree, red maple, shagbark hickory, witch hazel, and sassafras. The common vines are here, too: poison ivy, Virginia creeper, and wild grape.

At the top, the road loops past the various communications towers to the old fire tower. Leave Ninham Forest's herbaceous plant layer—the niche of ovenbird, towhee, and robin—with the first two steps up the fire tower. Climb to the first landing. You are above the shrub layer, the niche of sparrows. Keep climbing, up through the trunks of the understory, the niche of squirrels and woodpeckers. Toward the top, you emerge above the canopy layer, the tops of the trees spread out in the full sunlight, the niche of eastern oriole and certain butterflies. Each of these forest layers is distinct. Some animal species are adapted to living in only one layer and are seldom seen in the others. Keep climbing to the cab at the top.

Pine Pond is the larger pond to the east; West Branch Reservoir is the meandering lake. Lake Gleneida sparkles in Carmel. Look at all the open pastures, and the housing that spreads over an entire landscape. There is I-84, and the communications tower on Depot Hill; the Fahnestock plateau, Bull Hill, and the fire tower on South Beacon Mountain. To the southwest the steepest hills hunch over misty Peekskill Hollow. Power lines march across the hills. The Shawangunks and Catskills loom blue to the west. The wind's terrific up here when it blows!

Tree canopies form silhouettes that distinguish species: cones of evergreens, red maple swamps at the head of Pine Pond, the dominant oak forest over the rolling rounded hills.

This is the landscape we live on. Running around in our automobiles in the valleys, we seldom get up high enough to see that the majority of the land is hilltop and slope. These endless, low, rounded summits, once great mountain peaks, were eroded to their roots. Then glacial ice scraped, ground, plucked, and gouged the eroded roots. When the glacier receded, it dumped till and rock debris that became the parent material for our soil and the basins for our lakes, ponds, and swamps. Exfoliation and weathering further rounded the hills, while streams cut V-shaped valleys.

This was Sachem Daniel Ninham's land, his people's land, Wappinger land. Old papers of the day record the spelling as "Nimham." Ninham was a chief, a sachem, what Europeans of the day would have called a king. In 1756, various New England and lower–New York tribes joined a large group of Wappinger and Munsee Lenape or Delaware Indians led by Daniel Ninham. These Algonquian peoples were refugees in their own home. Their families and villages had been destroyed by smallpox, influenza, and other dread European diseases. The game that their way of life depended upon was gone from the shrinking forests. Their religion, the core of their being with its annual cycle of rituals, could no longer be maintained. Their men had gone off to fight for the British in the French and Indian wars only to find, upon their triumphant return, that their lands were occupied by British tenants of Adolph Philipse.

Ninham's refugee camp moved to the Housatonic Valley, then to Stockbridge, Massachusetts, where it established a Christian church. Sachem Ninham tried for years to regain the land you see from this fire tower. He filed suit in New York colony courts and clearly established that Philipse obtained his crown patent five years before he made his purchase of a small portion of Putnam County. European laws clearly stated that one must first show proof of sale before a patent could be issued. Furthermore, Ninham established that Philipse gained the rest of today's Putnam County simply by land squatting, with no purchase whatsoever. Despite the evidence, Ninham lost the suit. Not one to give up, Ninham next made an unprecedented and difficult journey over the Atlantic Ocean to the courts in London, England. He pleaded that his people be given back their stolen and defrauded lands. Proceedings from the case fill volumes of books. Promised that authorities would do all that they could to look further into the matter, Ninham returned to Stockbridge with high hopes.

The Revolutionary War canceled all British promises. Ninham and his men joined the rebels under Ethan Allen and fought in New York, Pennsylvania, and New Jersey against the British and the Iroquois. Sachem Ninham earned the rank of captain in the American Continental army. On August 30 and 31, 1778, in one of the fiercest battles of the war, Ninham's men and a company of Americans met British troops outside what today is Yonkers. When what is variously called the Battle of Tibbets Brook and the Battle of Cortlandt's Ridge was done, Ninham, his son, and forty native soldiers were dead. They were buried where they fell in a place that became known as Indian Field.

The entire Stockbridge community, into which Ninham's people had been absorbed, was forced to leave. Valley by valley they were pushed by the new Americans westward to Wisconsin, where Ninham's descendants live to this day as farmers. Others from that original refugee group kept on moving. Their descendants today live in Ontario and Oklahoma.

There are memorials to Daniel Ninham. Smalley's Hill was renamed Ninham Mountain. Within the triangle of grass at the intersection of NY 52 and NY 82 in Brinckerhoff near Fishkill, in 1937 New York State raised a monument to the memory of Daniel Ninham, and in the 1990s the Daniel Nimham Memorial was erected at the Putnam County Veterans Memorial Park off Gypsy Trail Road.

40 · James Baird State Park

Location: Freedom Plains, LaGrange
Distance: 3.3 miles, 2 hours
Owner: State of New York

In 1939, contractor James Baird donated his farm to become a recreational state park. Further land acquisitions brought the park to a total of 590 acres that today include a golf course, picnic areas, tennis courts, and ball playing fields. There's also a restaurant. The hills have reverted to woodland, and the trails cross a landscape of undulating knolls and ravines, brooks, woodland pools, and moss-covered outcrops of bedrock. In this park you can see red cedar or juniper in all stages of its life cycle, making this the perfect place to observe terrestrial succession, or how the old farm fields became forest. The park is also home to the threatened Blanding's turtle.

Access

James Baird State Park has its own exit off the Taconic State Parkway just north of the NY 55 exit. To pick up a trail map and a booklet on the rare Blanding's turtle, follow the signs to the park office. Then drive back to park at the restaurant. Open dawn to dusk. Dogs are not allowed in picnic areas. Information: 845-452-1489.

Trail

Cross the road to stand opposite the restaurant (the white building) beneath a giant of an old red cedar, also known as juniper *(Juniperus virginiana)*. More champions stand in front of the restaurant. Seldom are they so tall and mature in a forest. Junipers require full sunlight; in the parking

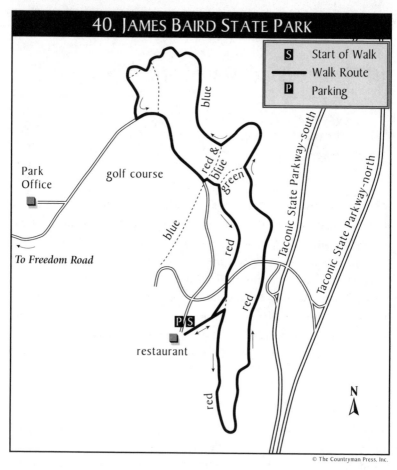

40. JAMES BAIRD STATE PARK

- **S** Start of Walk
- —— Walk Route
- **P** Parking

Park Office

golf course

To Freedom Road

Taconic State Parkway-south

Taconic State Parkway-north

blue

red & blue

green

blue

red

red

red

P S

restaurant

red

N

© The Countryman Press, Inc.

lot, they've gotten it for over half a century. No deciduous sapling has been allowed to overtop them, and the junipers have matured to a miraculous size. As you drive the roads in Dutchess County keep a sharp lookout and you'll find the same huge red cedars in every town, growing in what were once farm fields. In autumn and winter, they bear waxy blue berries. Keep some in your pocket, and the cedar-fresh smell will be with you for months. Put juniper berries in a crock with sugar and grain to ferment into the old-timers' sock-knocking gin. Or, add them to winter meat stews.

Juniper is also called red cedar because of its aromatic red heartwood that people build into chests and closets to repel clothes moths. Among Native Americans, cedar is a powerful and sacred purification plant.

Search the branches and you will find the cedar apple gall, the fruit of the rust fungus *Gymnosporangium globosum,* which alternates its years between juniper and apple and plum trees. After a warm rain in May, fleshy orange strings exude from these "cedar apples," mature, and release spores, which next infest apple trees, causing brown scabs on the apples. In an attempt to keep their trees free from this rust fungus, orchard owners kill all junipers near their orchards. If no apples grow near an infected juniper, *Gymnosporangium globosum* will host on any member of the rose family.

A sign points the way to the left edge of the lawn where the trail leads uphill. In the woods, the junipers grow as tall as those in the parking area. They are probably the same age, yet only their crowns are alive with needles, the only place where they get sunlight. The scraggly trees are crowded close. Deciduous species are overtopping them. Already, many of these junipers are dead. Soon, all will die. But this is no tragic thing. A short moment in the sun is the juniper's niche as a field pioneer species.

White pines *(Pinus strobus)* grow throughout Baird Park's forest. As with junipers, white pines require full sunlight and grow their needles only at the crown in the full sunlight of the forest canopy. The limbs below in the shade are dead. But, unlike juniper, these white pines are healthy and will live a long time. White pine is a dominant species in the north woods of New England. It grows as tall as (often taller than) any deciduous tree and can reach the sunlight it needs. At one time, white pine was an important component of Dutchess County forests, but debarking for the tanning industry reduced its numbers drastically.

Throughout the forest you will see hemlock. This climax conifer is shade-tolerant to the extreme. You'll find its lower limbs all alive and dark with needles (which will slowly become sparser as the tree succumbs under woolly adelgid attack). So here in one park, you see three conifers—red cedar, white pine, and hemlock—with three different adaptations to climate and light.

In streams such as this at Baird Park, the aquatic Blanding's turtles spend most of their days and nights.

At the dirt road turn left, go about 20 feet and take the right fork onto the green trail, then the left fork, still on the green. Off the trail to your right a small hemlock stand grows in the woods. Shortly, you'll top the rise and the green trail will fork right. Watch carefully for this turn as it is a bit obscure. In a few yards you intersect the new red trail. Turn right. If you miss the fork, you will find yourself walking a short section of the old red trail. It, also, will intersect the new red trail, so simply turn right. Either way, you are now headed right on the red trail.

Pass the wood-stave water tower, gradually climbing a hill. In winter, the views through the leafless oaks show fields and hills. Sedimentary layers of clay metamorphosed into red and green slate bend and fold in the bedrock outcrops, shot through with veins of weathered quartz. You'll find pieces of this rock in the trail. The stone walls are built of it. Chestnut and red oak predominate in the highest, driest sites. As the trail turns to head north and downhill, maple-leaf viburnum grows on both sides of the trail. It's rare to get to see the blue opalescent pearls of the berries of this common woodland shrub because so many birds and mammals eat them.

Keep straight across the paved entrance road. Pass hemlock knolls studded with the unusual red and green bedrock. Pass beech groves, the larger individuals carved with initials, the sad fate of smooth-skinned beeches that grow where people frequent. At the fork, beneath tall tulip trees, sugar maples, and white oaks, turn right, still on the red trail.

Follow past swamps and over brooks in the hollows. Now you're getting into Blanding's turtle habitat. Since they spend most of their days in the water, it is most possible to see a Blanding's turtle in April or May after they emerge from hibernation and are moving around looking for just the right, small wetland. It's also possible to run into one anytime during the summer when they decide to try out another small wetland. In June, the female Blanding's turtle will travel by night overland to lay her eggs in the warm lawn of the golf course or a field, so you might see her early next morning headed back home. You might also see the nestlings after they hatch. A mature Blanding's is a fairly large turtle, the black shell about a man's handspan in width. The yellow chin and throat identify it. These turtles have become so rare that Dutchess is the only county where they are still found in southern New York State, and they are disappearing even from here. In most other states and Canadian provinces where they occur, the Blanding's turtle is listed as endangered or threatened. But they have long been known at Baird Park. That sign you passed on your way to the park office, "Turtle Crossing," was no joke. Blanding's turtles have used that area for time out of mind. Unfortunately, they get squashed on the road, and the nestlings get run over by golf carts on the green. If by chance you find a turtle, observe it, note down its tag number if it has one, and then leave it where you found it. Carefully note its location. Notify the park superintendent as soon as possible after your walk. If you feel the turtle is in danger from vehicles, move it to safety in the direction in which it was traveling. Do not take the turtle home with you. Along with habitat loss and getting killed on the road, collectors are the next greatest threat to this species' survival.

When you meet up with the blue trail, turn right past a stand of old-growth red cedars and the stone walls of farm fields of the past. Keep straight (right) at side trails, staying on the blue trail. Toward the end, you pass through woods once familiar to those who grew up in the Hudson Valley at a time when agriculture had been largely abandoned and the fields left fallow for two or more decades: a stand of juniper interspersed with lush, deep mosses and patches of *Lycopodium* or club mosses where the sun falls in pools of light. This successional stage where the field has nearly disappeared, this type of pioneer woodland that once characterized the region, has now mostly gone from the Hudson Valley. The junipers are getting overtopped by deciduous saplings, and this stand will disappear with time. Already, the *Lycopodium* and mosses have decreased from what they were a decade ago as the shade from young maples and oaks increases. As mentioned before, this is no tragic thing. It is the natural process of terrestrial succession. As if walking back in time, as you approach the dirt road there is a vestige of the old field of poverty grasses, goldenrods, meadowsweet bushes, and seedling junipers.

At the road turn left, and left again at the paved road. Along with Blanding's turtles, Canada geese may be seen on the golf course. In winter, rather than migrating south, hundreds of the geese rest nights on the green, winging away each dawn to feed and returning at dusk.

Just past the picnic area, watch for the trail on the left. Follow it to the junction. Turn right onto the red trail. At the paved road, turn right and follow downhill on the pavement a few yards to pick up the red trail on the left. (This little detour avoids a wet area.) Watch carefully for the fork where the old red trail goes right and runs into the green trail. Follow the green back downhill to the parking lot (don't get confused by all the side roads). In the warm months of May through September, check under your car that no Blanding's turtle has stopped for a nap beneath your tires.

41 · Wappinger Creek Greenway Trail

Location: Pleasant Valley
Distance: 2.25 miles, 1 to 2 hours
Owner: Town of LaGrange

Applause for the Town Board, the Eagle Scouts, the LaGrange Conservation Advisory Council, and the property owners along Wappinger Creek for gifting the public with this beautiful riparian trail. A combination of town-owned land and of easements on private property gives access to the creek in its natural state for a good mile or so. No houses. No roads. Just golden, clear waters and sun-dappled woods, or untrampled snow and huge, stark trees. If you visit in summer be prepared for mosquitoes.

The trail is one-way, the return being back along the same route. As you walk the Greenway please respect private property rights by keeping to the trail. That you can walk here at all is due to the kindness of the landowners.

Access

From Poughkeepsie, drive east on NY 44 past Adams Fairacre Farms (on the left) for 0.2 mile. Turn right at the stoplight onto Degarmo Road. Turn left onto Overlook Road/Dutchess County 46. Drive 0.5 mile to a left turn onto Sleight-Plass Road. In 0.7 mile see a split-rail fence on the left with a sign for the trail entrance. Park in front of the fence. Dogs allowed on leash. Information: Town of LaGrange Recreation Department, 845-452-1972.

Trail

Sign in at the kiosk and take a look at the map display, then walk toward the creek. The trail curves left past a wet meadow of tall purple loosestrife, then into a bottomland forest of ash. Once at the streamside, you have a

271

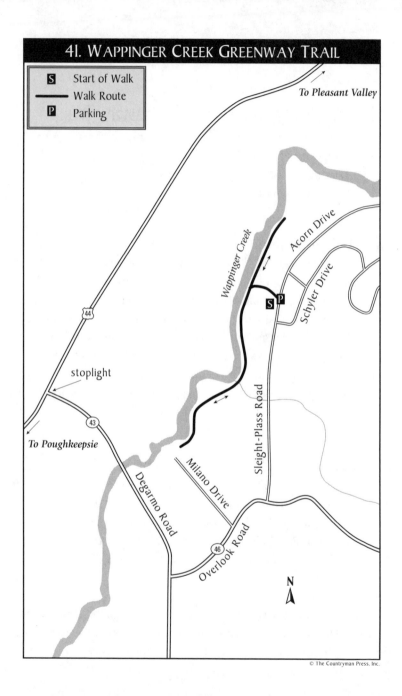

41. WAPPINGER CREEK GREENWAY TRAIL

S Start of Walk
— Walk Route
P Parking

To Pleasant Valley

Acorn Drive

Schyler Drive

Wappinger Creek

S **P**

44

stoplight

43

To Poughkeepsie

Sleight-Plass Road

Degarmo Road

Milano Drive

46

Overlook Road

N

© The Countryman Press, Inc.

choice of either left or right. The left turn is the longer of the two, nearly a mile long, while the right is very short, just under a quarter of a mile.

Ah, it's beautiful here! The swift-running creek water is clear and golden in summertime. Dutchess County's main riverway is named for the Native people who used to live on its banks and knew its entire length inside and out. The 1683 deed of sale of the Rombout Patent records the original name as "the Great Wappings Kill, called by the Indians Mawenawasigh." The Wappinger were an Algonquian people culturally similar to the Mahikans, who lived to the north, and to the Munsee Lenape or Delaware, who lived west and south. During the early colonial era the Wappinger became an important political group with a territory that extended east into today's Connecticut and west past the Catskills.

Here are the riverside woods of sycamore, basswood, sugar maple, ash, and box elder. Sycamore ranks as many people's favorite tree; they like the way the upper limbs gleam stark white. Others say this makes it look like a blighted tree worthy of being cut down. Some of the sycamores in Dutchess County reach formidable trunk diameters easily over 6 feet. Naysayers dislike the cavities that tend to form in all that girth and foster all manner of nesting wildlife. The trunk's brown bark scales off in whorls and rolls that I used to hang as mobiles. Messy, some say, the way they drop all over the lawn, along with those annoying pom pom balls of seed heads and veritable thick plates of leaves. But then there are all those soulful songs about sitting beneath sycamore trees . . . .

I think, however, everyone can agree with pleasant *Tilia americana:* sweet, heart-shaped leaves, pretty red buds, fragrant blossoms absolutely *smothered* in humming insects in spring. Basswood, whose European species is known as linden, is the river tree of Dutchess County, appearing on nearly every bank of every major stream, including the Hudson River. Native peoples used it for many household purposes. Strip the bark off in spring (which of course kills the tree) for wigwam shingles. Collect the stringy, brown, inner bark for twisting into cordage. Split the straight logs, char the heartwood with burning coals and hollow it out into dugout canoes, big corn-grinding mortars, or cooking troughs. Mmmm, in springtime, the smell of fresh maple sap boiling around heated stones dropped in basswood troughs! In spring you can hear the hum of insects and smell the bewitching perfume before you even notice the yellow-and-cream blossoms. Mmmm, basswood honey! In France there are whole festivals for the picking of the flowering sprigs of basswood for linden tea, and we can do the same here. Pick them before the blooms wither. Dry completely before storage. Do not crumble. To make tea, just place several whole sprigs in your cup, pour boiling water to cover, and let steep a few minutes. Mmmmm . . . .

Ash is an interesting tree. Famous for its white, fine-grained wood, its ability to absorb shocks makes it the choice for baseball bats. Native peoples stripped fresh-downed trees for their bark and inner bark, then beat the tree, causing the rings to pull apart in long strips, which they used to weave baskets of superior strength and longevity, suitable as heirlooms. Box elder (*Acer negundo*), a small tree of Dutchess County's rivers and rich, moist soils in general, is actually a species of maple, with an arrangement of leaflets similar to that of an ash. Its soft, white wood is used to make boxes.

The trail is marked in yellow diamonds. Take the left turn following downstream. In about half a mile, the path crosses a footbridge over a tributary. Notice how this small brook has undercut its banks downstream of the bridge. On the other side of the bridge the trail builders have protected the bank with stones. Streams are dynamic creatures. They erode their banks, deepen and widen their valleys, and move their main channel this way and that in their floodplain over time. Even little brooks like this one can form formidable ravines, especially if the land is cleared upstream, as has happened here. A housing development just upstream sheets huge quantities of storm water off its impermeable driveways, roofs, and roads, swelling this "little brook" to a raging torrent 6 feet deep. This hastens both erosion and undercutting of stream banks, and silts the bed of the creek, interfering with the life cycles of native stream insects and fishes.

Follow the yellow diamonds along the edge of a vast cornfield. Throughout these riverside woods you'll find dark, silty soil, rich and moist. In such soil grows wild ginger, bloodroot, and wild leek—mainly springtime

Wild ginger

herbs; bloodroot and wild leek largely disappearing after they bloom and fruit. Wild ginger *(Asarum canadense)* can grow in dense patches of dark green leaves that sheen slightly with light as you walk by (due to silvery hairs). They have the most intriguing May-month flowers that you have to part the leaves to find: a small, burgundy colored, fleshy cup, with three pointed lobes, hung on its own hairy stem below always *two* leaves. Sometimes these flowers are so low they bloom underneath the mat of the forest's dead leaves and you have to lift them up out of the leaves to find them. There is no odor I've ever detected, but the roots taste just like gingersnaps.

Perhaps because the stocky root bleeds a red, bloodlike substance, bloodroot *(Sanguinaria canadensis)* has been used for millennia for all sorts of ailments. It was also used wherever a red color was desired, on baskets, bark, skin, wood, you name it. A dangerous, toxic medicinal, an overdose of the root causes death by paralyzing the heart. The "blood" rubbed on hairless skin can raise a blister.

Wappinger Creek Greenway Trail

Moist, rich, riparian soils such as these used to host entire woodlands thick with blooming wildflowers in spring. Whole stream banks sprung up in bloodroot looking like a drift of snow. Entire hillsides were dense with wild ginger, rue anemone, wood anemone, hepatica, spring beauty, toothwort, trout lily, Canada mayflower, and many others. There was a time, say, from the late 19th to the mid-20th century, when it was fashionable to walk the spring woods and return home to city or village with armloads of spring blooms. Our native species are susceptible to harvest, even be it just the plucking of the single, gorgeous bloom that required years of photosynthesis and storage of energy to produce. It may well be the flowers never recovered from that decimation. Now, facing additional stresses on their depleted ranges, including, as reported by Hudsonia, the environmental research center at Bard College, overbrowsing by overpopulated deer, disturbance by the non-native earthworms that populate our soils, and competition from aggressive alien plant species (especially garlic mustard, which chemically alters the soil to suit its own dominance), they are reduced to a remnant. Pretty as the woods are today, the loveliness, the sweetness, of spring is diminished from what it once was. What remains requires safeguarding. The cry to save the wildflowers that began in the early 1900s should still echo today: look, enjoy, but don't pick! Bloodroot is so ephemeral, anyway. The spotless white petals last perhaps only a day or two. Pick one, and the petals fall in minutes, the naked stem no longer desired is tossed away, and the precious seed never develops.

Notice the dry channels that may bear the silty mark of floodwaters from heavy rains. This is an old oxbow that once was the bed of Wappinger Creek. The trail leaves the creekside to skirt the floodplain of this low-lying area.

The trail ends when the cornfield ends at the twin holes of a woodchuck burrow. You'll know the woodland marmot is living there if you find fresh dirt and stone thrown up. While a fox might get the woodchuck and the hole may disappear, it is just as likely that the woodchuck and its descendants will inhabit this ancestral hole for generations to come. Return back to the T-intersection and try the other fork past cottonwood and black willow, the other trees of Hudson Valley riversides. Retrace your steps to your car.

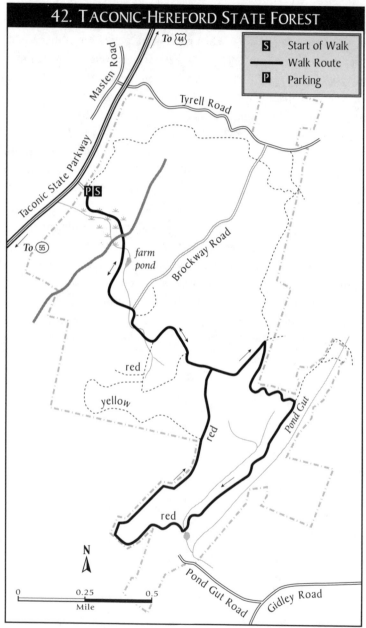

42. TACONIC-HEREFORD STATE FOREST

S Start of Walk
— Walk Route
P Parking

Masten Road

To 44

Tyrell Road

Taconic State Parkway

To 55

P S

farm pond

Brockway Road

Pond Gut

red

yellow

red

red

red

N

0   0.25   0.5
Mile

Pond Gut Road

Gidley Road

© The Countryman Press, Inc.

42 · Taconic-Hereford State Forest

Location: Pleasant Valley
Distance: About 4 miles, 3 hours
Owner: State of New York

A great park for hikers and mountain bikers, its system of dirt roads and marked footpaths wander all over its 909 acres. Basically, the park can be divided into two sections: the upland forest of chestnut oak woodland and red maple wetland, and the Pond Gut hemlock ravine.

The word *taconic* is a corruption of a native Lenape or Delaware Indian word, originally pronounced *tek-HA-nek*. *Tek* means "cold," and *hane(k)* is "river," so *taconic* in both Munsee and Unami Lenape dialects means "cold river."

Access

From NY 55 in Freedom Plains, go north on the Taconic State Parkway. The park entrance is just north of Rossway/Drake Road, directly off the northbound lane of the parkway. There is no marked access from the southbound lane, so you need to go one exit south and get in the northbound lane. Park just inside the tree line at a designated lot. If you own a vehicle with a high carriage, and if the gate is open, you can drive through the park. Primitive car-camping is allowed throughout (bring your own water). Dogs are allowed.

There are two other parking areas for this park, which may be handy if you want to explore other trails, one off Tyrell Road and another at Pond Gut Road.

Trail

From the parking lot, walk down the dirt road marked as a red-orange snowmobile trail. In summer, this is one of the most inviting woodland walking roads I know. Pass through sugar maple and mixed deciduous woods of rich, medium-moist soil full of diverse edibles and medicinals, and most of our common plants.

In summer, watch the verge for a native wild legume, the hog peanut, especially after you've passed a brook tinkling on your right: a light green, low-lying vine with three delicate, pointed, oval leaves on a gold-green stem twining up nearby grasses. Trace the fine roots through the soil (granted, a bit difficult) to locate the edible "peanut" nodules. Lovely purple wild geranium also blooms here, along with a foot-high, frilly green plant, each one looking like a miniature Christmas tree. This is horsetail or *equisetum,* a species that occurs throughout the northern hemisphere. If you walk here in spring, you may see what looks like bamboo, erect as porcupine quills. These are the fertile fronds of the horsetail that produce spores. They disappear in summer while the frilly sterile fronds remain. Without picking them, scratch two horsetail stems together (this works best with fertile fronds). The coarseness comes from crystals of silica in the stems. Horsetail stems in a colonial housewife's hand could scrub a pot of burnt barley clean in seconds, which lent the plant its other name of scouring rush.

The road passes a red maple swamp grown up in skunk cabbage then gradually rises uphill past sugar maple woodlands. Champion specimens of poison ivy vines rope up the trees, furry with rootlet hairs. Delicate rue anemone and the popular jack-in-the-pulpit populate the verge. The sound of highway traffic has been left behind, replaced by birdsong and the tinkling of the brook. Old sugar maples line the road, and sometimes so does an old stone wall. At one point the brook crosses under the road through a handsome, handmade culvert. There is no metal pipe. Step off the trail to see this original road stonework; the best view is on the downstream side. I once spooked a large bobcat drinking here early

Taconic–Hereford State Forest

one morning. A bit beyond this watch on your left for a small green field, actually a marsh with sunlight shining on the plants growing in what was once a farm pond. The stone dam covered with earth has been breached.

To imagine how this land looked eighty or so years ago, when it was under agriculture, remove all the trees except the old sugar maples and Norway spruce lining the road. Replace the woods with fields. Fill the pond with water and one of the fields with cows standing in the shade beneath a single, large sugar maple or oak.

Continue gently uphill on the old road past many spur roads. Oak becomes more predominate. Chestnut oak *(Quercus prinus)* is the dominant species in well-drained, rocky soil, which makes up much of this park. Chestnut oak bark is distinctive, with its deep clefts and ridges. The acorns are unique: smooth polished brown, red, and yellow wood shells slippery as marbles.

Should you visit in fall during hunting season (perhaps not the wisest choice of time), you'll find these acorns. Crack one open with a rock and gingerly take a tiny bite. Yugh! Now hold on, give the thing a chance. Taste that meaty nut flavor? A bit bitter, yes, but all acorns contain tannic acid. Chestnut oak acorns contain the least. Acorns are the mainstay of several upland game mammals and birds. They used to be the major wild vegetable component in the diet of the Native people. If you've fallen in love with the taste of these chestnut oak acorns, take them home. Soak or boil them in a few changes of water to leach out the tannic acid (such stuff is better kept as an astringent medicine for curing, say, bouts of diarrhea). Dry your acorns and pound them into flour for acorn nut bread.

Arrive at a major fork. This is old Brockway Road. On the right are the remains of a house and on the left a cellar hole of what perhaps was a barn. Keep on the orange-marked main road, the right fork, which will shortly jog left. This leads uphill and becomes lined on both sides by stone walls. Pass more trails and side roads. Finally, the walls stop and turn to follow the crest of the hill, but the road continues down the other side. New walls appear. Watch carefully on the right for a small parking area. Take the next right after this on a washed-out dirt road that starts up over a knoll, still the orange snowmobile trail. Climb into hillcrest chestnut oak, lowbush blueberry, and green mosses. Hemlocks and white pines stand to the right. You are on the lip of the Pond Gut ravine.

Down into the ravine you go. Halfway down, hemlock—healthy in appearance but infected with woolly adelgid insects—mixes in among the oaks. When the leaves are down you can see the opposite ridge is an entire slope of hemlock. When the trail reaches the T-intersection, turn right into dense hemlocks. Thick. Cool. The very air smells moist. Dark with hemlocks, the ravine wall plummets downward to Pine Brook far below. The trail turns southwest and follows along at a height. The hemlocks have taken a beating. Damage from storm and windfall, trampling by off-road vehicles, and the deadly woolly adelgids endanger this ravine. Once the norm, just as chestnut trees were once king of our forests, just as declining tender native wildflowers, amphibians, and songbirds were once prevalent, the hemlocks are disappearing. As one friend said to me, soon we will not be able to say, "hemlock ravine." If you've read the Pawling Reserve chapter, you know why the oaks of Taconic–Hereford grow on top of the hills and why the hemlocks grow in the ravine. The question is, once the hemlocks are gone from the ravines, what species will take their place?

Watch on your left for a side trail that leads to an overlook of an old beaver meadow. This is the stage that comes after beaver have exhausted the food supply around their pond and abandon it for new territory. Eventually, the dam is breached by natural causes, the pond drains, and bright green growth proliferates in the rich silt. Deciduous shrubs and trees are sprouting, which will probably prove attractive to future beaver who wander into the area. They will investigate and probably build their dam in exactly the same spot as before, forming the pond anew and rearing their young for many seasons until they, too, deplete the available food sources. This cycle of pond to meadow to pond again can go on for centuries.

While exploring the hemlocks, you may be scolded from the treetops by red squirrel, the squirrel of coniferous woods. If you stand still and scold back with similar noises, you may get quite a show of squirrel fury. Try shaking one leg in the same movement as a squirrel does his tail, and you'll get even greater screams of indignation.

The hemlocks deepen and darken. The land bends into many ravines and hollows. The ravine bottom and the opposite hill lie within land privately owned by Rockefeller University Field Research Center. Their land in turn surrounds Innisfree Garden of Millbrook (open to the public; for information call 845-677-8000). Between the three contiguous properties there are 2,221 acres of valuable wildlife habitat.

Just before the woods road ends at the paved road, another dirt road leads uphill on the right marked as the red footpath. Follow this through mixed deciduous woods past many stone walls. This is another old road and will lead you to an old farm site marked by foundations and a huge, old sugar maple tree. Keep bearing left/straight at all intersections until you start up hill. Then keep right/straight until the "end" sign for off-road vehicles. The red trail levels off and leaves the old road, turning right. Simply follow the markers; sometimes they are white. The trail meanders along the hill slope keeping just below the crest, slowly gaining height despite a few ups and downs. Eventually, the red trail forks right to meet up with the main road. Turn left and you're on your way home. If you are itching for more miles, you can take the left fork of the yellow trail instead, which will wind you around before intersecting the main road.

43 · Mary Flagler Cary Arboretum

Location: Millbrook
Distance: 2.5 miles
Owner: Institute of Ecosystem Studies

Melbert and Mary Flagler Cary, heirs to the Standard Oil Company fortune, bought fourteen farms on 1,800 acres in the 1930s. In 1971, the estate became the Cary Arboretum. The Institute of Ecosystem Studies, formed in 1983 and incorporated in 1993, uses this property as a field research laboratory studying how land recovers from disturbance. Therefore, most of the land is closed to the public, but you may walk the trails described below, most notably the woodland bank of Wappinger Creek. You can also partake of a public education program and visit display gardens and the greenhouse (especially nice for a breath of green air in the dead of winter).

Access

From the Taconic State Parkway, exit onto US 44 east toward Millbrook. Go nearly 2 miles to a left onto NY 44A. Drive 1 mile to the Gifford House on the left, to park and obtain a free access permit. Hours are April to September: Monday to Saturday, 9 AM to 6PM, Sunday 1 PM to 6 PM. October to March: Monday to Saturday 9 AM to 4 PM, Sunday 1 PM to 4 PM. Permits are available up to 1 hour before closing. The greenhouse closes at 3:30 PM daily. The arboretum is closed on public holidays. Trails are closed during deer hunting season and in extreme weather conditions. No dogs allowed. Information: 845-677-5359 or visit www.ecostudies.org.

Trail

Stop in at the Gifford House and obtain the required (free) visitor's pass to the arboretum, as well as a historical and ecological guide to the trails. Walk out the back door and stroll the perennial gardens, abloom each summer week with something new. Come in late May for the lilac collection. Any time of year, right off the bat, keep your eyes peeled for bluebirds. They sit on phone wires like hunched old men, a unique silhouette of rounded shoulders. Or you may hear their sweet, short *cher-wee* call. You can get quite close to them before they fly a short distance off. Our New York State bird with the red breast is blue not because of pigment in its feathers, but because the microscopic structure of its feathers scatters and reflects the light, making it appear a brilliant metallic blue. Pulverize a blue bluebird feather, destroy its structure, and it turns gray. The bluebird, like the robin, is a thrush; the young hatch from pale blue eggs and bear speckled breasts.

Bluebirds were common in the 1800s when the land was mostly fields divided by post-rail fences. Holes in the fence posts were used by bluebirds as nesting sites. Since the forests have grown back and the fence posts have rotted, the bluebird has become rare. Tree holes made by woodpeckers would do, but these usually get taken by aggressive starlings, English sparrows, tree swallows, or house wrens.

It has been proven that placing out nesting boxes increases bluebird populations. An entrance hole of less than 1.5 inches diameter keeps out starlings, and a location no higher than a fence post discourages English sparrows. The Ralph T. Waterman Bird Club maintains forty bluebird boxes in the Cary Arboretum. The club reports that during the 2003 nesting season 118 young bluebirds were fledged.

Head to the barn out back and begin on the Cary Pines Trail through the Scotch Pine Allée planted in the 1930s. The orange upper branches and trunks look just like they do in the glens of Scotland, although these trees are straight while those in Scotland twist and lean. At the woods edge turn left on the Cary Pines Trail and walk the ecotone line between field and forest. Shortly, our trail (marked as "C") enters the woods.

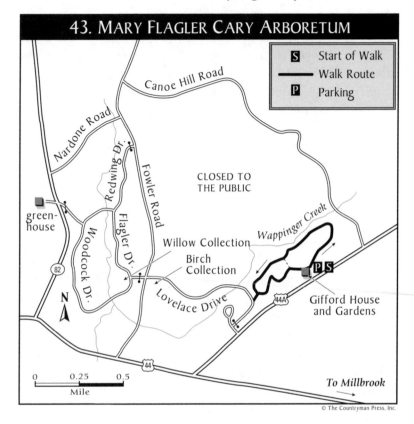

43. MARY FLAGLER CARY ARBORETUM

S Start of Walk
— Walk Route
P Parking

Canoe Hill Road

Nardone Road

Redwing Dr.

Fowler Road

Flagler Dr.

Woodcock Dr.

CLOSED TO
THE PUBLIC

green-
house

82

N

Willow Collection

Birch
Collection

Wappinger Creek

Lovelace Drive

44A

P S

Gifford House
and Gardens

0   0.25   0.5
Mile

To Millbrook

© The Countryman Press, Inc.

Did you notice the stone wall just inside the woods line? These shrubby woods were a field not so long ago. Stop mowing a lawn and it will come to look somewhat like these woods, perhaps with just as much tartarian honeysuckle heavy with red berries in summer. Follow the "C" trail markers through mixed deciduous woods with white pine shade overhead and haircap moss underfoot. At the next intersection, turn left and then right at the paved road. Look back at the trail and the conifers to either side of the road. The ones with short needles over the trail are hemlock. To their left grows white pine, then the sweeping branches of Norway spruce with needled branchlets hanging down. Walk down the hill.

Halfway down a few red cedars or junipers grow atop the bank. Their needles are so short they are scales and cannot be seen individually except close up. Compare these four conifers, their silhouettes, needle colors, and the different way their branches move in a breeze. Once you've learned these characteristics, you can identify these conifers from far away, say, as you stand in a valley looking up at them on a mountain, or from a peak top as you survey the panoramic landscape.

Continue along the paved road to the Fern Glen, planted with over 130 ferns, fern allies, and wildflowers, mostly native to Dutchess County. Because the plants are labeled, this is the perfect place to learn ferns, shrubs, and wildflowers of moist soils. Relax in the Adirondack chairs on the deck overlooking Wappinger Creek.

If you feel like taking a long walk (about 5 miles), you can continue on this paved road up and over the hill to the white house and visit the birch and willow collections, then turn right onto a town road, Fowler Road. You'll pass fields, woods, brooks, ponds, marshes, and a handful of private homes. Pass Nardone Road, keeping straight on pavement, then turn right onto the dirt Canoe Hill Road. This winds through the woods. At NY 44A turn right to return to Gifford House. Since these roads are quiet and mostly level they make for great walking, and the fields and split-rail fences of Millbrook's hunt country are the perfect habitat for the bluebird, more bluebirds than I've seen in my entire life. You may also often hear the loud double squawk or horn-honk of courting male ring-necked pheasants, released by an adjacent sportsmen's club.

Or, if you wish to continue the shorter Cary Pines and Wappinger Creek Trails, then simply climb back up the hill from the Fern Glen and return to the trail. At the fork, bear left to continue on Cary Pines Trail. The forest floor grows both Virginia creeper with its five leaves and the three-leafed poison ivy. Now that you are walking beneath conifers, from your previous observations can you tell which species they are? The one with all the dead branches along the trunk is Norway spruce.

Arrive at a hemlock ravine on the left and a white pine plantation on the right. Keep on "C." Pass "E" on the right. At the T-intersection, turn

Mary Flagler Cary Arboretum

left on "W," the Wappinger Creek Trail through the hemlocks to the East Branch of the creek. Tall hemlocks cloak the ravine slope. As you walk the streamside, listen for a rattling call and you may see a steel-blue bird wing swiftly past. This is kingfisher, who dives beak-first into the stream to catch fish.

As the ravine wall ends, so do the hemlocks, abruptly. Step into sunny deciduous woods and the sparkle of the creek. Watch deeper pools for blacknose dace, the common minnow of cold-water streams. A black stripe can be seen to run from nose to tail, *if* they hold still long enough for you to see it. The creek here has grown sizably from the little brook you may have visited in Pine Plains, where Wappinger Creek is born from Thompson Pond. Yet, the creek is not so large as it looks in Pleasant Valley on the Wappinger Greenway Trail, nor when the creek grown to full size waterfalls into its estuary mouth on the Hudson in Wappingers Falls village. Right here in Millbrook the creek is grown to about its "mid-width."

Follow "W" for the entire loop along the creek then back into hem-locks. The trail climbs the slope and leads into a successional field area of dogwoods, red maple, and lots of juniper. Turn left at the intersection through a red maple swamp grown up in skunk cabbage and tussock sedge. The trail leads out into old hay fields, the lawn, and, straight ahead, the lilac collection at the parking lot.

44 · Buttercup Farm Sanctuary

Location: Stanford
Distance: Variable, 1 to 3 hours
Owner: National Audubon Society

Alastair Martin's donated farm allows us all to enjoy old farm roads and cow paths through pastoral fields, wetlands, orchards, and forests. This 640-acre park is excellent for birding, viewing wildflowers, or just wandering around in. There are numerous loop trails through diverse habitats. Celebrated are the views of the Pine Plains valley floor at the foot of tall and broad Stissing Mountain. Part of the property also has abandoned railroad beds along the little brook of Wappinger Creek.

Access

Take the Millbrook exit off Taconic State Parkway and go east on US 44 for about 1 mile. Turn left onto NY 82 north for 10.3 miles, passing through Stanfordville. At this point you'll pass on the left the Stissing Lane entrance to the west parcel of the park. Keep on NY 82 for another 0.7 mile, around a curve where the view on the left opens up to fields, red barns, and Stissing Mountain. Slow down. The preserve's main entrance will be a very sharp right into a small driveway. If need be, you can continue just past the entrance to the intersection with Dutchess County 88, turn around, and come back. No dogs allowed. Information: 518-325-5203 or visit http://ny.audubon.org.

Trail

In spring and summer, head straight into the hay fields of tall grasses and find a spot to sit in the sun. The air smells sweet with pine and grass

44. BUTTERCUP FARM SANCTUARY

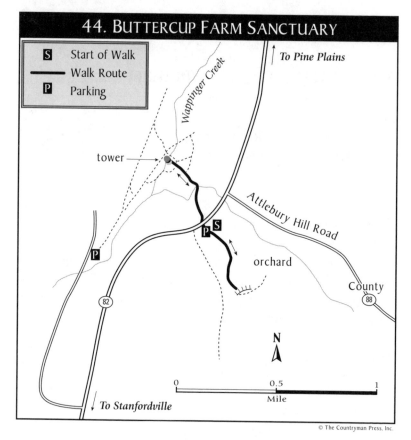

S   Start of Walk
——   Walk Route
P   Parking

tower

Wappinger Creek

To Pine Plains

Attlebury Hill Road

orchard

County 88

82

N

0   0.5   1
Mile

To Stanfordville

© The Countryman Press, Inc.

pollen and the fragrance of multiflora rose in bloom. See any butter-cups? A fitting symbol for this bucolic sanctuary, the buttercup: shining golden in the grasses knee-high up to where the cows once stood.

Truth to tell, I have a hard time finding any buttercups at Buttercup Farm Sanctuary, which is good news for past farm usage; buttercups are poisonous.

The common buttercups of the fields are both European plants: common buttercup (*Ranunculus acris*) and bulbous buttercup (*R. bulbosus*). Have you ever noticed how, if you pick them and get their juice on your hands, your fingers burn? All buttercups, also known as crowfoots, alien and native, contain acid irritants that in large doses cause paralysis, convulsions, then death. Cows who browse in a field of buttercups and eat the pretty, bright things get blisters in their mouths and intestinal tracts. The acids pass into their milk, which must be discarded. Fields full of buttercups are useless to farmers, so Buttercup Farm—devoid of buttercups—had fields worthy of pasturage for livestock.

Undeniably, they're pretty, the buttercups. Held close to the chin, the glossy petals reflect yellow light onto any color skin even on an overcast day, regardless of whether or not the chin's owner likes butter.

From the parking area, climb the hill to your right for the view of Stissing and Little Stissing (to Stissing's right) mountains. In some years these fields are home to nesting bobolinks and meadowlarks. The plains of the valley floor once produced most of the milk for New York City, which accounts for all the rail lines that you can visit on the other side of NY 82. The trails of Buttercup Farm wind through a high diversity of closely packed habitats. There are so many ecotones that birding is excellent throughout the sanctuary. It is easy enough to find your way along the many paths, not all of which are shown on the map. From the hilltop as you gaze out upon the view, you can choose trails to your right, and keep choosing right at every fork to tour the perimeter of the entire parcel this side of NY 82. To cut your walk short, take any left and then choose lefts to return to your car. You will wend past stands of sugar maple and hickory, a hill of paper birch and chestnut oak, along clear spring-fed brooks, and through old fields in various stages of succession. The fruit of the apple orchard is the old barrel variety meant for winter storage. Each apple trunk is riddled with lines of bullet-size holes from yellow-bellied sapsuckers drilling for sap.

To visit the west parcel of the sanctuary, cross NY 82 and go straight ahead into farmfields. Take a close look at the mound of dirt on your left by the barn. Here is the chance to see, out in the open, the glacial outwash that underlies and is the parent material for many soils. Made up of gravel and water-rounded cobbles, this mound was dumped by the last glacier. Climb to the top to see how the mound continues. More of these

Buttercup Farm Sanctuary

glacial outwash mounds are scattered throughout the undulating valley floor.

The trail winds past fields and views of farms to a stone tower. Have a seat on the bench behind the tower with the view of the pond and the friendly dragonflies. Hold out your hand with the index finger extended and wait patiently. Sooner or later a dragonfly will alight to rest for a bit. Not to be afraid; it won't bite you, and dragonflies do not sting.

Trails that head downhill from here cross Wappinger Creek and pass into more fields of tall grasses and wildflowers. Here find excellent old field botanizing, the sweet smell of sun on pollen, the glossy seedheads of grasses waving in the breeze. Pass a tussock sedge swamp and intersect the long green tunnels of the old railroad beds. At open pools of water you may start up wood ducks with a whine of a whistling cry.

In the fields, especially those near brooks or swamps, the male woodcocks dance for their mates in spring. Inquire when a guided dusk-time walk will be held so you can see this: the male woodcock—neckless, chunky, his bill ridiculously long—spirals upward. Wind whistles through his stiff short wings. Trilling, the wind-song warbles louder until in a final burst he plummets, stately and absurd, starlight on his wings and the moon in his eyes, to his mate on the dark moist soil.

And, sometime later in early summer, when you are leaving the park when it closes at dusk, there are few better places to be enchanted by the myriad sparkling of fireflies.

45 • Stissing Mountain State Forest

Location: Pine Plains/Stanford
Distance: 2.7 miles, 2 to 3 hours
Owner: State of New York

Stissing Mountain State Forest straddles the border between Pine Plains and Stanford and includes a corner of Milan. Half the park's 450 forested acres is developed with trails. The remainder comprises the southwest slope of Stissing Mountain with only a single trail, so most of that acreage is bushwhack country.

If you want to climb Stissing Mountain, this is not the best place to start. The shortest access is described in the Thompson Pond and Stissing Mountain Preserve chapter. But, for those who like long hikes, there is a trail at Stissing State Forest that links up with a path that begins from the end of Mountain Road and then runs the entire length of Stissing Mountain's crest for 2.5 miles all the long way to the fire tower. There is no longer parking or access to the trail available from the end of Mountain Road other than what is described below. If you want to attempt this long hike, perhaps the best arrangement is to have two cars, one parked at Hicks Hill Road and the other at Thompson Pond Preserve.

For the beaver dam fun described in this chapter, in summer you may want to bring stream sneakers or water-sport shoes.

Access

From the Taconic State Parkway, exit east toward Pine Plains on NY 199, and go just a short distance to a right onto Dutchess County 53. Go 2.8 miles to a left onto Hicks Hill Road. The parking pull-off is 0.7 mile down the road on the right. Dogs are allowed. Information: 845-831-8780.

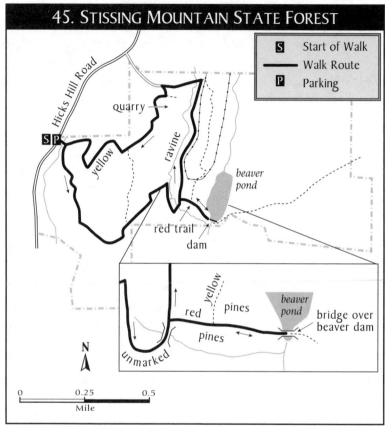

45. STISSING MOUNTAIN STATE FOREST

S — Start of Walk
—— Walk Route
P — Parking

Hicks Hill Road

quarry

yellow

ravine

beaver pond

red trail

dam

yellow

red

pines

pines

beaver pond

bridge over beaver dam

unmarked

N

0   0.25   0.5
Mile

© The Countryman Press, Inc.

If you haven't much time or would enjoy a shorter walk to see only the pines and the beaver pond, then continue on Hicks Hill Road beyond the first parking area for another 0.4 mile. Watch carefully on the right for a sign for the preserve and a rough dirt road that leads downhill (which may not be passable for all vehicles). Follow this road to its end. Walk beyond the gate, following the road to the pines, where you can then follow the chapter directions up to the small bridge, with a left turn that leads to the beaver pond.

Trail

From the parking pull-off, your way begins over a footbridge. Bear right (the left fork is your return route, marked as a yellow cross-country ski trail) through sugar maple woods that soon open out into a small field. Note the junipers, cropped by deer as high up as their lips can reach. These ruminants digest their food with the help of bacteria in their stomachs. Research at the Institute of Ecosystem Studies at Cary Arboretum shows that juniper can make up to twenty percent of a deer's total food intake with no ill effect. But when the juniper reaches thirty percent of the total food intake of the deer, the volatile oils in the juniper—the same chemical that repels clothes moths—inhibit the stomach bacteria. A deer with a full stomach of juniper will starve to death.

Stissing Mountain State Forest is deer habitat heaven. The stone walls, old red cedars, and large, dead, field-shade trees are all that's left of the pastures and fields of what was once a working farm. You'll see these signs as you walk the woods grown into a mosaic of field, shrub, and vigorous young deciduous forest full of tender leafy shoots and buds for deer to browse and dense cover in which to hide. What more can a deer ask for? These excellent conditions have led to a large deer population, as indicated by the close-cropped junipers, not a deer's first choice in food.

Giant dragonflies zip over the grasses, clashing their wings. These insects maneuver so expertly that the United States Air Force has for years copied them for jet design. The long abdomen is for balance and contains no stinger. If you visit after a frost or in early spring, the dragonflies will be absent.

You may see in this field a giant mound of fine dirt. This is an ant hill of mound-building ants. These mounds can get large. See all the tunnel openings? Not a place to sit for a rest. Mound-building ants manicure their nest to keep it clear of plants, and thus clear of shade. Any day the sun shines on their mound, warming it, they are active, even in winter.

The trail leads into a mixed deciduous woods of more deer habitat heaven. This is a good place to come to learn the common tree species

Stissing Mountain State Forest

because there are so many of them present. Medium-moist soil communities intermixed with field species in sunny openings and with upland
species also make for good birding. Mostly, the remnant field openings
are simply the centers of what were wide fields bounded by stone walls. In
fact, when you come to a stone wall and intermittent stream (one that
runs only in times of rain), note how the sugar maples are all young,
tall, and straight, equal in girth, being of an age. And the shrubs and
herbaceous cover are gone, replaced by only the brown litter of fallen
maple leaves. Can you read what the land is saying here about its past use?
Why does it look the way it does? Recall the times you have walked in
abandoned fields that are still open and grassy. Where, for the most part,
do the trees first begin to invade once field maintenance is neglected?

Most of the time, trees begin to grow on the edge of the field, delineated by the stone wall. And, in this particular case, perhaps they were further fostered by the moisture of the intermittent stream. Continue on
the trail. At one point, the path dips slightly into a shallow hollow, all oak
and mixed deciduous trees on moist ground. Why is this spot so well

wooded? The trees appear to be older. Was it left to reforest earlier than the farm fields? Did it have a better supply of available water, or nutrients, and so grew more? Or was this just caused by chance? There are too many variables to really know. But, as you proceed, the woods become more mature, a sign of great age, and you are definitely out of the more recent farmland/successional mixture. How long will it take until the old field areas come to look like these mature woods?

At the intersection keep straight. Upon topping a rise, you will hear a stream off to the right down in a small valley. Soon you arrive at the woodland stream and cross it at an old home site, now just a clearing in the woods. Turn right onto the red trail. Follow the brook into a white pine plantation planted by the state when it took over the farm property. No green plant grows on the dark, needled floor; no needles grow on the dead lower pine limbs. Only the tops of the white pines are alive, where the sunlight shines. The circular holes you see are from deer probing their noses into the red needles on the floor for mushrooms. Just past the pines you may find the trail flooded, and you may want to take off your shoes to wade to the bridge. As you are wading, if you spy any clear sand, walk around it: it is a sunfish nest filled with eggs.

Beaver have dammed the brook that drained the swamp and created the pond before you. The dam is a nice one, semicircular, built of saplings and mud. From the center of the bridge you can see the beaver lodge—the living quarters—out in the middle of the pond. If you like and if you are already wet, you can get a better look at the dam by carefully walking along its crest and down the other side, stepping into the sticky blue clay deposited in the brook bed. From here you can appreciate the height of the dam, at least 4, maybe even 5, feet high. The deep pool behind the dam makes for an inviting swimming hole on a hot, summer's day, but I found the tea-brown pool to be well populated with leeches. AHHHH! Aw, no big deal if you get some on you; just dunk them off underwater with a light brush of the hand. Still, it's best not to swim in pools of stagnant water heated in the summer sun and populated by *Giardia*-carrying beaver. If nothing else, the bridge is the perfect spot to sit and watch the scenery, the birds, the insects, and the swimming newts. The trail continues up the slope of Stissing Mountain, eventually intersecting Mountain Road. If you are headed to the fire tower, turn left and hike Mountain Road nearly to its end. Rudy of Stissing Sawmill has given permission for hikers to access the trail via his property (no parked cars, please). Stop in, say hello, ask to see his turtle. If he's not there, just head straight on back past his office and you'll pick up the trail.

For those of us not attempting the long hike to the fire tower, return back to the old house clearing. (You will pass the yellow ski trail on your right that runs along the white pine plantation.) At the footbridge, turn right on an old road, also the red trail. If you look carefully in the black walnut woods you will find an old barn foundation and old apple trees. Soon you will pass a red pine plantation, then travel along a ravine wall with a succession of conifer plantations opposite. When it looks deep and dark and beckoning, feel free to walk into the pines. Since this is a state forest, you do not have to keep on the trail and can leave to explore anytime.

Continue on the road across the stream on a bridge and past the metal gate. Here is the alternate parking mentioned in the access section above. This road will take you all the way to Hicks Hill Road, or, instead, walk past a brook and then take your next left past another metal barrier and a warning against promiscuous shooting. Keep straight and you'll come to a pit of gravel and rounded cobbles dragged from the north ten thousand years ago and dumped by the Wisconsin Glacier. Humans have excavated it and now use if for a shooting range. Young cottonwoods shimmer on the banks. Backtrack to just before the quarry and find the yellow ski trail marker tacked on a huge, old, farm-field sugar maple. With your back to the quarry, turn left onto this trail that climbs up and over the glacial till "hill" mound. The mosaic of successional field and woods returns.

Watch carefully for a right turn that leads downhill; it is unmarked. (If you miss this turn, then just keep straight and turn right at the next intersection for your car.) This continuation of the yellow ski trail will loop you back to your car.

46 · Thompson Pond and Stissing Mountain Preserve

Location: Pine Plains

Distance: 2.75 miles, 3 to 4 hours, for the preserve; 1 mile, 1 hour, for the mountain

Owner: The Nature Conservancy, Friends of Stissing Landmarks, and private

I f you're going to visit one, visit the other, too, pond and mountain; the view from each lends reciprocal understanding. Both are celebrated in a permanent exhibit at New York City's Museum of Natural History.

Imagine ice a mile high, stretched across North America in a blue-white sheet to the North Pole, moving slowly southward grinding everything in its path as it rounds the mountains and scours the valleys. Then, ten thousand years ago, the Earth warmed. The great glacial sheet melted slowly, starting in the south and proceeding north raggedly. Some areas of ice were thicker than others. Some were covered with more rock debris, which temporarily protected the ice from melting. Protected areas harbored relict ice blocks after the great ice sheet itself melted away. Outwash streams deposited sand and gravel around and over these blocks. When the ice blocks finally melted, they left steep-sided holes or kettles in the outwash plain.

The irregularly shaped kettle in the sand and gravel outwash plain of Pine Plains filled with water and became a lake with two natural constrictions. Peat and sediments built up over centuries, dividing the one into three lakes. Humans in the 1900s added fill and roads to form Twin Island or Mud Lake, Stissing Pond, and Thompson Pond. Thompson Pond is the headwater for Dutchess County's mighty Wappinger Creek.

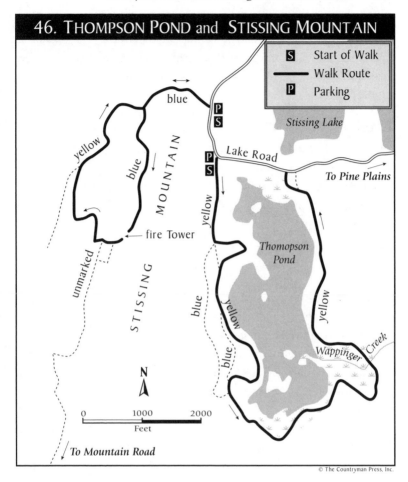

46. THOMPSON POND and STISSING MOUNTAIN

The best way to see that the three ponds were formed from one kettle
is to climb Stissing Mountain, which contains rocks 1.1 billion years old,
the oldest in New York State. The 1,403-foot-high Precambrian gneiss-
granite is an island of the same rock that makes up the Hudson Highlands way at the other end of the county. One theory is that the mountain
got pushed and isolated here 350 million years ago when the North American and African continental plates collided. Such a formation is called a

"klippe." Another theory says the mountain traveled only, say, half a mile, and it didn't get pushed; it slid downhill from the continental collision to the east. At the trail's end (actually not quite the summit) is a fire tower with fabulous views (which will be obscured in humid summer afternoons).

Access

From NY 82 just south of the village of Pine Plains, by the firehouse, turn west onto Lake Road. Drive 1.5 miles, passing a sign for the preserve (your return route) and a cattail marsh to parking against the flank of Stissing Mountain in dirt pull-offs on the left. A parking lot for Stissing Mountain is just another couple hundred yards down the road on the right. No dogs allowed. Open dawn to dusk. Information: 914-242-3271.

Trail

The yellow entrance trail to the 507-acre Thompson Pond Preserve leads through black birch woodland bright with sunlight on sedges and ferns. The lake lies to the left; Stissing Mountain rises steeply to the right.

Pass the monument that states, "Thompson Pond, 1973 registered natural landmark, National Park Service." Sign your name at the kiosk register (be careful of possible wasps in the register box) to help the park committee keep track of use. Such data is highly useful in determining park maintenance and future usage plans. Take the left blue trail for a short loop to the pond shore.

You can smell the lake ahead on the breeze. Pass a spur trail on the left, down which you have a view through the trees of Little Stissing Mountain. Continue on the blue trail where you are now walking along the top of the kettle wall. When you get views across and down the length of the pond, you will see a beaver lodge and a trail that leads down to it. Come to this spot about an hour before dusk in the summertime to see the beaver. If you hit it right, you'll see them swimming away as they leave their lodge to begin the night's activities (beaver are nocturnal). Once out of the lodge, they could be anywhere on the pond. Look for chew marks on downed trees along the shore as you walk, and listen for the tail-splash alarm that means they've sighted *you.*

You may find standing at the water's edge by the lodge squishy with damp sphagnum moss. Here grow tall cinnamon fern, sensitive fern, tussock sedge, and blue iris. Then it's cattails and phragmites, and all sorts of floating vegetation. Thompson Pond is not a pond or a lake in the normal sense. It is a circumneutral bog, which differs from the typical northern bogs of New England and Canada. Under Thompson Pond's central open water is a false bottom of soupy peat. Peat is centuries' worth of dead sphagnum moss, undecayed. Organic material usually decays relatively quickly when there is enough oxygen for the bacteria to work. Therefore the presence of peat usually indicates cold, acid waters with little oxygen present. But the open pond waters of Thompson Pond are neither sterile nor cold, so why is there so much peat? It is thought that the peat was left by an earlier ecosystem.

Beneath the entire surface of Thompson Pond lies an extensive and deep peat deposit. The pond's vegetation grows by peat rafting. In spring, as the water warms, masses of bottom peat in the central pool are buoyed to the water surface by the gases of decomposition. Most sink come fall, but on many, plants take root: first white water lily, then spikerush and, in one to two years, cattail. The marsh is growing inward toward the deep water on these floating mats so slowly that aerial photographs from fifty years ago show little change, yet it is occurring.

Follow the blue trail until it rejoins the main yellow trail, where you turn left. If the swampy edge is flooded, at dusk you might find the beaver here foraging among the speckled alder shrubs and hop hornbeam. Keep on the yellow trail to circle the pond. Now and then come views through the hemlocks and paper birches of the stands of cattails and floating vegetation on the water.

The overlook knoll is a good spot to sit and take in the view. Stissing Mountain is now visible, and there's another beaver!—chewing on a downed sapling half in the water. The blue trail leads on along a steep straight bank that plunges down to the water: the kettle wall. The steep

Thompson Pond and Stissing Mountain Preserve

slope is the natural angle of repose of the glacial outwash gravel and sand, buried beneath ten thousand years of soil accumulation. You could easily expose it with a stick. Descend off the wall. You'll see the glacial till in the path, the rounded cobbles and gravel.

The trail takes you around a cove. Open water disappears from sight behind a red maple swamp. The trail continues on the edge of the kettle bank. The father you walk from the pond, the older the red maples become. The trail narrows to a footpath. Bear left at the fork. The brightness of cornfields through the trees and the lowing of cows in the distance have been common occurrences in a valley under agriculture for centuries. You'll pass well-trod deer paths leading from the fields to the pond.

Descend the steep kettle wall and cross the red maple swamp on a boardwalk. On the other side you are back on the kettle wall, and have great views through the trees of the pond and Stissing Mountain. On this side of the pond I always see ducks. The trail stays away from the swampy pond shore. Still, if it's been raining, the trail may be wet and muddy. The wettest sections have boards for you to cross. Smell the cows?

Once you pass their barnyard, you can see what a mess they make of the sucking mud. Imagine if they had access to the pond? The shore would be hopelessly mired, and a cow could get stuck and succumb. That is why practically every wetland in the Hudson Valley is protected by a historic stone wall, and why there was old barbed wire back the other side of the boardwalk, by the cornfields, embedded in the trees. Farmers know livestock must be kept out of swamps.

If you got your own hoofs muddy, not to worry. Soon you come to the newborn Wappinger Creek as it issues out from Thompson Pond, and you can clean up. As I sat cleaning my feet one recent visit, a beaver attracted by my splashing startled me with a loud tail slap, and then unhappily eyed me over, since I was sitting above its dam.

Continue on. When the trail goes uphill slightly, there's a knobby white-oak-like tree with beautiful corrugated bark smack beside the trail. The leaf looks and feels like an elm. It is hop hornbeam *(Ostrya virginiana)* with catkins that fuzz out in spring, and seeds that look like party decorations. It's one of the heaviest (a cubic foot weighs 51 pounds), strongest, and hardest (unsplittable) of timbers.

This next section can get a bit tall along the verge, making for good botanizing in summer. Hope you've got on long pants. You'll pass a scraggly stand of Norway spruce. Now, *that's* the way Norway spruce is supposed to look, like a wild evergreen of the mountains. *That's* the way it looks in its native land. Transplanted to America, Norway spruce takes on a grand and sweeping appearance. This is a benevolent example of how a plant species, taken from its native habitat and set loose in a new ecosystem, can change in both appearance and behavior.

The footpath will join with an old woods road. Turn left, following the trail markers. Soon you arrive at the paved road and turn left to return to your car.

You can either walk or drive the few hundred yards farther down Lake Road to the Friends of Stissing Landmarks (FOSL) Lake Road trail, which begins opposite the parking area. The blue trail climbs right off. Note how the rocks exposed in the trail are angular, broken off with edges or in layers. These are not the rounded cobbles of glacial till as seen around Thompson Pond.

Climb straight up until you encounter one of the many old woods roads that run all over the mountain (mostly onto private property). Actually, you're on private property now, so please respect the kindness of landowners who allow hikers to use just the marked trail. Follow the markers, turning left to follow the ridge at a height in a saddle between Stissing and Little Stissing mountains. At the fork, the choice of enthusiasm is to the left. It's a stiff climb. Hiking shoes are strongly recommended. If you have the breath to notice, the medium-moist woodland will change to xeric, stunted chestnut and black oak, hop hornbeam, and lowbush blueberry. A climb in a "mast autumn" (one with a heavy mast crop, occurring every seven years or so) may be slippery with acorns in the trail.

Climb all the way to the old fire tower, which stands not on the top, but on Stissing Mountain's north slope. From the cab you view the outwash plain, a rich aquifer of drinking water, and beyond from the Catskills to the South Taconics to Albany. Imagine that block of glacial relict ice: it may have stood higher than where you are now.

At the bottom of the tower take a look at the Hudson Highlands granite bedrock. You may find a few of the scrub oaks that are so numerous in the Highlands and Beacons. Behind the fire tower find the trail that passes a perched wetland of swamp blueberry and swamp azalea. In late June, this pool of black water swarms alive with tadpoles. Bullfrogs sit atop Stissing Mountain!

A yellow trail marker points the way straight ahead and downhill. On the left is an unmarked woods road. This is the level, crest trail (no views) that leads the length of Stissing Mountain (all private property) for 2.5 miles to Mountain Road, which can be accessed (permission has been granted) at the end through the property of Stissing Sawmill. Stop in and say hello to Rudy, the mill's owner. More likely you're ready to head home. Take the downhill path. This gentler grade will return you toward your car, but it's still steep. Bear right at all forks (caution: keep alert for these).

47 · Wilcox Park

Location: Milan
Distance: 2 miles, 2 to 2.5 hours
Owner: County of Dutchess

The long drive entering this 600-acre county park highlights what a pretty place it is, with its evergreen plantations, steep wooded hills, views across a pastoral valley. The swimming and boating ponds and camp and picnic sites are centered on the valley floor. Marked trails climb up and down the valley walls of knobby hills to form a ring of trails. The blue loop is about 3 miles long. The red loop, which is described below, is about 2 miles long. Both are real workouts because of the constant ups and downs. If you'd like a shorter walk, try the half-mile-long yellow trail that loops around the campground. Even easier and very pleasant is a stroll along the level valley floor on an abandoned dirt road, just past the old mansion. Whichever you choose, in summer bring along your swimsuit and leave it in your car for a dip in the lake upon the trail's end, and some cash for a snack at the concession stand.

Access

From the Taconic State Parkway travel east on NY 199 toward Pine Plains. The park will be on your right. Follow signs to parking in the big lot by the office. Hours vary and the park may be closed in winter. Generally, in summer the park is open seven days a week from 9 or 10 AM to 7 or 8 PM. Entrance is free to county residents (proof of residency required), $5.00 per car for out-of-county visitors. Dogs allowed on leash. Picnicking, swimming in pond with lifeguard, camping, paddle- and rowboat rental on pond, miniature golf. Reservations for camping and group pavilion rental available at office. Information: 845-758-6100.

47. WILCOX PARK

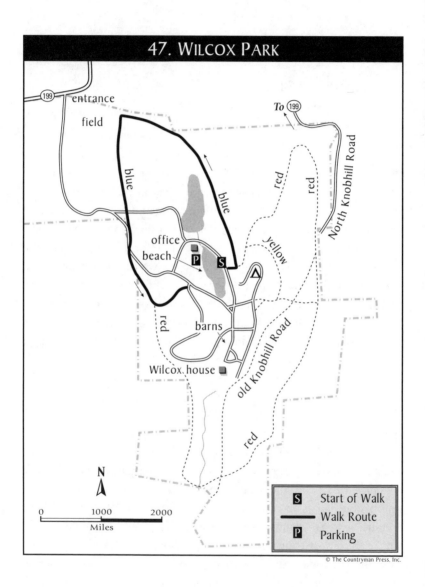

199 entrance
field

To 199

North Knobhill Road

blue
blue
red
red

office
beach
P
S
Yellow

red
barns

old Knobhill Road

Wilcox house

red

N

0   1000   2000
Miles

S   Start of Walk
—   Walk Route
P   Parking

© The Countryman Press, Inc.

Trail

Pick up a map at the office, an old farmhouse. Down the valley past lawns you can see barns and buildings. Currently used for maintenance and therefore closed to the public, this complex is the original farm estate of Frederick Wilcox located on what was Old Knobhill Road. Mr. Wilcox bought four or five small farms to form Oakdale Farms, his gentleman's estate. He kept horses, cows, sheep, bees, chickens, and pigs. He grew vineyards and orchards, watering them with an elaborate irrigation system. He built a state-of-the-art mansion with all the modern conveniences of its time, such as a refrigerator, the type with its motor on top. Frederick fell in love with his cook, Irene, 37 years his junior, and married her. Upon her husband's death, the heiress built Wilcox Memorial Hall, Milan's well-known town hall west of the park on NY 199. Sadly, their son died before his time. In 1963, Irene Wilcox donated Oakdale Farms to Dutchess County for all to enjoy. If you walk toward the barns and bear left, you will come to the abandoned Old Knobhill Road and can stroll past the mansion and the marshy remains of Mr. Wilcox's ice-cutting pond.

To hike the hills, from the parking lot walk back along the paved road beside the swimming pond. Watch on your right for a tiny graveyard from the mid-1800s. You may also see the white, shriveled eggs of snapping turtles dug up from their nests and eaten by raccoons. Halfway down the pond, find the trailhead on your left, marked for the red, yellow, and blue trails. Begin up a knoll under oaks, hop hornbeam, and hickory. Follow the blue blazes. Reindeer lichens grow atop the rocky knoll among lowbush blueberry bushes and mosses.

The blue trail is well marked and keeps on top of the ridge through a xeric community of chestnut oak floored in sedges and blueberry. Some people think this "grassy" appearance means it is a young woodland recently pastured with cows. But no, the "grasses" are really sedges and the oaks are as old as the taller ones in the valley, if not older. It's just harder to live here what with the bedrock and the dry soil, so the trees simply never get all that big. And some of the scattered short ones are actually a dry-adapted species, scrub oak, not found in the valley at all.

Now and then you pass single, huge, old oaks four times the girth of the others, with thick and low limbs swept horizontal to the ledge-prone ground. Soon off to the left see a low, old stone wall of the type found throughout the region weathered gray and coated with green and gray lichens. These single, big, old trees once stood alone on the hillside, and the stone wall is part of a network of walls that can be more clearly traced when the leaves are down. Ghosts of past land usage, these are signs of the original farms when nearly the entire region was clear-cut for crops and pasture.

Soon you come upon an evergreen stand of red pine and Norway spruce, signs of Mr. Wilcox's outdoorsman activity, reclaiming the pasturage for wildlife. Fields he did not plant in evergreens simply grew back over time into oak woods.

Can you "read" the stone wall? See the opening for a gate? Both sides of the gap are dressed—this is not just a gap made of missing stones. Why would there be a gate in this spot? Where did it lead to? As you continue the trail goes right through the stone wall, but the edges of this other gap are not flush. The stones were simply pushed aside to make room for the park trail. Rubble lies within the opening and to the side. As you walk, keep an eye out for what we've talked about to "read the land" for yourself. Not every sign has an answer. Sometimes the walker can only guess what a sign means. Once the living memory of land use is gone, the artifacts can be difficult to interpret correctly. For one who has lived the farming life, the answer can be absurdly simple. At one point, there's a pile of rocks beside the trail getting overgrown by haircap moss (the type beloved by children who love to sink their fingers into its "fur"). It's a small, farmer's rockpile, over 100 years old, maybe 150 years old or more, where a farmer tossed the rocks he cleared from each spring's fresh plowing. These fieldstones, some also brought to the surface by alternating thaw and freeze, were the raw material for the stone walls.

What do you think will happen to Mr. Wilcox's conifer plantations? To

Wilcox Park

see their future, look at what species of seedling and sapling trees are growing in their shade. The trail passes along the park border along a hillcrest, then steeply downhill to join an old woods road subtly delineated by an edge cut into the bank. Pass through a tall, dark Norway spruce stand, long cones frosted with white, spruce sap on the needled floor. You may also find deer droppings. Deer favor Norway spruce plantations where the dense dead branches provide good cover. Blazes cut into the spruce trunks and painted blue dissolved in the natural turpentine. Follow the blue blazes past fields, across the entrance road (where a left turn can shorten your walk and lead you back to your car), through woods and more conifer plantations.

Eventually, you intersect with the red trail and can lengthen your hike. Otherwise, continue on the blue up and over the hill past a failing Scotch pine plantation overmastered by black birch and sugar maple. Imagine what this hill looked like 50 years ago when the pines were at the height of health. Perhaps it was a sunny pine wood just like in its native Scotland

and floored in ferns. Imagine the same site 50 years before the pines were planted in the old farm field. And imagine what it looked like before it was a field. How many times in the past two centuries was the hill used as a wood lot? Its deciduous growth was lumbered time and time again as the woods grew back in between cuttings. Trees and plants of some sort kept coming back, at one point quite different when the dominant American chestnuts were lost to foreign disease. We see these woods today; pretty and seemingly natural yet, simply put, an artifact of human use.

48 · Other Parks in the Inland Hills

Nuclear Lake

A marked trail loops around this public, picturesque, man-made lake once the site of a nuclear research facility (since removed). The total trip is about 1.5 miles long. There are two parking sites, both unmarked. The easiest is to travel from NY 292 (Whaley Lake turnoff) east on NY 55 toward Pawling. At the bottom of a long hill, turn left onto Old Route 55 and proceed about 50 feet to the first dirt lot on the left. Park here and walk in on the paved road, past the caretaker's house, and on to the lake in about half a mile. Keep straight on to the head of the lake. When the road ends, keep straight on the Appalachian Trail (white blazes), watching for the yellow trail turnoff on your right that loops round the lake's other side and back to the entrance road. The blue trail you encounter in the beginning is a cutoff to the other parking lot on top the hill on NY 55 opposite the gun shop. Information: New York–New Jersey Trail Conference, 201-512-9348.

Putnam Trailway

Along eleven miles from Baldwin Place to Brewster Village, the trail leads past lakes and reservoirs, country villages, and the Putnam County hills. Three marked parking lots are at Baldwin Place, off Old Route 6 between Stoneleigh Avenue/Putnam County 35 and US 6 in the hamlet of Carmel, and off Mine Lane just south of the intersection of US 6 and Dykeman Road/NY 312, on the way toward Brewster. Remarkably, from Baldwin Place, the trail simply continues into Westchester County all the way to the Bronx and 225th Street. Plans call for extensions from Lake Mahopac to Goldens Bridge and Mahopac Falls to Baldwin Place. Information and brochure: Putnam County Department of Planning 845-878-3480.

Putnam Land Trust

This organization owns and manages several beautiful natural and historic properties throughout Putnam County. Those with trails are listed below. For a full description visit www.pclt.net.

Tophill, Carmel, 19 acres. From US 6 in Carmel take Stoneleigh Avenue 1.7 miles to a left on Cherry Hill Road. Go 0.8 mile to a right onto Columbus. Go 0.3 mile to a right on Bucyrus Avenue. Preserve on right at dead end.

Glenda Farrell–Henry Ross, Brewster, 36 acres. From NY 22 in Brewster, take Dean's Corne Road for 1.7 miles. Turn right on Field's Lane. Go 0.3 mile to a right into entrance for Brewster Ice Arena. Preserve at top of ramp.

Peach Lake Natural Area, Brewster, 138 acres in three preserves: Birdwood, Paul Fitchen, and Cedar Swamp. Take US 6 east from Brewster to a right onto Starr Ridge Road. Go 0.5 mile to a left onto Cobb Road. Go 0.2 mile. Preserve entrances on right.

Doansburg, Southeast, 13 acres. From NY 22, take Doansburg Road for 1.5 miles to a right onto Mill Farm Lane. Preserve is past third house, on left.

Sterling Farm, Patterson, 37 acres. From NY 22, take Putnam County 164 to Cornwall Hill Road. Go 0.8 mile to a right onto Couch Road. Preserve in 0.4 miles on right.

Twin Hill, Patterson, 33 acres. From Putnam County 312, take Farm-to-Market Road for 1.1 miles to a left onto a dirt road alongside the pond. Go over bridge. Preserve on left, by stone chamber.

Ice Pond Conservation Area, Patterson, 104 acres. From Putnam County 312, take Ice Pond Road for 1.2 miles. Preserve on right.

Appalachian Trail

As if Dutchess and Putnam counties were not already rich enough in history and walking trails, here is also the internationally famous Appalachian Trail. Conceived in 1921 by forester Benton MacKaye, the AT stretches for over 2,150 miles—maintained solely by volunteers—from Maine to

Georgia along the crest of the older Appalachians. It is one of the longest marked footpaths in the world. Thirty-two miles of the AT run through Dutchess County, 24 miles through Putnam.

The trail enters Dutchess from the Schaghticoke Indian Reservation in Kent, Connecticut, with views from Schaghticoke Mountain, reenters Connecticut, and emerges into Dutchess again at Duell Hollow. It then traverses southwesterly to the Bear Mountain Bridge at the foot of Anthony's Nose. Along the way, it encounters several of the parks covered in this book. Since there are shelters along the way, you could take a weeklong backpacking trip.

The AT is well-documented by many publications. The New York–New Jersey Trail Conference publishes an excellent free brochure, *Getting to Know the Appalachian Trail in Dutchess and Putnam Counties, New York*, complete with suggested walks, campsites, and points of interest. Information: 212-685-9699 (24 hours a day).

New York State Forests

Most state forests are under the jurisdiction of the New York State Department of Environmental Conservation, Forest Service Resource Management Office, which is headquartered at Stony Kill Farm in Wappingers Falls. For information call 845-831-8780. Dogs are allowed.

California Hill State Forest

A new acquisition in Kent between the existing California Hill State Forest and Pudding Street State Forest has created a 1,000-acre preserve now known as California Hill State Forest. From Gordon Road, a dirt road, closed to traffic, once called Mungers Road, leads from the parking area in the valley of Peekskill Hollow up a ridge to what was once a farm and is now all woods. A lower road leads along the slope within earshot of Peekskill Hollow Creek. Most of Wawayanda Lake is now included in the preserve, along with the abandoned California Hill Road, which makes for fine walking. To reach this, drive Pudding Street, turn off onto Wawayanda Road and drive to the end.

MICHAEL TURCO

New York State Forest's Big Buck Mountain

Lafayetteville State Forest

Located in Lafayetteville/Milan, the 718 acres are mostly for bushwhackers and sportsmen. Wilbur Flats Road, a seasonal dirt road (not maintained from December to April) makes for a good walk and good birding past wetland, woodland, and old fields with numerous ecotones. There are no maintained or marked trails, although hunters and fishermen have formed herd trails. Since this park is undeveloped, the visitor will enjoy seclusion, primitive camping, and exploration. Access: There are a few marked parking lots. The best for hikers are either at the intersection of NY 199 and Wilbur Flats Road, opposite the lake (which is part of the park, so you can canoe there); or halfway down the length of Wilbur Flats Road, where herd trails lead into the woods on both sides. There is also parking along NY 199 at the lake and at the head of the fields.

Depot Hill State Forest

These 260 acres are located in Beekman near Stormville. Shortly after the parking area, old Depot Hill Road turns to dirt and makes for very pleasant walking on a sunny day, especially in autumn (early October) when you smell the thousands of witch hazel blossoms on the breeze. The Appalachian Trail crosses at one point, a narrow footpath with white blazes; you need to watch for it carefully. You can stroll it in either direction for as far as you like. There is also an old woods road (it'll be on your left, with a metal gate) that eventually leads off the property. Great botanizing. Access: From the intersection of Dutchess County 7 and NY 216 in Poughquag, take NY 216 west 0.6 mile to a left turn onto Depot Hill Road. Follow for 2 miles, up the hill. Park opposite the communications tower.

Castle Rock Unique Area

The castle, the winding entrance road, and the land immediately surrounding the castle are private property strictly off-limits to hikers. Trespassing by the curious has led to problems. Since most of the trails on the

129-acre state property in Garrison are old carriage roads that lead to the castle it is difficult for the hiker to traverse much of this parcel other than the fields at the foot of the ridge (where there is a rewarding view). There are two loop trails on top of the ridge that can be accessed from Osborn Preserve trails. (See Sugarloaf chapter for more information.)

Big Buck Mountain State Forest

This park is located in Kent. An unmarked path, all that remains of a dirt road, climbs Big Buck Mountain. There are views of the surrounding hills when the leaves are down. Keep on the main footpath that curves left and leads to the old woods road to the top of the hill. The park's 146 acres are seldom used, and are good for a short nature walk in the woods. Access: Ressique Road can be found off Farmers Mills Road in Kent. Ignore the first parking lot on the right, which is marked (alternatively, check to see if the yellow footpath has been maintained and is walkable). Better, continue on Ressique Road for another 0.1 mile to an unmarked, dirt parking lot on the left. This lot is on a blind curve and its driveway leads down a bank to a locked metal gate with a stop sign.

Night Walks

At least once in a lifetime, if not once every season, walk the woods on a moonlit night. There is no more bewitching woodland experience than a midsummer night's walk past a meadow of moving mist and fireflies. As for a fur-clad, full-moon-lit walk after fresh snowfall . . . it's like walking in a dream.

In the summer, the evening of your moonlit walk is best after a hot day, so that the fireflies will be at their peak, and the grasses humming with crickets. The coolness of the evening air will feel delicious on the skin after a 90-degree day. A round, full moon is best, the sky at least partially clear (or dramatically flying with clouds). Don't bother with a flashlight; it spoils the magic and ruins your night vision. It takes a full 30 minutes for your eye to manufacture the photochemicals necessary for peak night vision, but they are destroyed by a single light beam. Afraid? Choose a park with a dirt road or an old woods road so you need not fear tripping or stray branches. On a wide dirt road there's plenty of room. You can feel the road through the soles of your feet, so you'll know it if you start to wander off onto the verge. Choose a level road to avoid ruts and washouts. Walk the same as you always do, as if it were daylight. Bring along a walking stick to help you, if need be.

As the sun sets the meadows cool and the mists form over the grasses. This magical mist is why you must choose an uncut meadow: a field that has been mown for hay holds not half the enchantment. Choose a field of tall grasses with woods nearby. Approach your walking site an hour after sunset, at dusk. Even the name of this time sounds magical, the crepuscular hours of dawn and dusk, when many mammals and birds are most active. As the sky turns white with diminishing light, the birds sing anew and the deer come out. Foxes may be seen, skunks, opossums, and raccoons emerge. Northern gray tree frogs trill in the trees. In late summer,

MICHAEL TURCO

Night Walks

the katydids sound deafening by dark. As you wait for full darkness to start out on your walk, play with the bats, throwing pebbles high in the air for them to chase. Let your eyes adjust to the darkness. Do not strain to look directly at things. Instead, see the whole picture out of the sides of your eyes. Perhaps it is this inability to see things straight-on in the dark that gives rise to the enchantment and to night's fears, seeing shifting shapes in the shadows and floating fog, the moonlit mist that cascades the dew. The fireflies begin to flash, so many of them that the darkening woods and fields sparkle. The earth and trees turn black, gleaming, shimmering with light. It is bewildering, the flashing and twinkling. It is mesmerizing. The cares and fatigue of the day fall away, the enchantment begins. You won't want to leave such meadows.

Walk past water to see the sheen of the moon on a stream or the stars reflected in a lake. Walk the night road to a black conifer grove, stand perfectly still and quiet, and hoot like a barred owl (or use a tape of a real one). Don't get frightened when the assembly of owls gathers unseen and hollers back. Don't worry about crashes in the bushes or, more likely, the rough, sudden snorts seemingly right at your shoulder. It's just the deer. There's nothing to be afraid of, there's nothing to hurt you. Even if you run into a black bear (highly unlikely) because you are so silent and wraithlike in the woods, you needn't fear; just scream and it will run away. Whatever you do, if you see something black and white waddling along in front of you, don't step on it.

Best night hikes:

- ◆ Full moon at midsummer in a wild meadow to see the fireflies.
- ◆ Full moon in spring to a wet meadow to see and hear the woodcock mating dance.
- ◆ Full moon in winter when snow blankets the ground—bright as daylight, then.

Some of the best places for these enchanting walks are closed after dusk. If you ever hear of the chance to walk Burger Hill or Poets' Walk in Rhinebeck at night, take advantage of it. Places where you can park legally and walk at night:

Lafayetteville State Forest (park at the intersection of NY 199 and Wilbur Flats Road and walk Wilbur Flats Road)

Harlem Valley Rail Trail

Putnam Trailway

Ninham Mountain State Forest

Big Buck Mountain State Forest

Cranberry Mountain State Forest

Stissing Mountain State Forest

California Hill State Forest

Wassaic State Forest

Depot Hill State Forest

West Mountain State Forest

Taconic–Hereford State Forest, from the Taconic Parkway entrance

Any quiet country road sans street lights

If you camp at a park, such as Wilcox, Fahnestock, Mills–Norrie, or Rudd Pond, you can walk the park trails after dusk.

Selected Bibliography

Adams, Arthur. *A Guidebook to the River*. Albany: State University of New York Press, 1981.

Appalachian Mountain Club. *In the Hudson Highlands*. New York: Walking New, Inc., 1945.

Beers, F. W. *Atlas of New York and Vicinity*. New York: Beers, Ellis and Soule, 1867. Available at certain historical societies and public libraries. This atlas covers the entire Hudson River shoreline with a map for each town.

Boyle, Robert H. *The Hudson River, A Natural and Unnatural History*. Exp. ed. New York: W. W. Norton, 1979.

Bruce, Wallace. *The Hudson*. Cent. ed. New York: Walking News, Inc., 1982.

Carmer, Carl. *The Hudson*. The Rivers of American Series. New York: Holt, Rhinehart and Winston, 1939.

Cronon, William. *Changes in the Land: Indians, Colonists, and the Ecology of New England*. New York: Hill and Wang/Farrar, Straus and Giroux, 1983.

Gekle, William F. *A Hudson Riverbook*. Poughkeepsie, NY: Wyvern House, Hamilton Reproductions, 1978.

Glunt, Ruth R. *Lighthouses and Legends of the Hudson*. Monroe, NY: Library Research Associates, 1975.

Howell, William Thompson. *The Hudson Highlands*. New York: Walking News, Inc., 1982. Reissue of 1933 and 1934 volumes.

Jameson, J. Franklin. *Narratives of New Netherland, Original Narratives of Early American History, 1609–1664*. New York: Barnes and Noble, Inc., 1967.

Kraft, Herbert C. *The Lenape: Archaeology, History, and Ethnography*. Newark, NJ: New Jersey Historical Society, 1986.

Lossing, Benson. *The Hudson, From the Wilderness to the Sea*. Somersworth, NH: New Hampshire Publishing Co., 1972. Facsimile of the 1866 edition.

O'Brien, Raymond J. *American Sublime, Landscape and Scenery of the Lower Hudson Valley*. New York: Columbia University Press, 1981.

Parker, Arthur C. *The Archaeological History of New York*. Pt. 2. Albany, NY: The University of the State of New York, New York State Museum, 1922.

Van Zandt, Roland. *Chronicles of the Hudson: Three Centuries of Travelers' Accounts*. New Brunswick, NJ: Rutgers University Press, 1971.

Wyckoff, Jerome. *Rock Scenery of the Hudson Highlands and Palisades*. Glens Falls, NY: Adirondack Mountain Club, 1971.

Index

G